PONYO

Original story and screenplay written and directed by
HAYAO MIYAZAKI

2

MAIN CHARACTERS

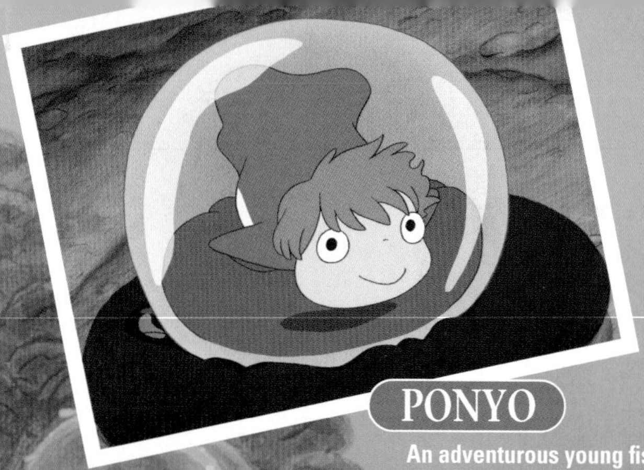

PONYO

An adventurous young fish who came from the sea. She meets Sosuke, who gives her the name Ponyo.

SOSUKE

The boy who finds Ponyo. He walks to the beat of his own drum, but is polite and has a strong sense of responsibility.

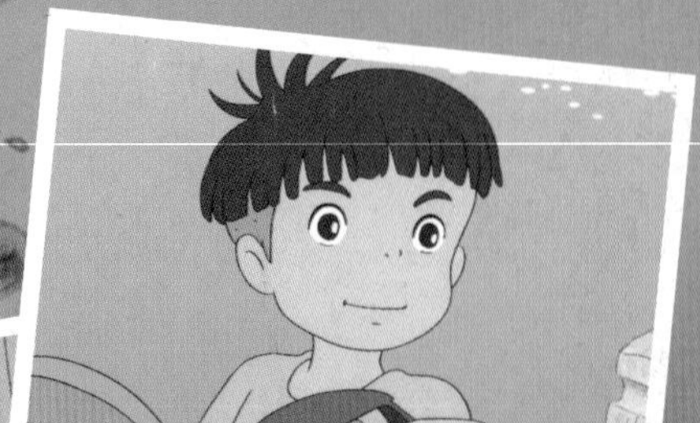

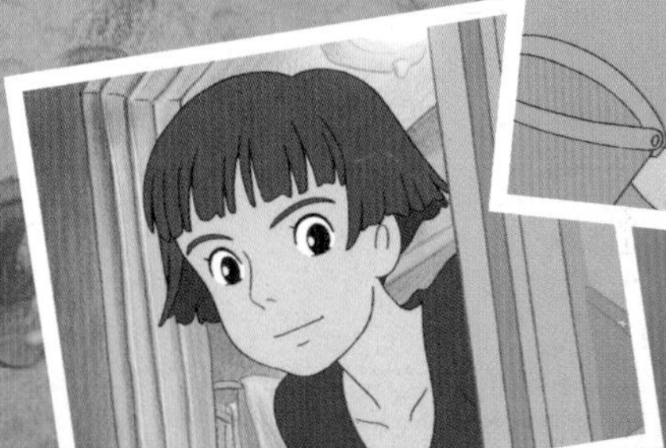

LISA

Sosuke's mother. She is strong, capable and caring.

KOICHI

Sosuke's father. He is the captain of the ship *Koganei Maru*.

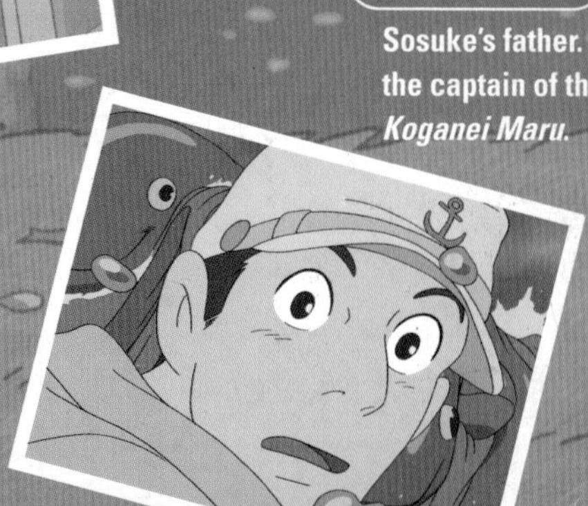

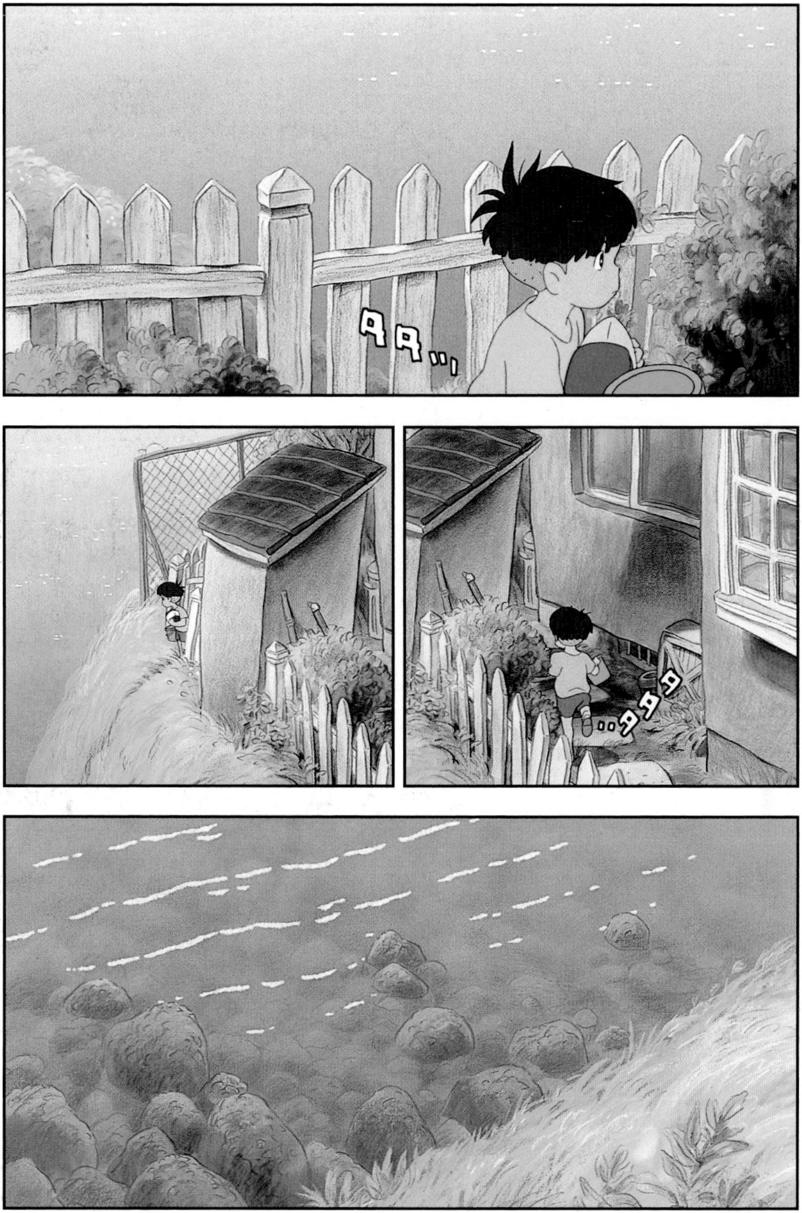

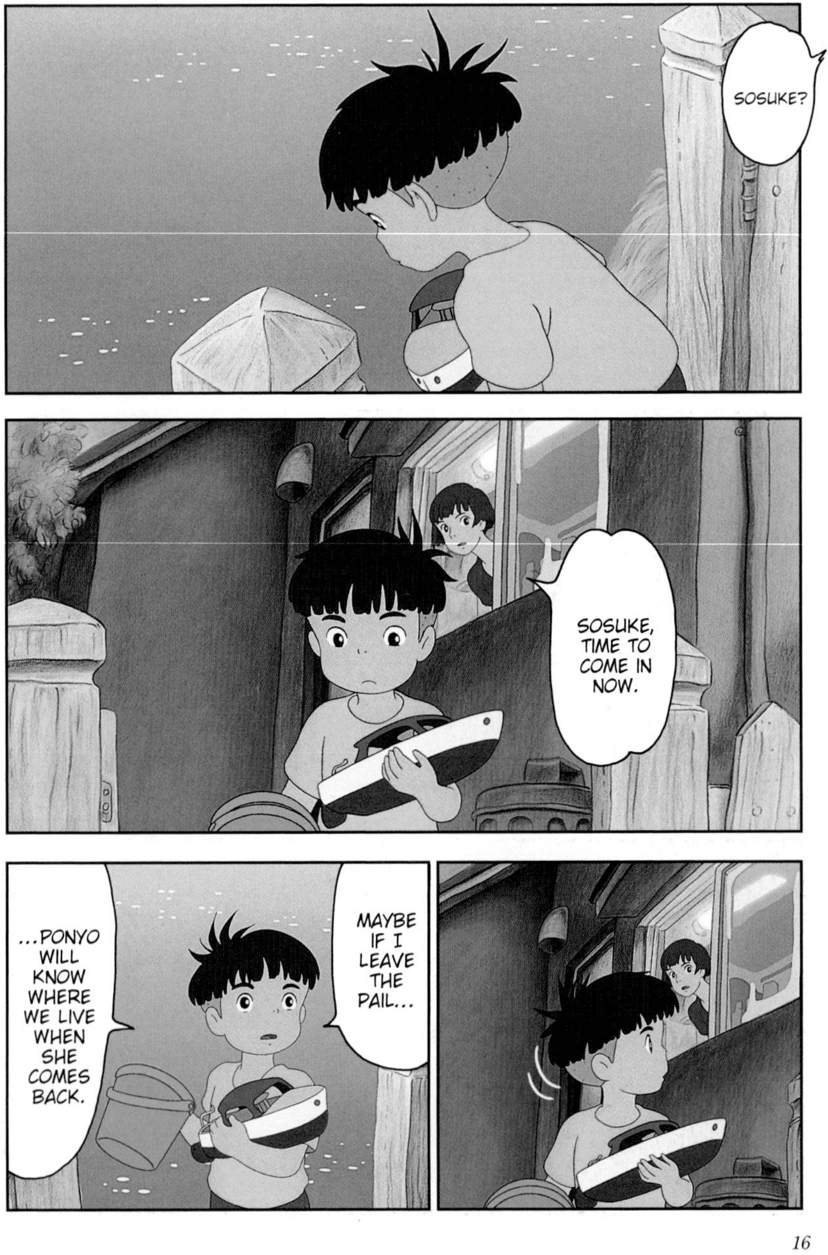
SOSUKE?
SOSUKE, TIME TO COME IN NOW.
MAYBE IF I LEAVE THE PAIL...
...PONYO WILL KNOW WHERE WE LIVE WHEN SHE COMES BACK.

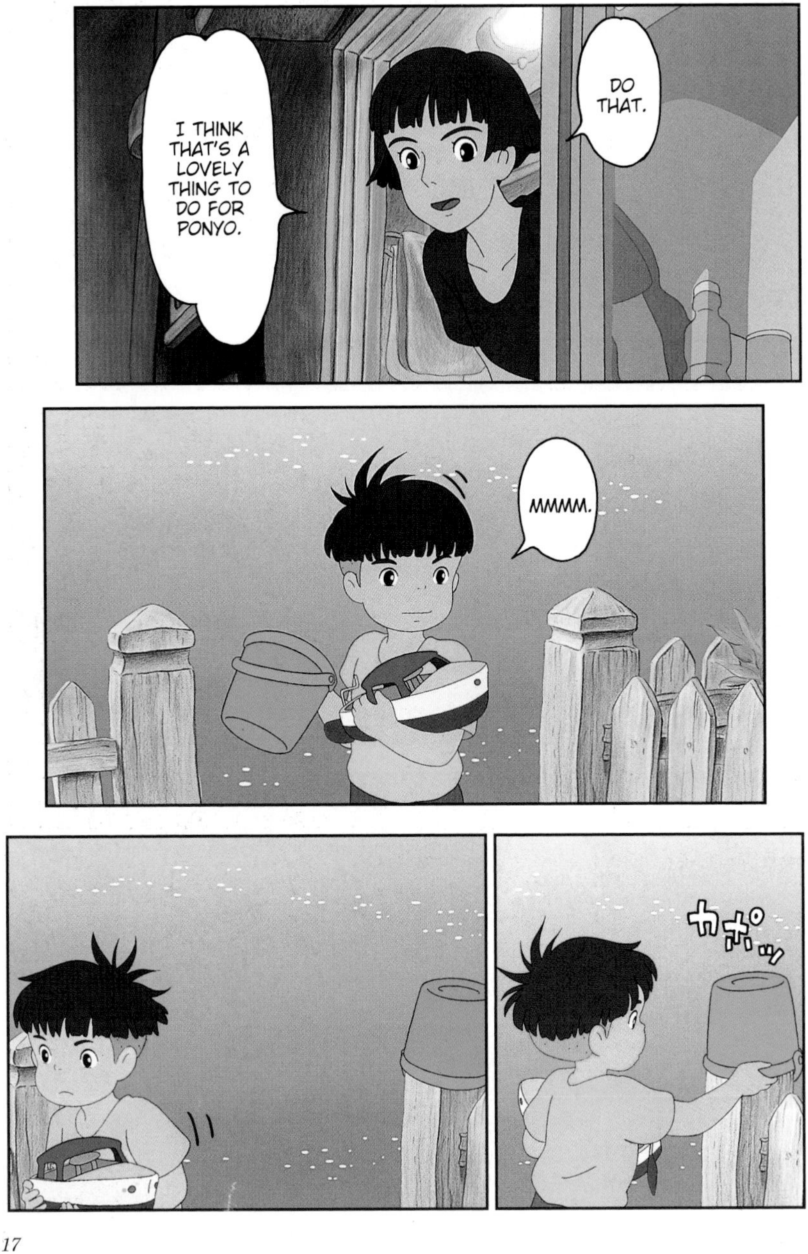
DO THAT.
I THINK THAT'S A LOVELY THING TO DO FOR PONYO.
MMMM.
カポッ

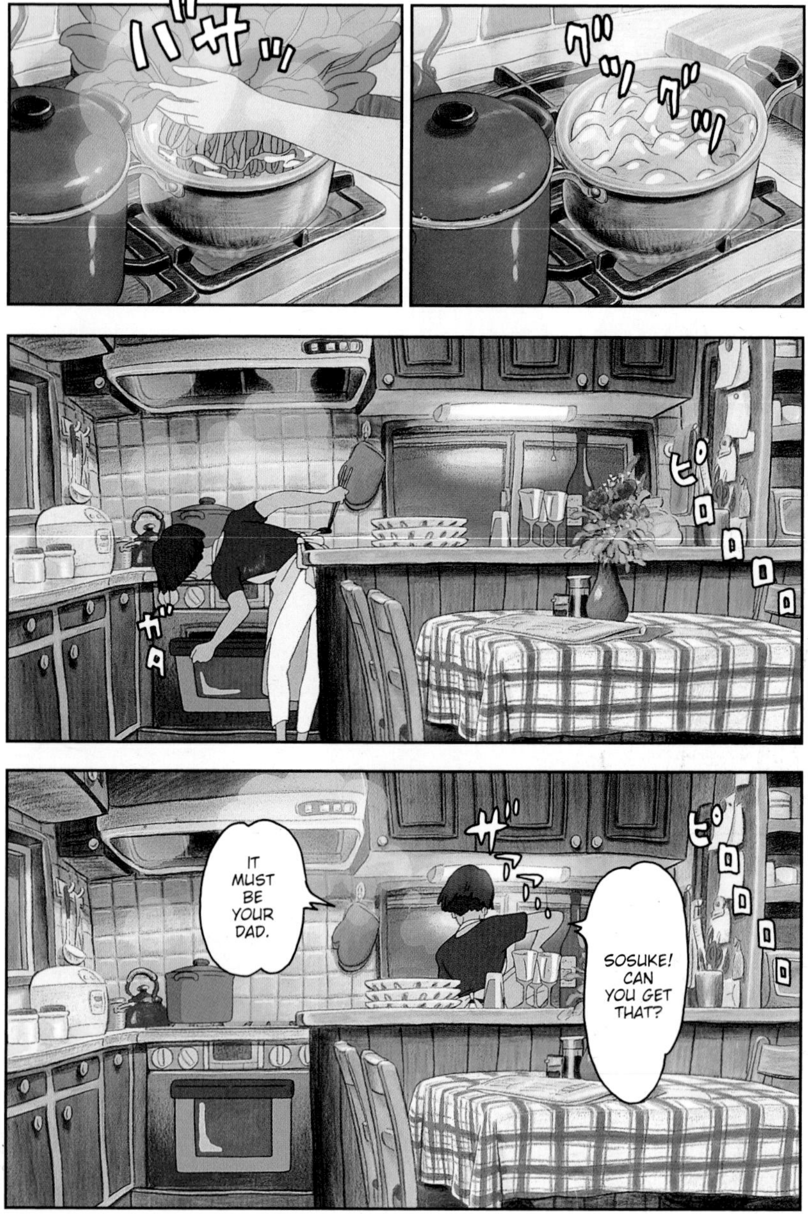

グツグツ
バサッ
ピロロロロ
ガタ
ピロロロロ
ザァァ
SOSUKE! CAN YOU GET THAT?
IT MUST BE YOUR DAD.

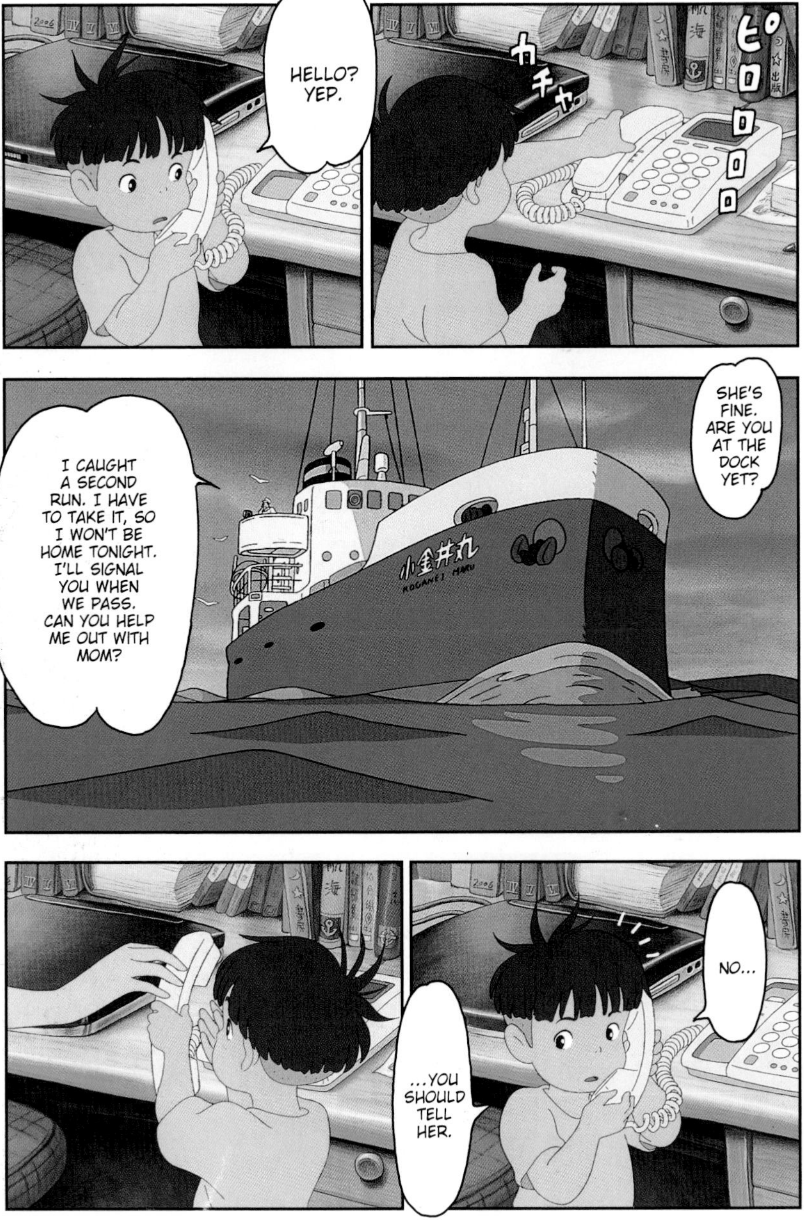
ピロロロロ
カチャ
HELLO? YEP.
SHE'S FINE. ARE YOU AT THE DOCK YET?
I CAUGHT A SECOND RUN. I HAVE TO TAKE IT, SO I WON'T BE HOME TONIGHT. I'LL SIGNAL YOU WHEN WE PASS. CAN YOU HELP ME OUT WITH MOM?
小金井丸
KOGANEI MARU
NO...
...YOU SHOULD TELL HER.

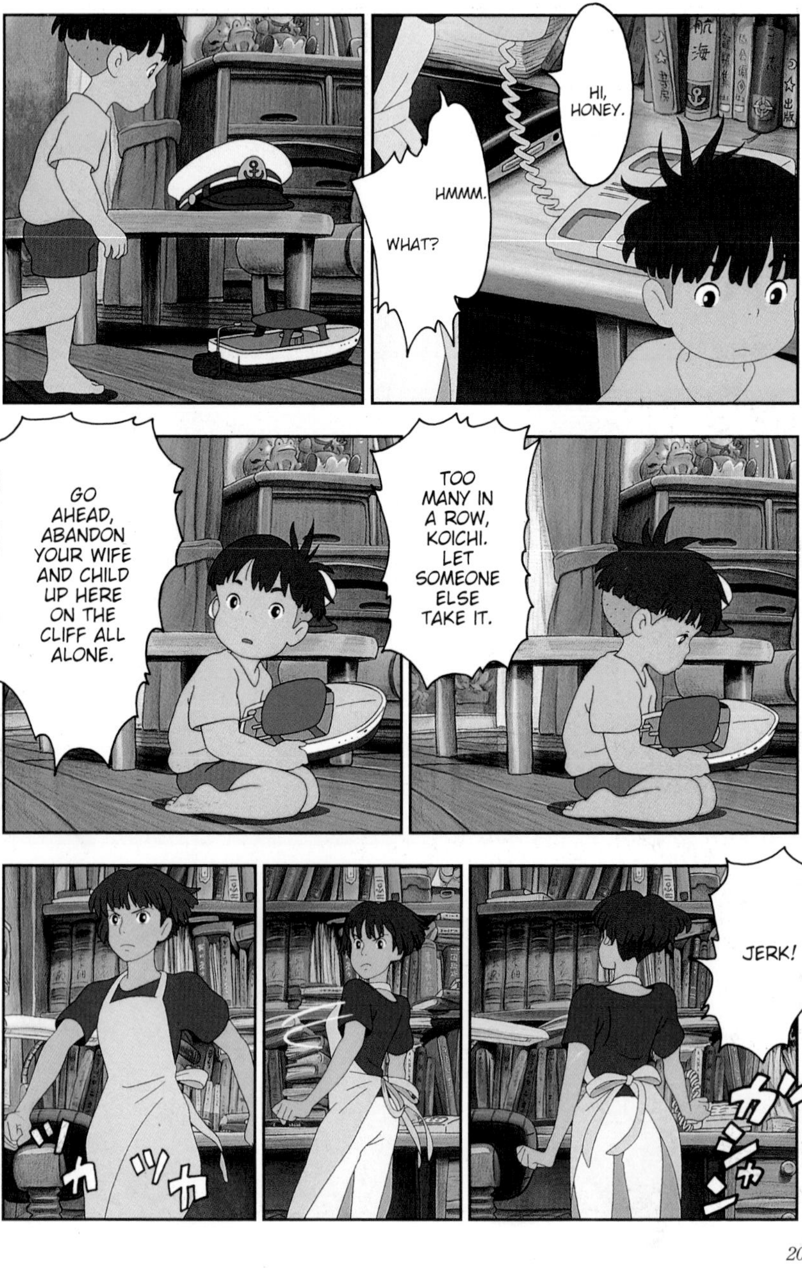
HI, HONEY.
HMMM.
WHAT?
TOO MANY IN A ROW, KOICHI. LET SOMEONE ELSE TAKE IT.
GO AHEAD, ABANDON YOUR WIFE AND CHILD UP HERE ON THE CLIFF ALL ALONE.
JERK!
ガシャン
ツカツカ

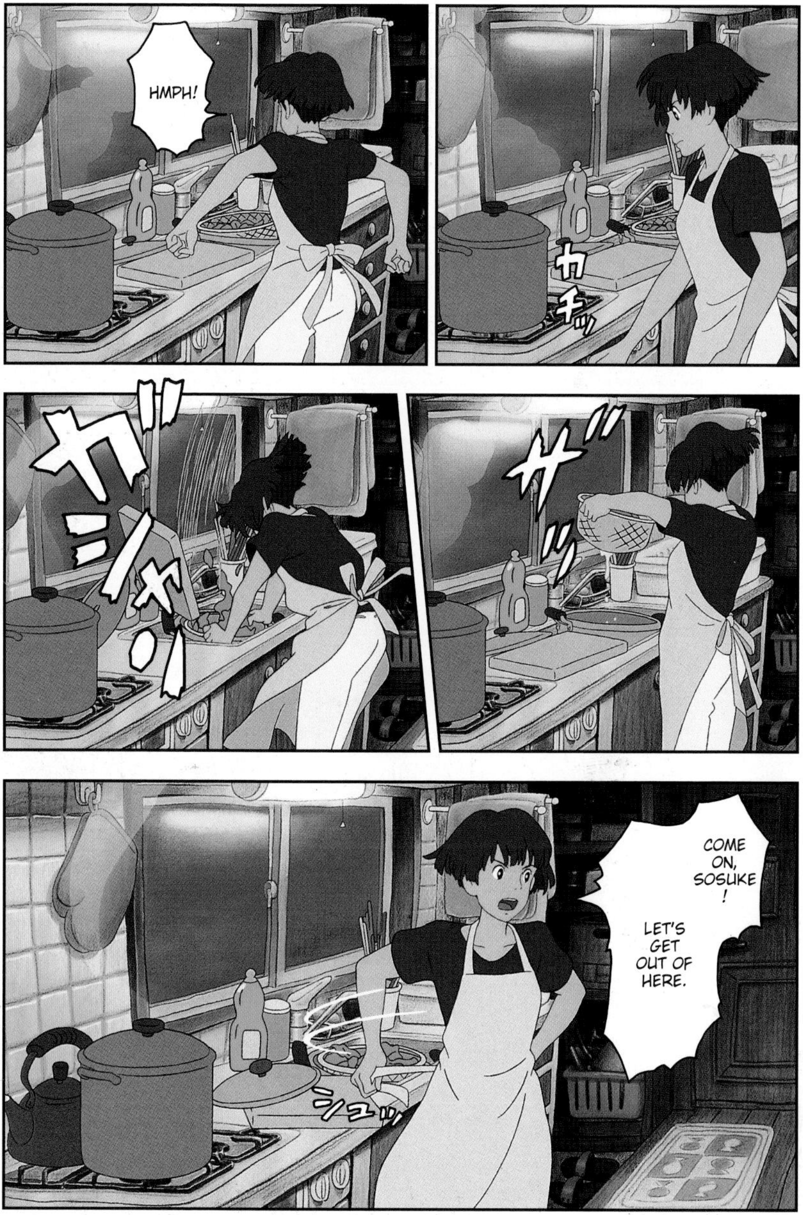
カチッ
HMPH!
ザザッ
ガシャン
COME ON, SOSUKE!
LET'S GET OUT OF HERE.
シュッ

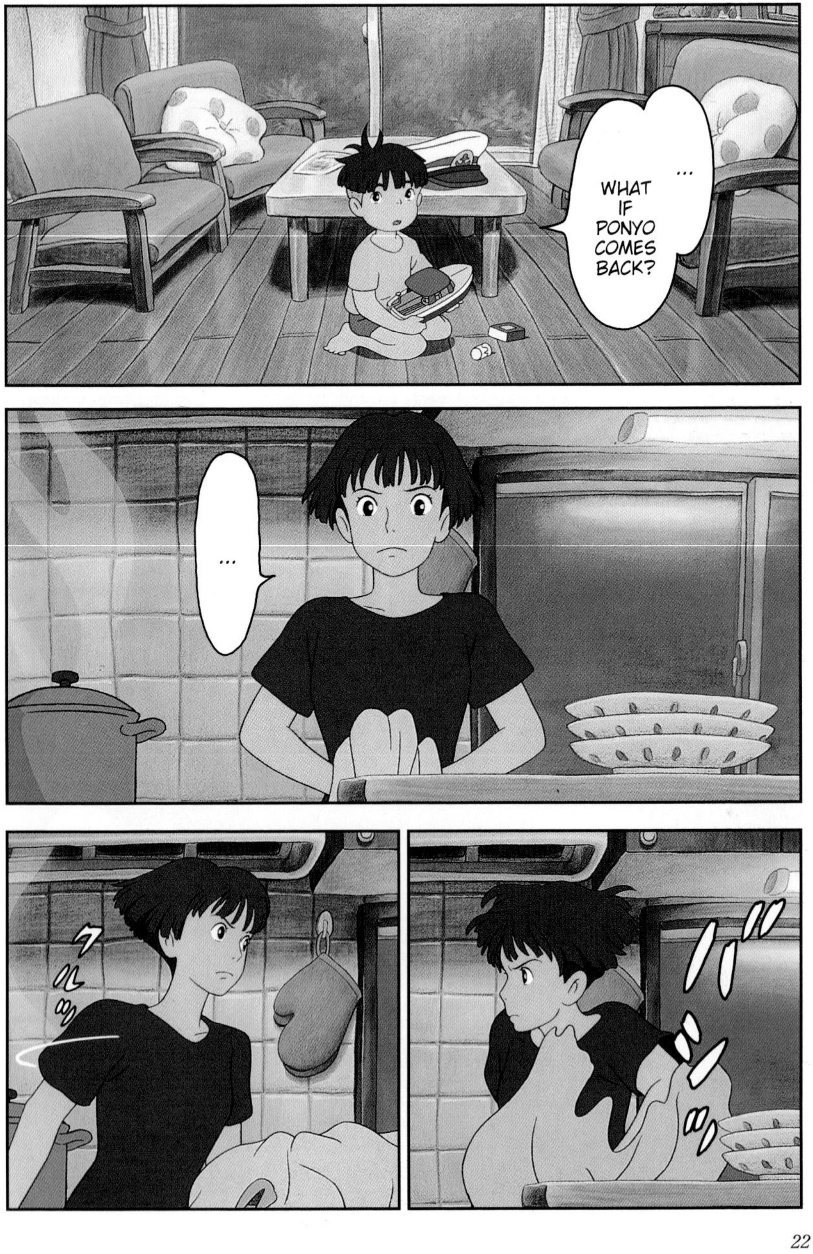
...
WHAT IF PONYO COMES BACK?
...
クルッ

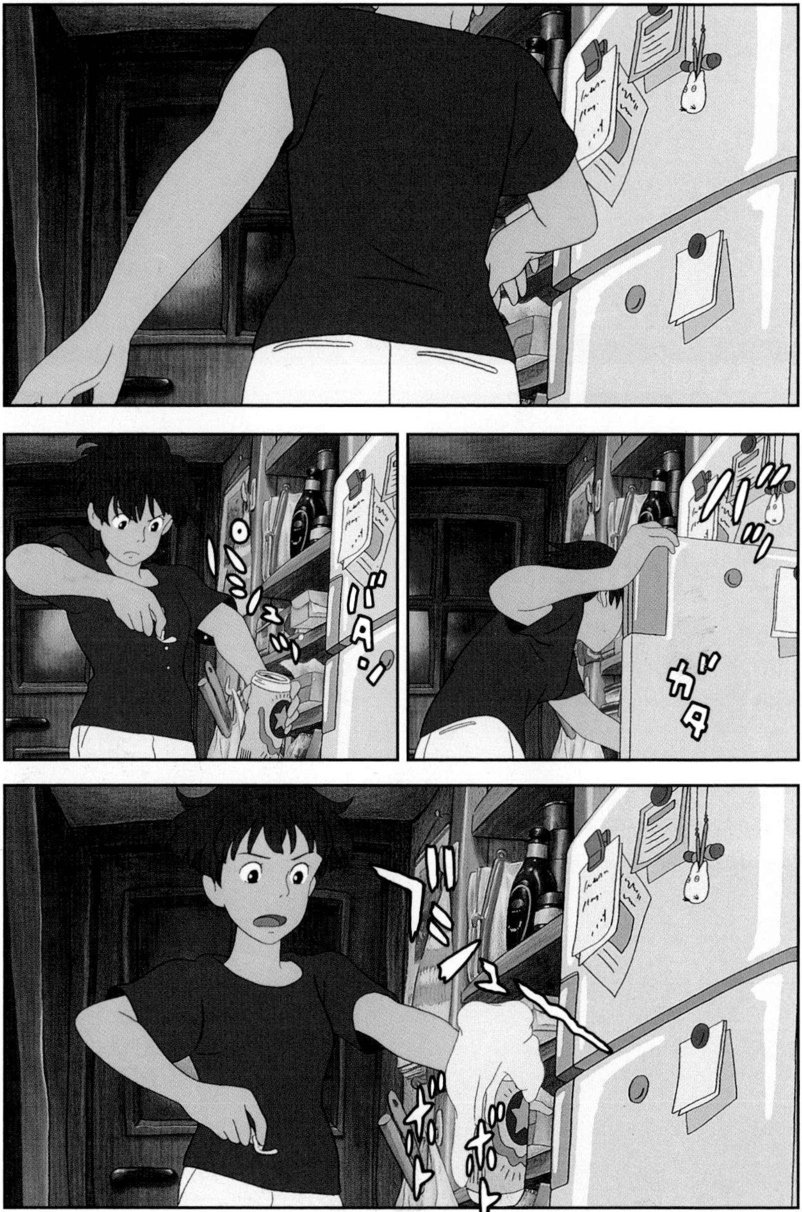
ガタ

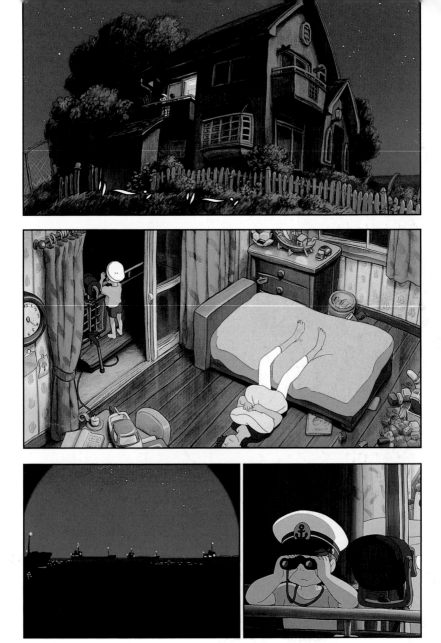

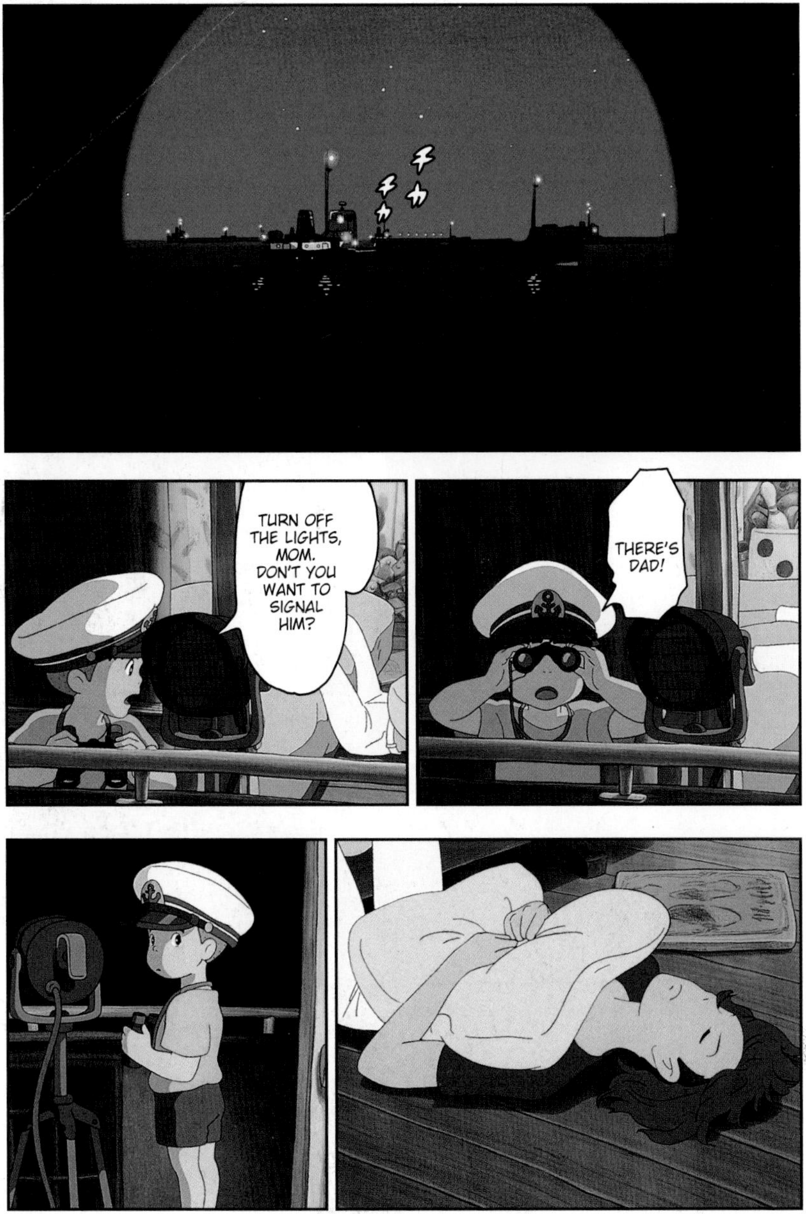
チカ
チカ
THERE'S DAD!
TURN OFF THE LIGHTS, MOM. DON'T YOU WANT TO SIGNAL HIM?

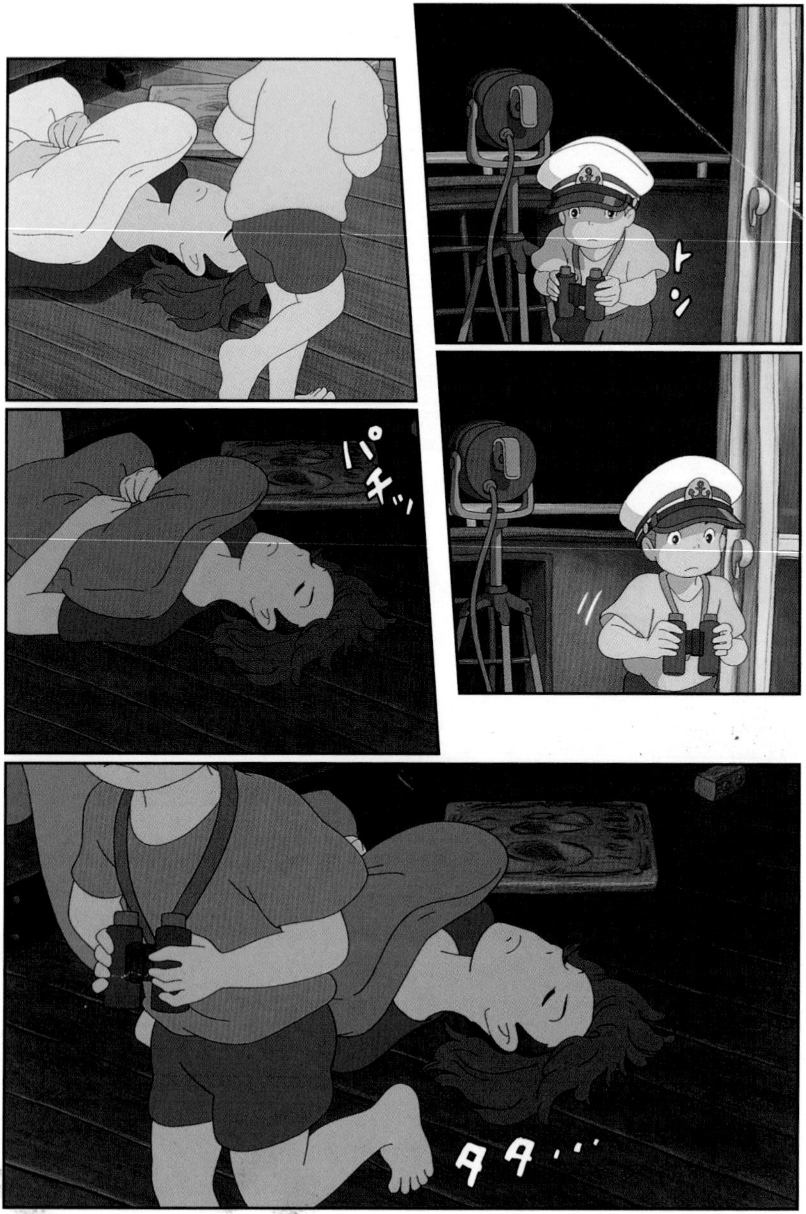
トン
パチッ
タタ…

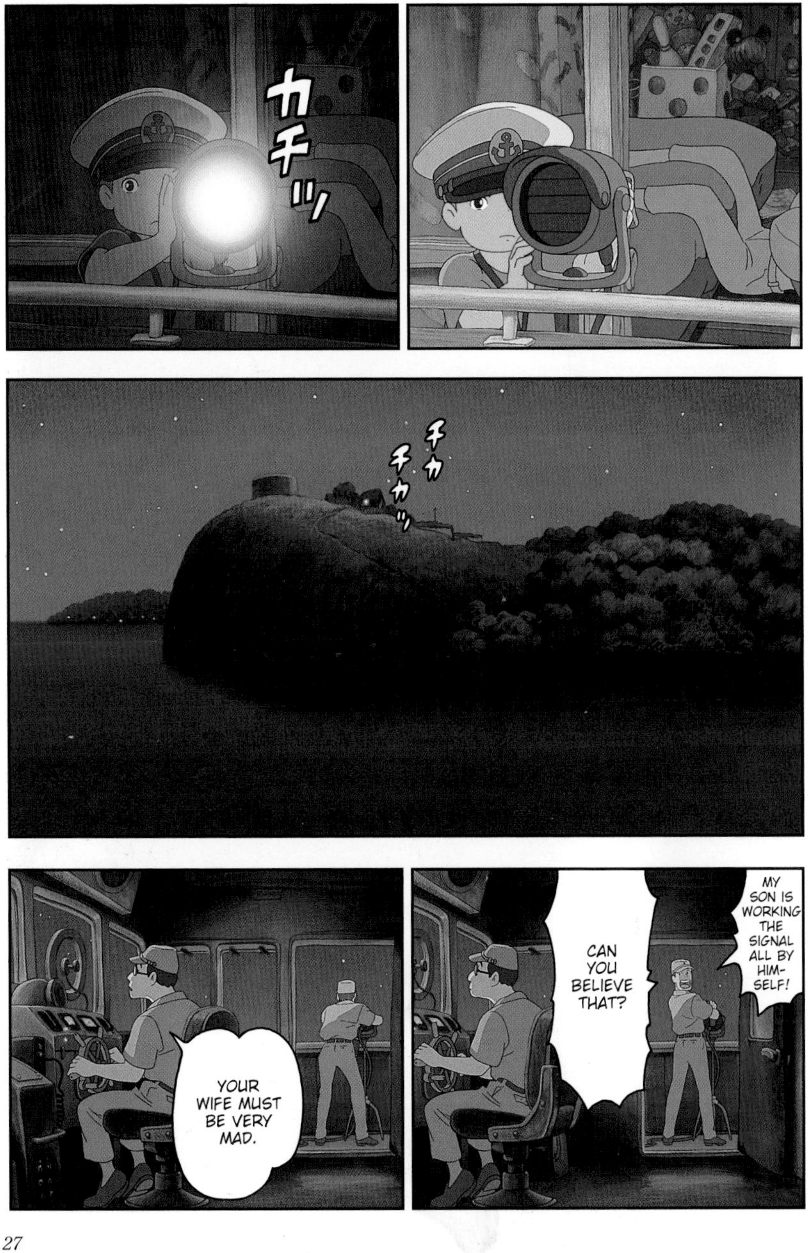
カチッ
チカチカッ
MY SON IS WORKING THE SIGNAL ALL BY HIM-SELF!
CAN YOU BELIEVE THAT?
YOUR WIFE MUST BE VERY MAD.

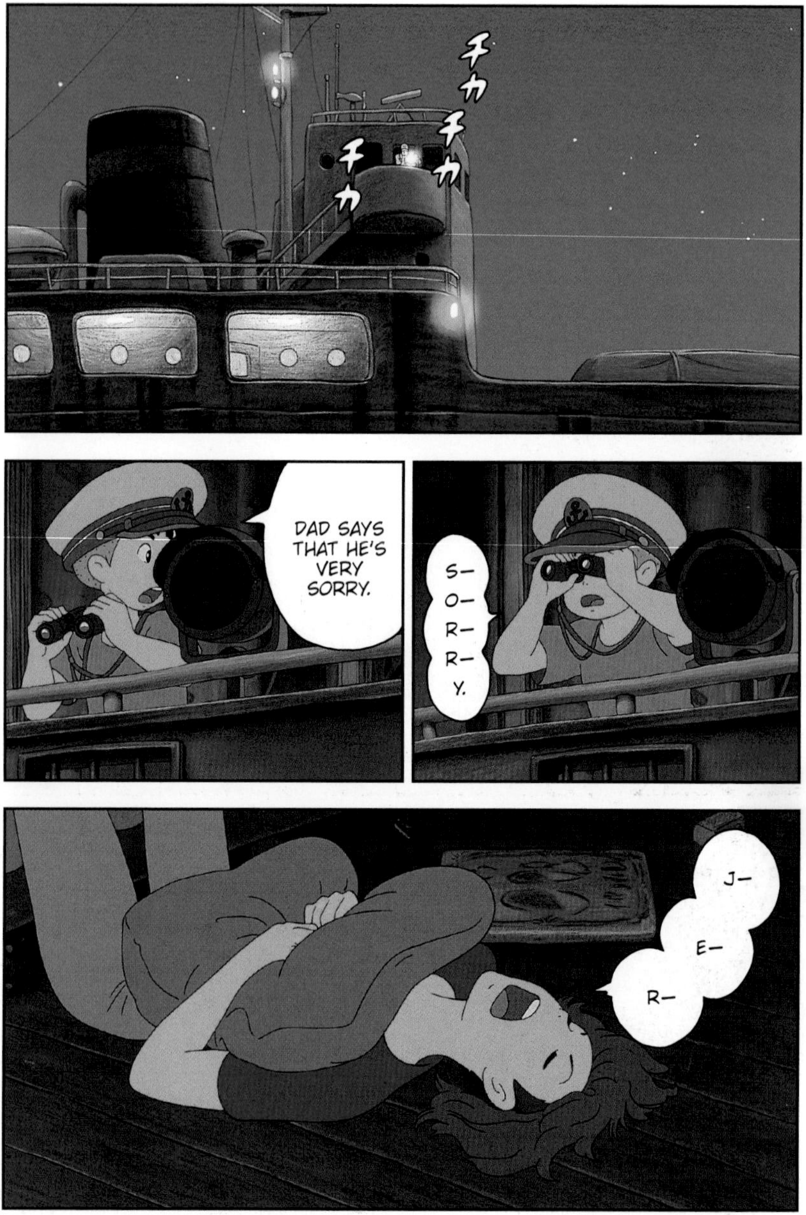
チカ
チカ
チカ
S— O— R— R— Y.
DAD SAYS THAT HE'S VERY SORRY.
J— E— R—

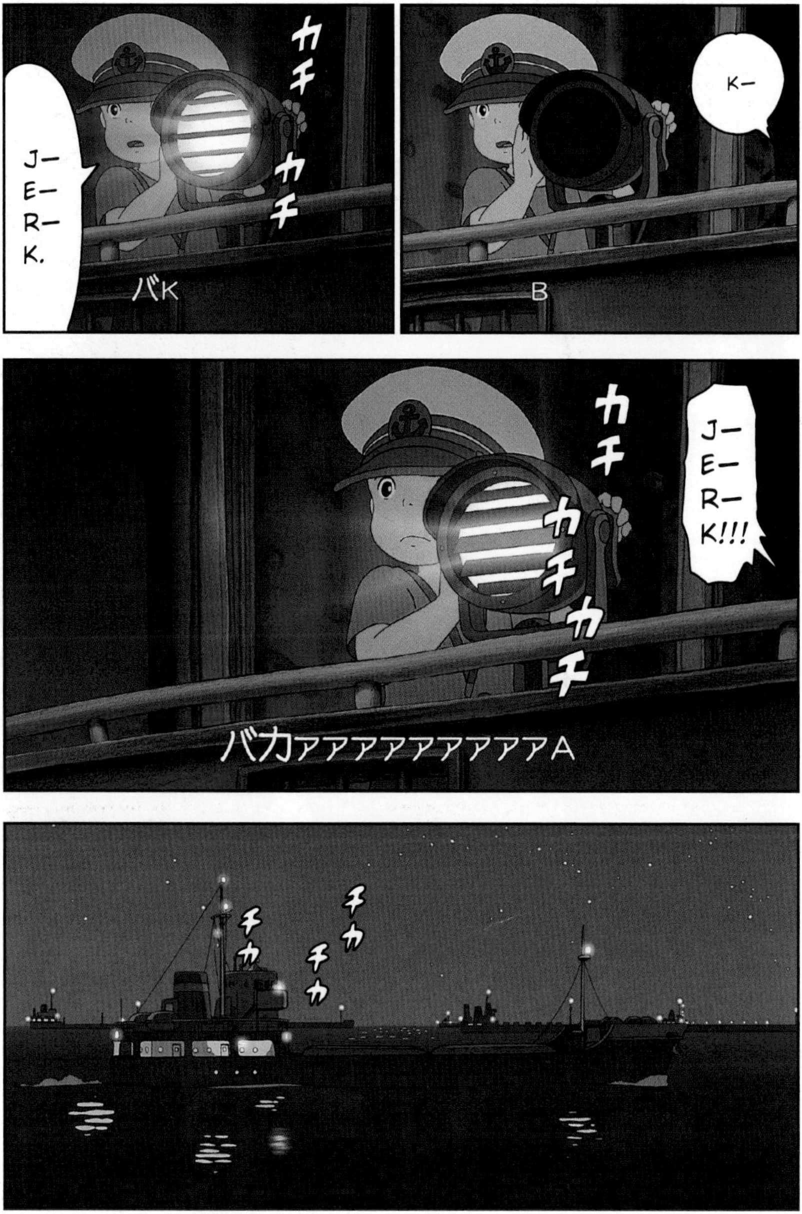

K–
B
カチ カチ カチ
J– E– R– K.
バK
カチ カチ カチ カチ
J– E– R– K!!!
バカアアアアアアアアアアA
チカ チカ
チカ チカ

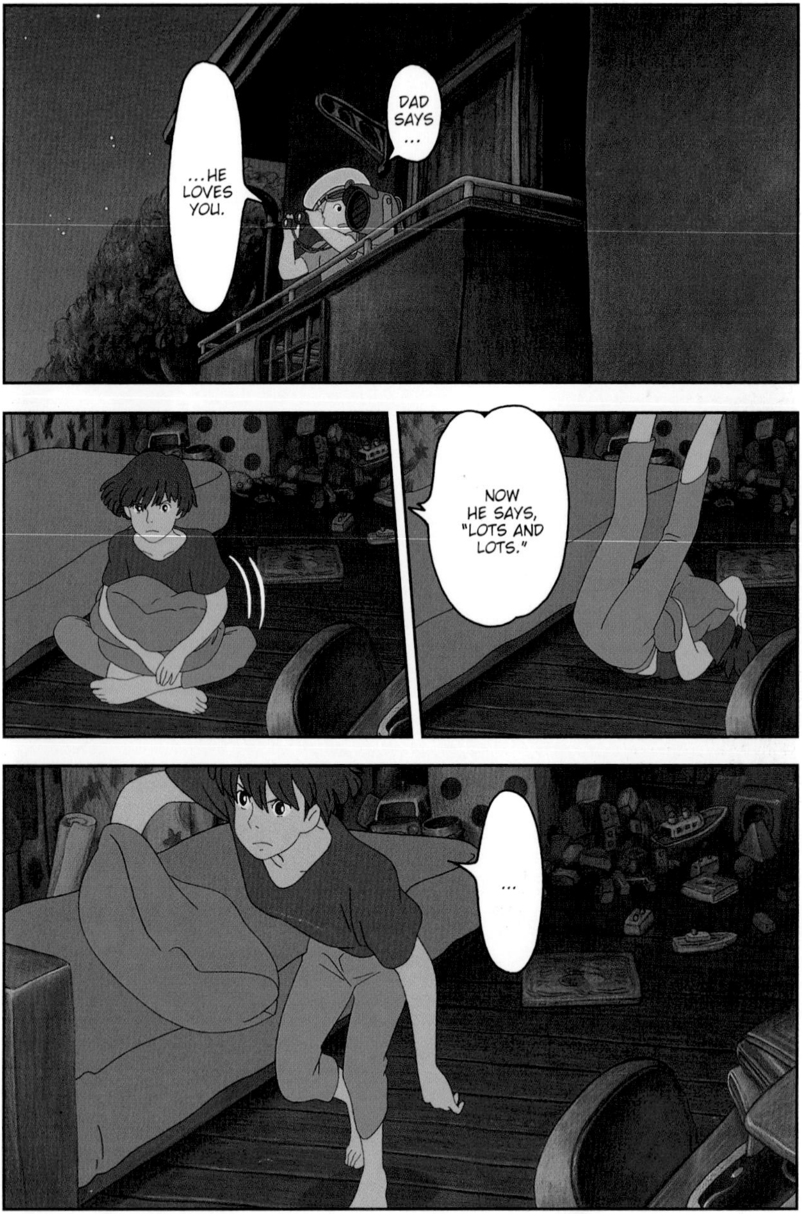
DAD SAYS ...
...HE LOVES YOU.
NOW HE SAYS, "LOTS AND LOTS."
...

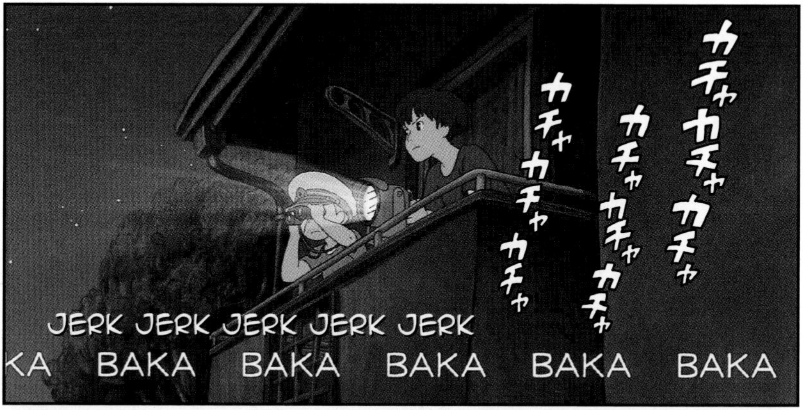
カチャカチャカチャ
カチャカチャカチャカチャ
カチャカチャカチャ
JERK JERK JERK JERK JERK
KA BAKA BAKA BAKA BAKA BAKA

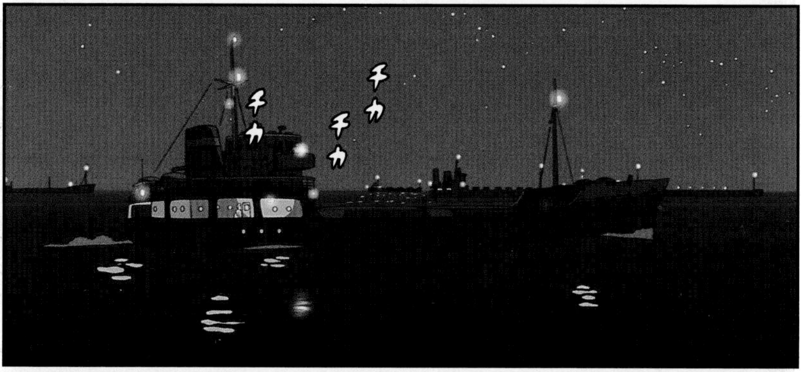
チカ
チカ
チカ

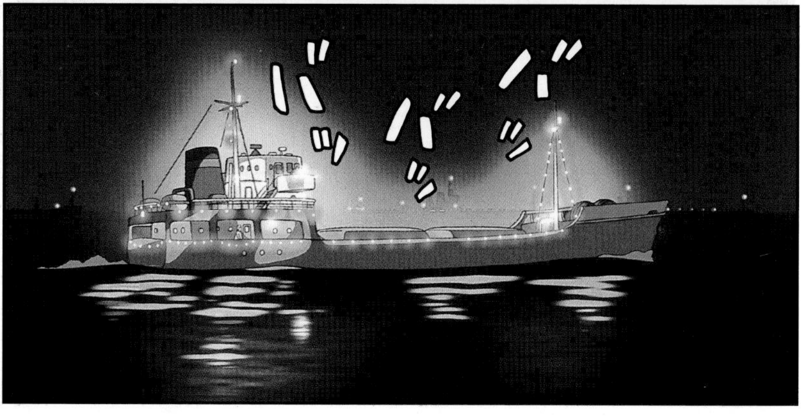
バッ
バッ
バッ

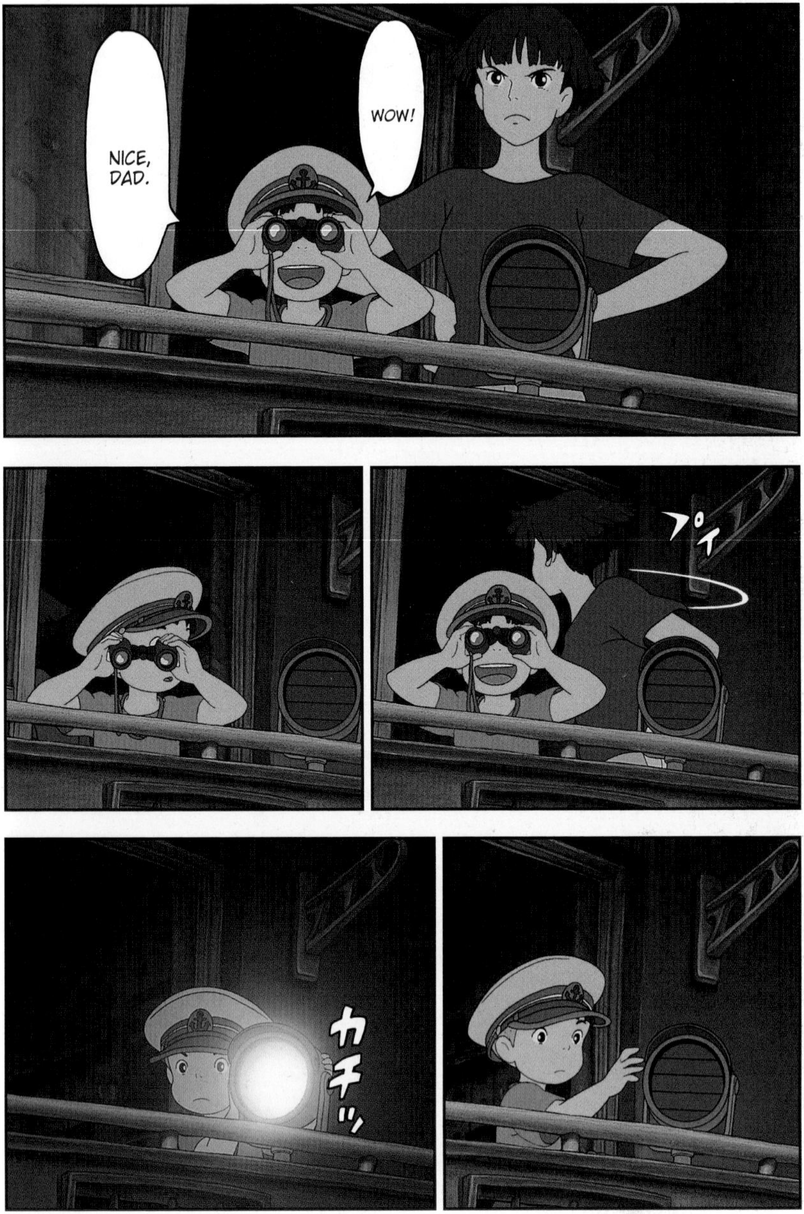
WOW!
NICE, DAD.
プイ
カチッ

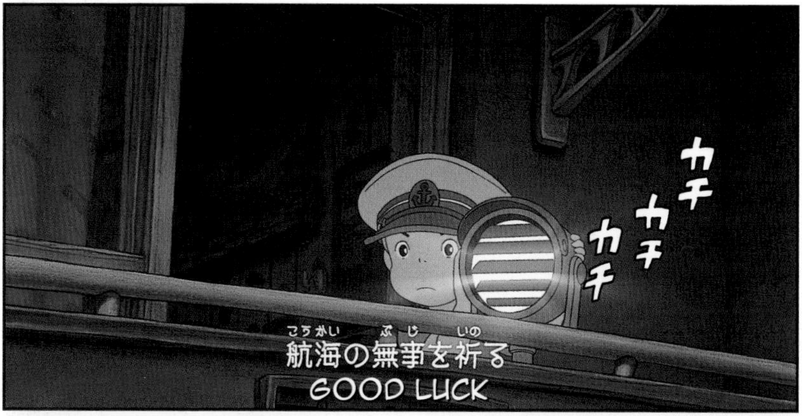
カチ
カチ
カチ
航海の無事を祈る
GOOD LUCK

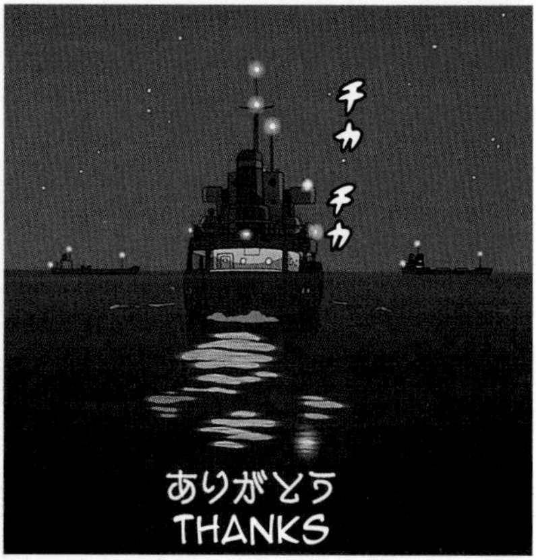
チカ
チカ
ありがとう
THANKS

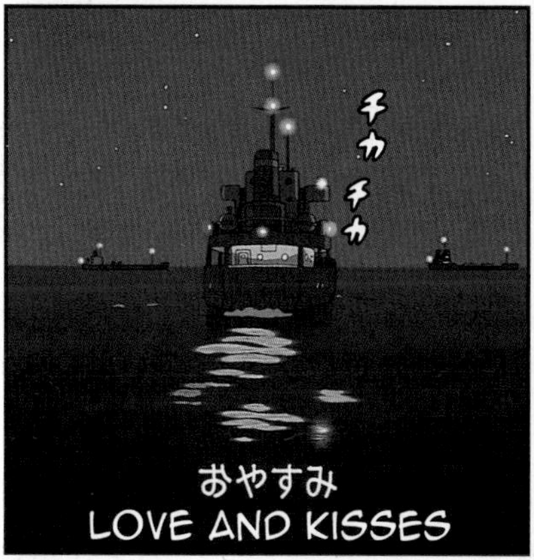
チカ
チカ
おやすみ
LOVE AND KISSES

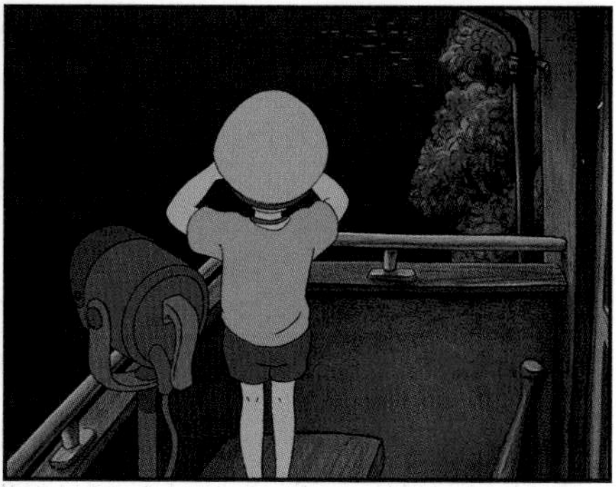

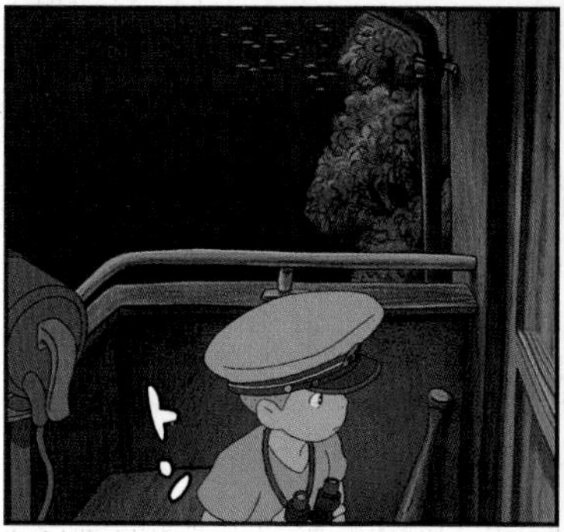
ト・・

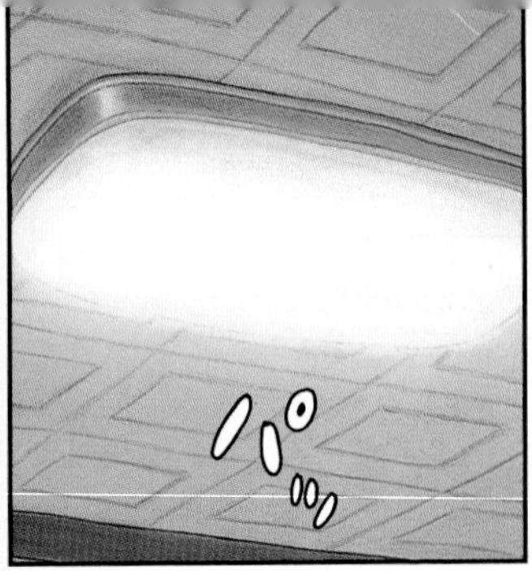

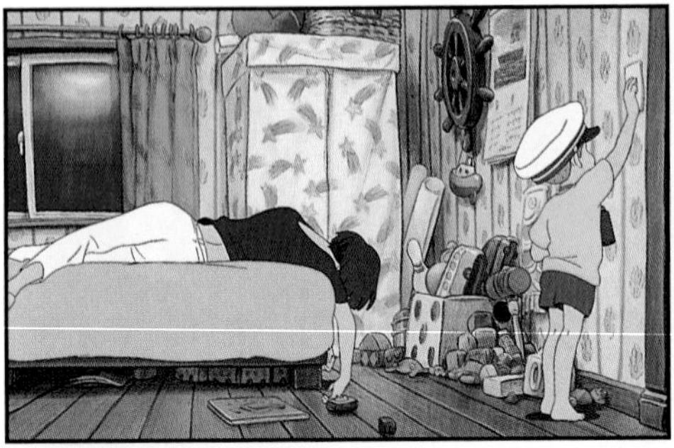

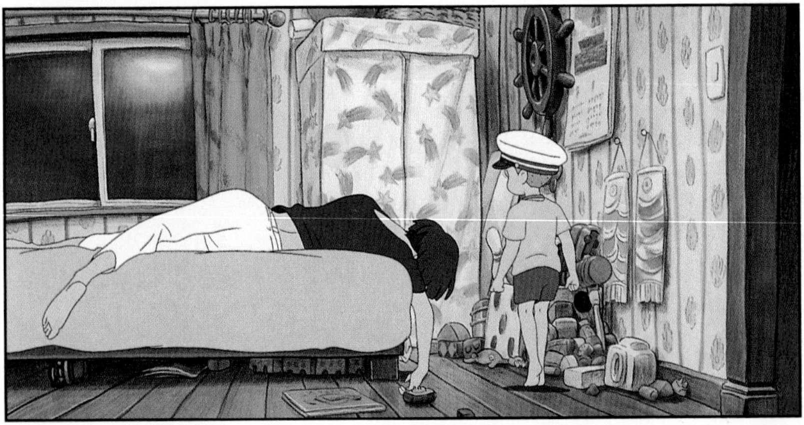

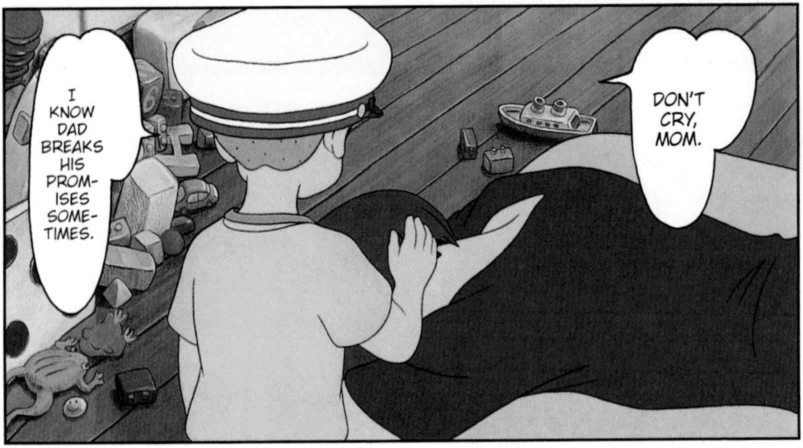
DON'T CRY, MOM.
I KNOW DAD BREAKS HIS PROM-ISES SOME-TIMES.

BUT
HE DOES HIS
BEST FOR US.
I PROMISED
PONYO I'D
TAKE CARE
OF HER,
THEN I
LOST
HER.

I
WONDER
IF
SHE'S
CRYING
NOW.

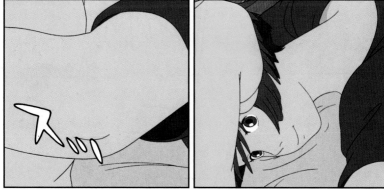

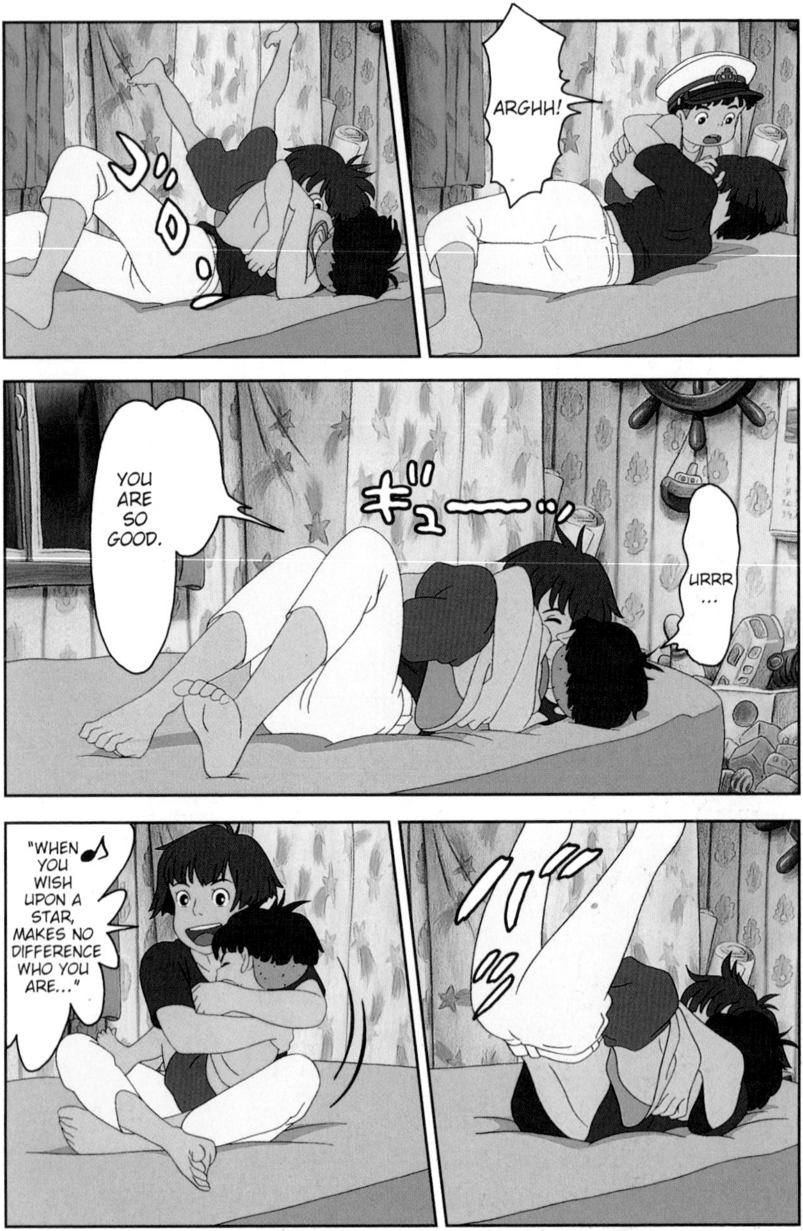
ARGHH!
URRR...
ギューーッ
YOU ARE SO GOOD.
"WHEN ♪ YOU WISH UPON A STAR, MAKES NO DIFFERENCE WHO YOU ARE..."

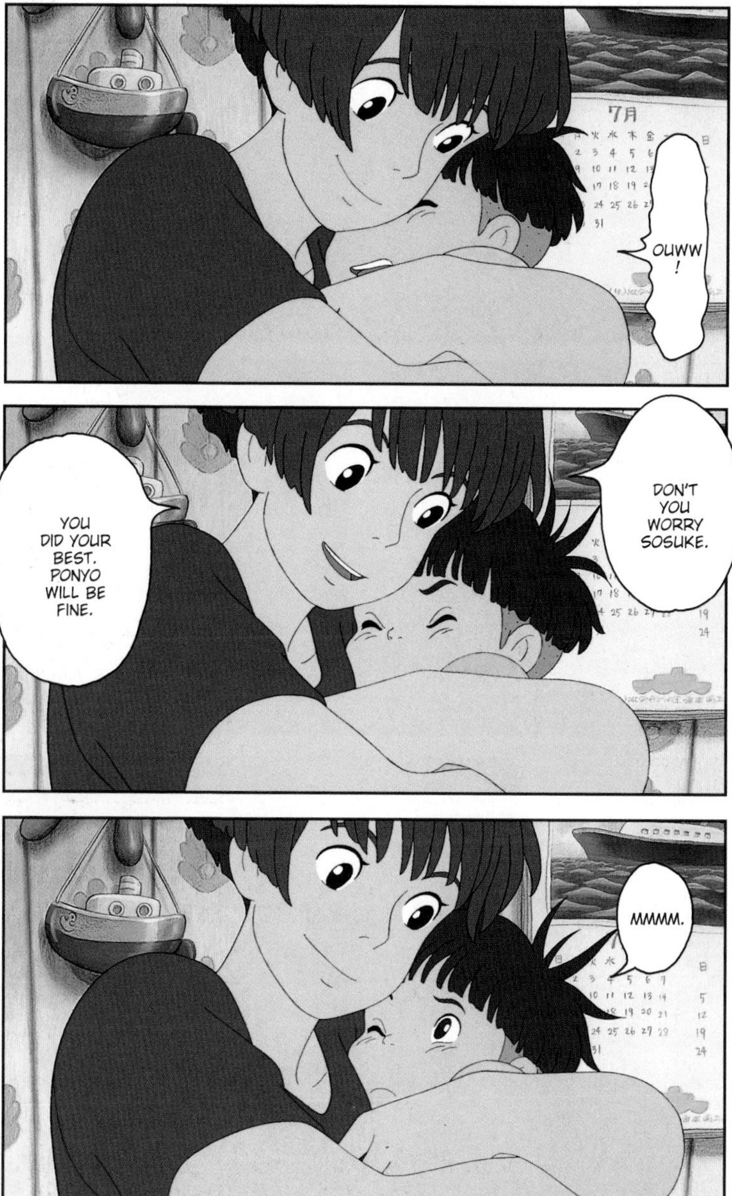
OUWW!
DON'T YOU WORRY SOSUKE.
YOU DID YOUR BEST. PONYO WILL BE FINE.
MMMM.

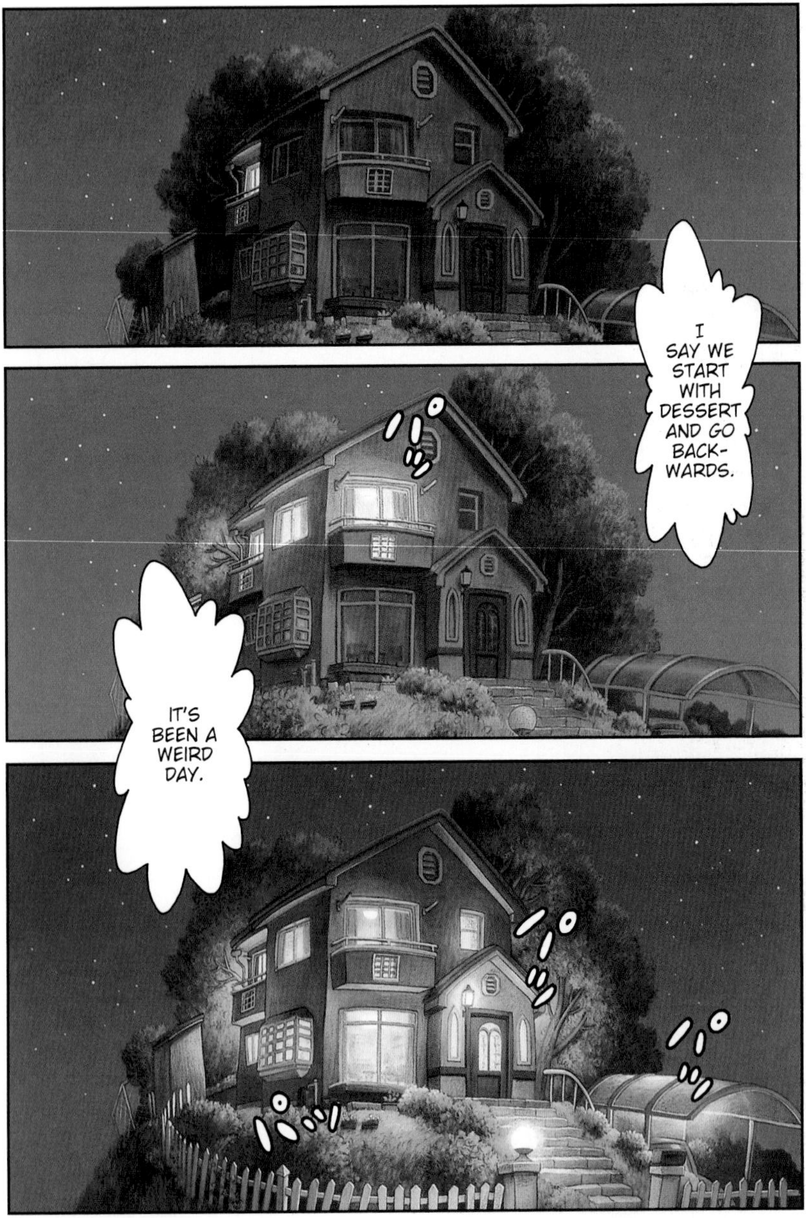
I SAY WE START WITH DESSERT AND GO BACK-WARDS.
IT'S BEEN A WEIRD DAY.

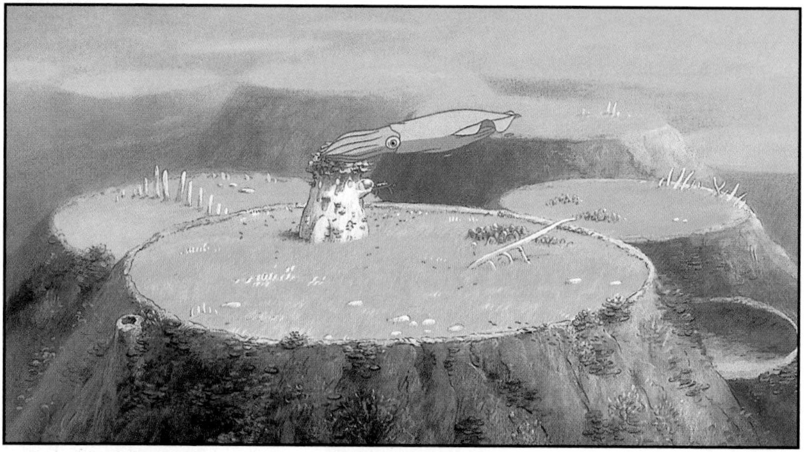
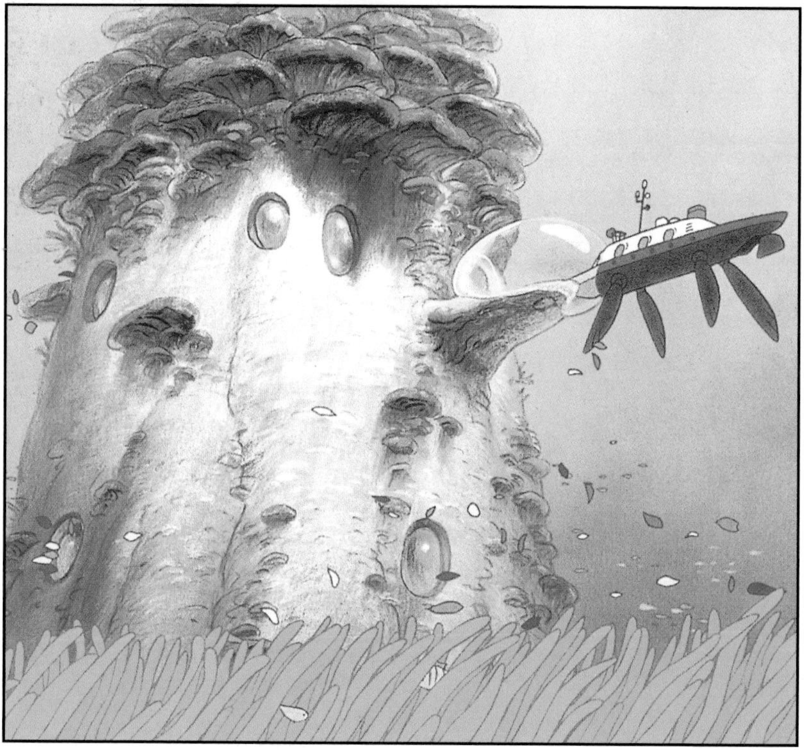

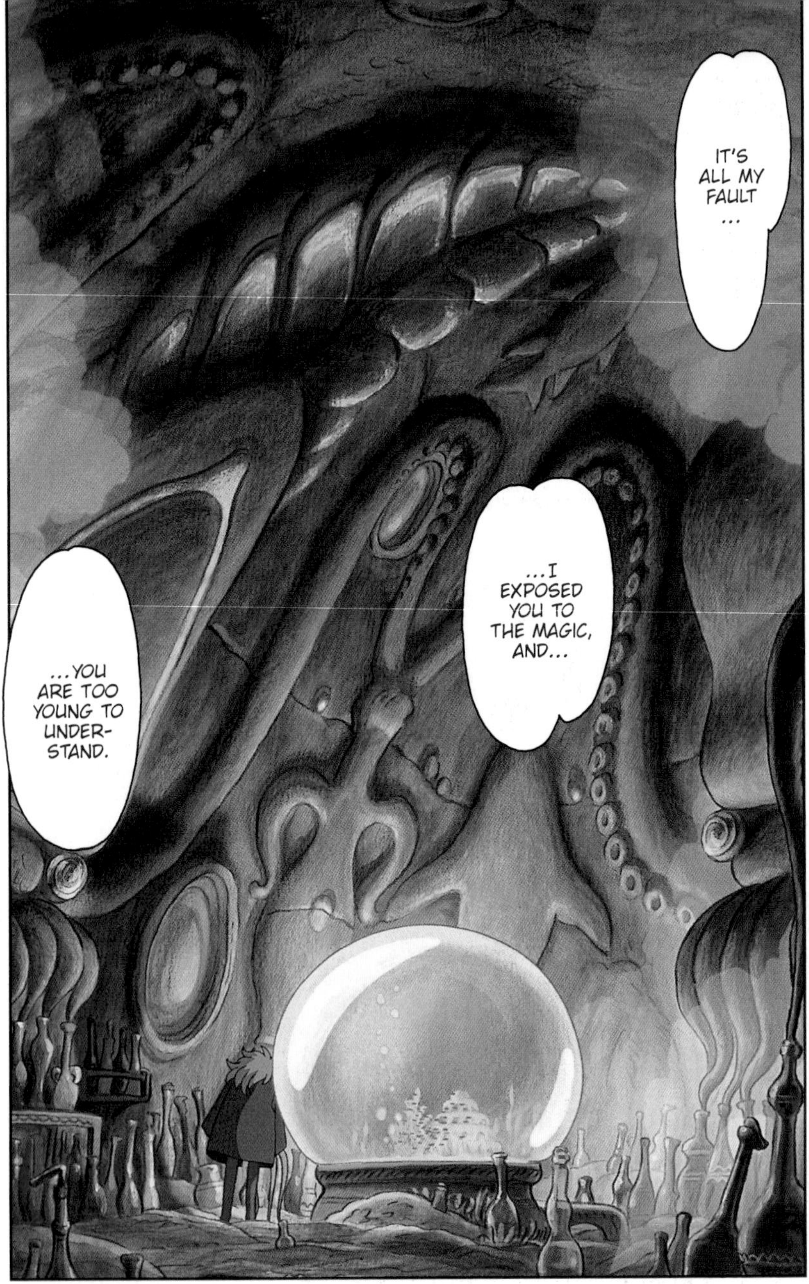
IT'S ALL MY FAULT ...
...I EXPOSED YOU TO THE MAGIC, AND...
...YOU ARE TOO YOUNG TO UNDER-STAND.

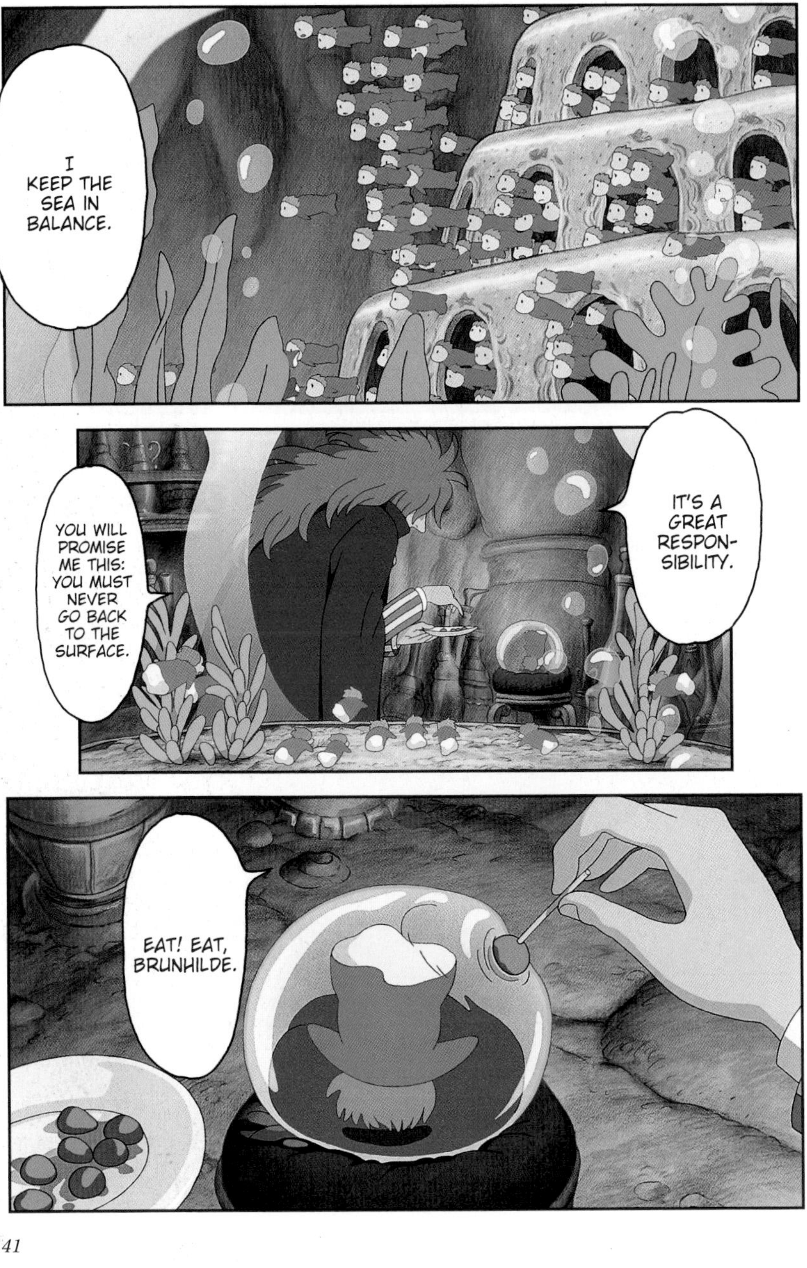
I KEEP THE SEA IN BALANCE.
IT'S A GREAT RESPON-SIBILITY.
YOU WILL PROMISE ME THIS: YOU MUST NEVER GO BACK TO THE SURFACE.
EAT! EAT, BRUNHILDE.

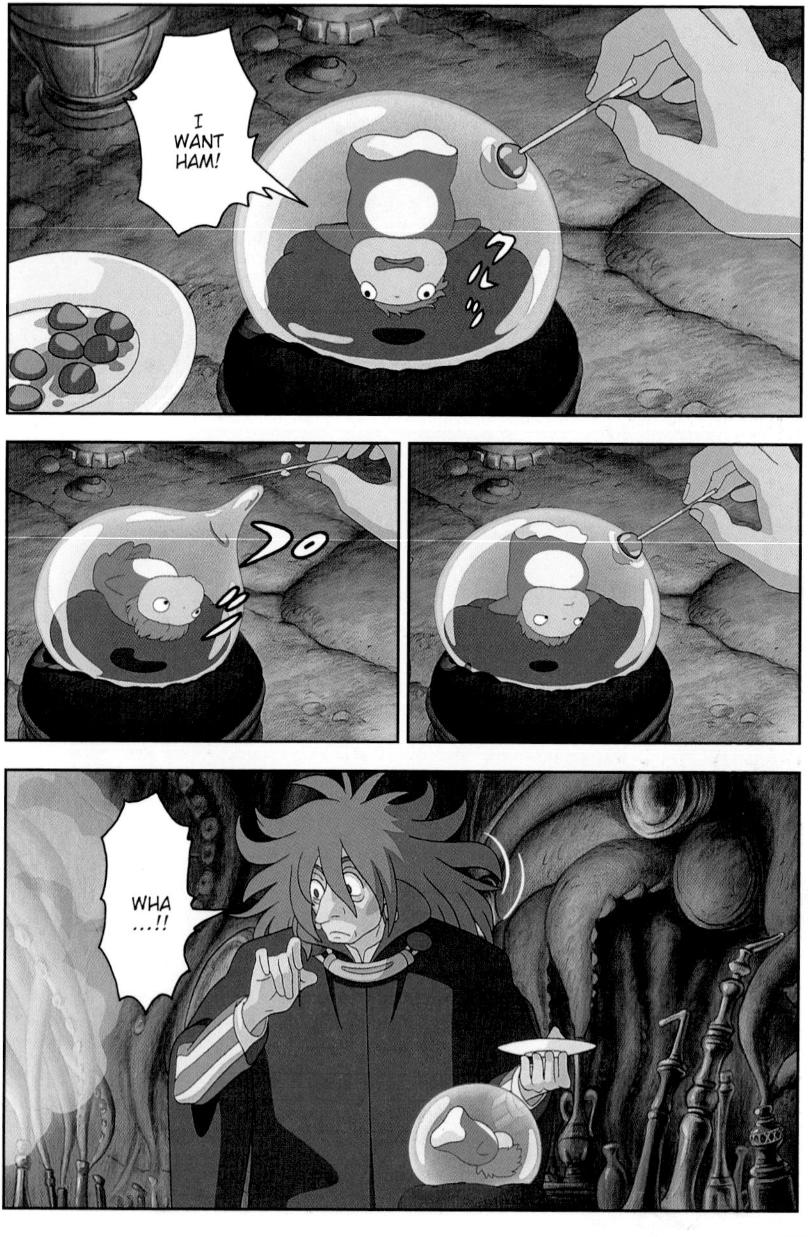
I WANT HAM!
WHA ...!!

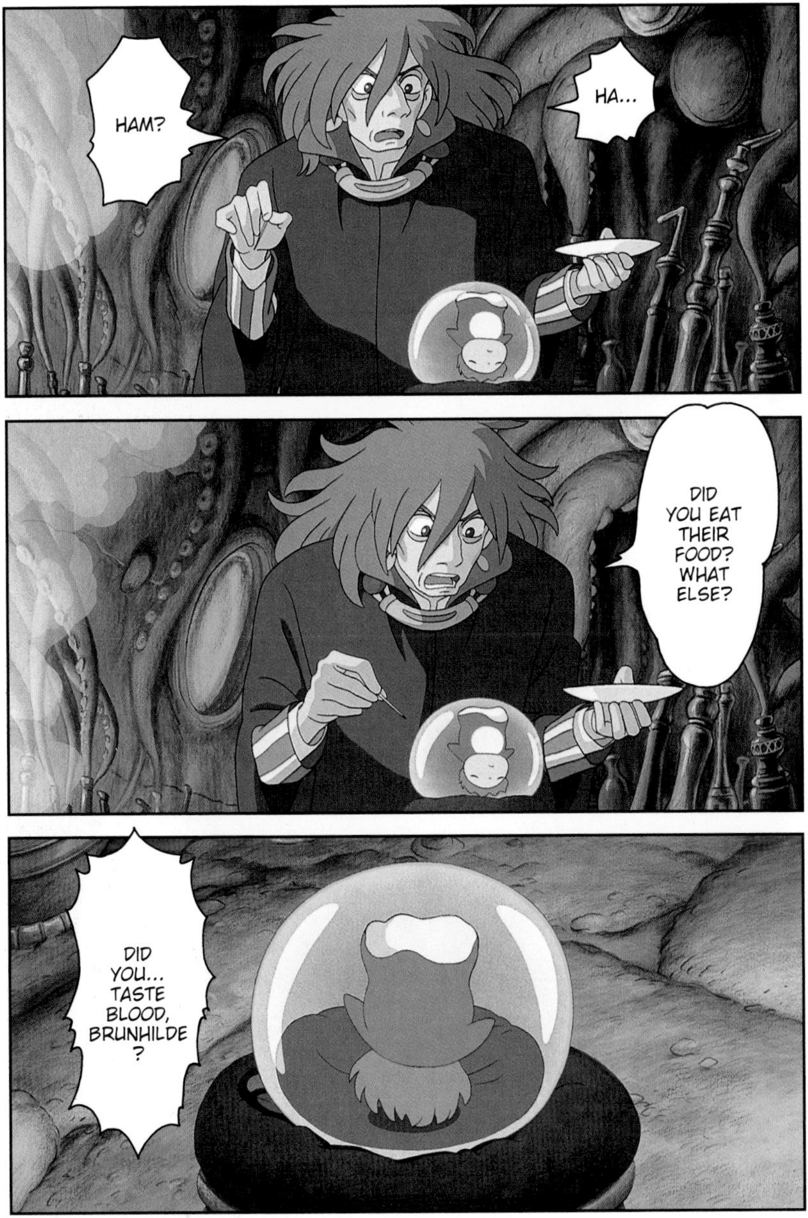
HA...
HAM?
DID YOU EAT THEIR FOOD? WHAT ELSE?
DID YOU... TASTE BLOOD, BRUNHILDE?

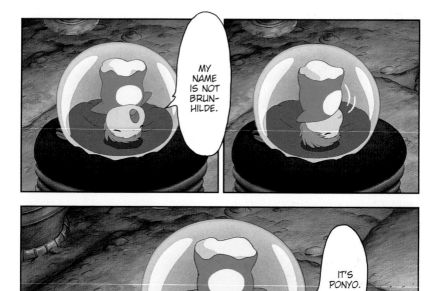

MY NAME IS NOT BRUN-HILDE.

IT'S PONYO.

PONYO?!

PO... PO...

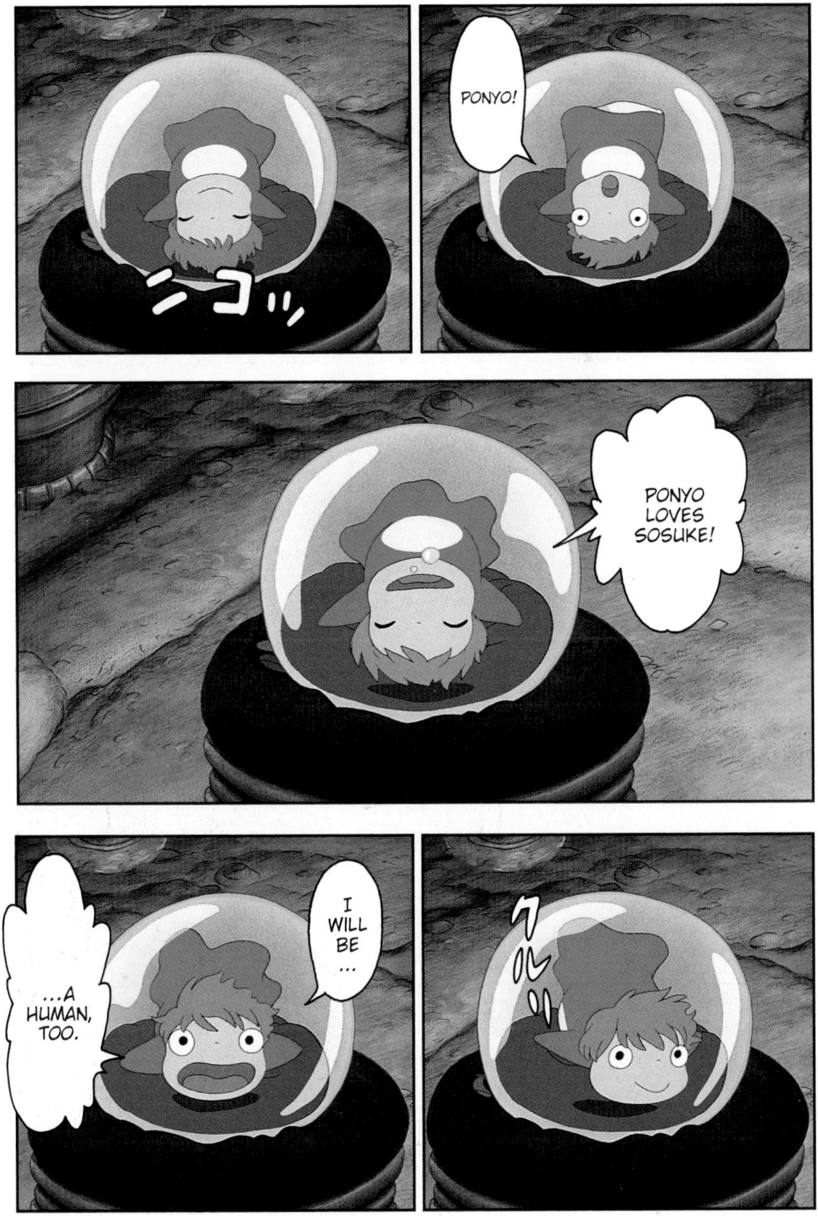
PONYO!
ニコッ
PONYO LOVES SOSUKE!
クルッ
I WILL BE ...
...A HUMAN, TOO.

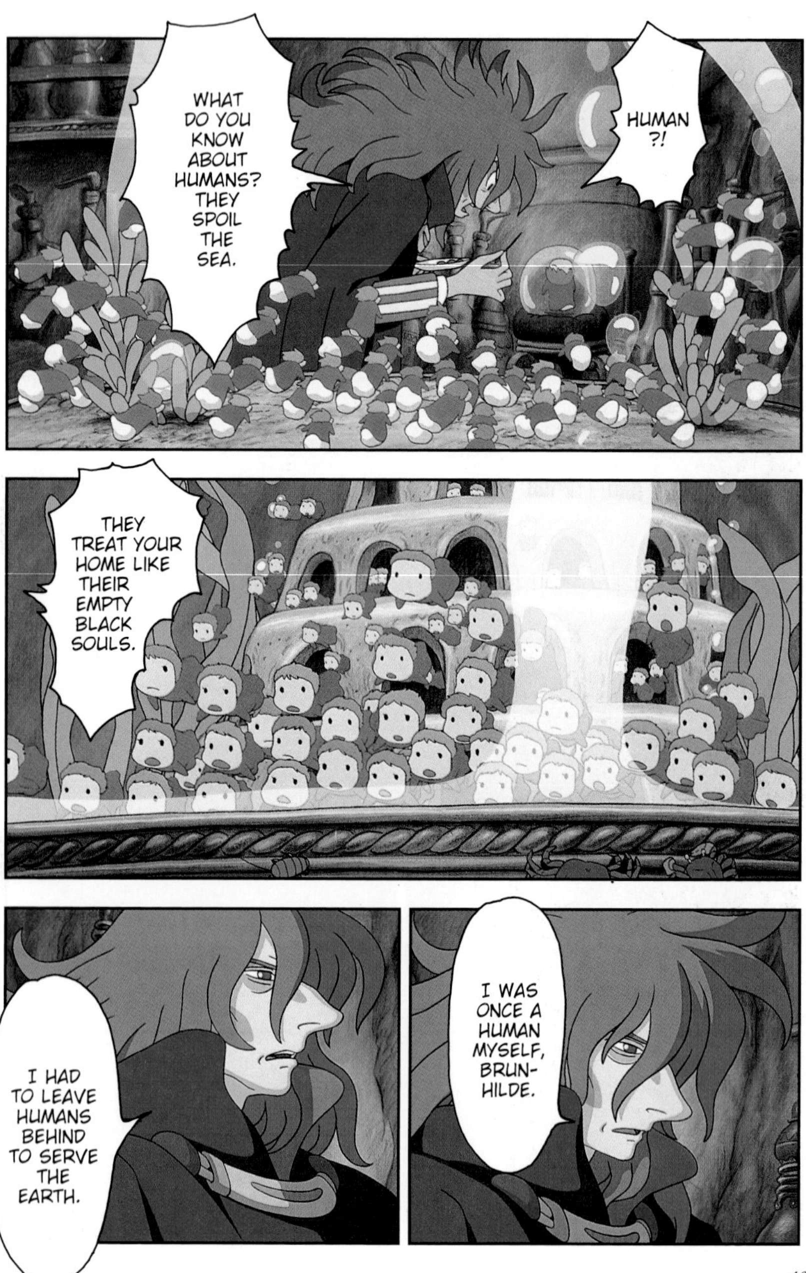
HUMAN ?!
WHAT DO YOU KNOW ABOUT HUMANS? THEY SPOIL THE SEA.
THEY TREAT YOUR HOME LIKE THEIR EMPTY BLACK SOULS.
I WAS ONCE A HUMAN MYSELF, BRUN-HILDE.
I HAD TO LEAVE HUMANS BEHIND TO SERVE THE EARTH.

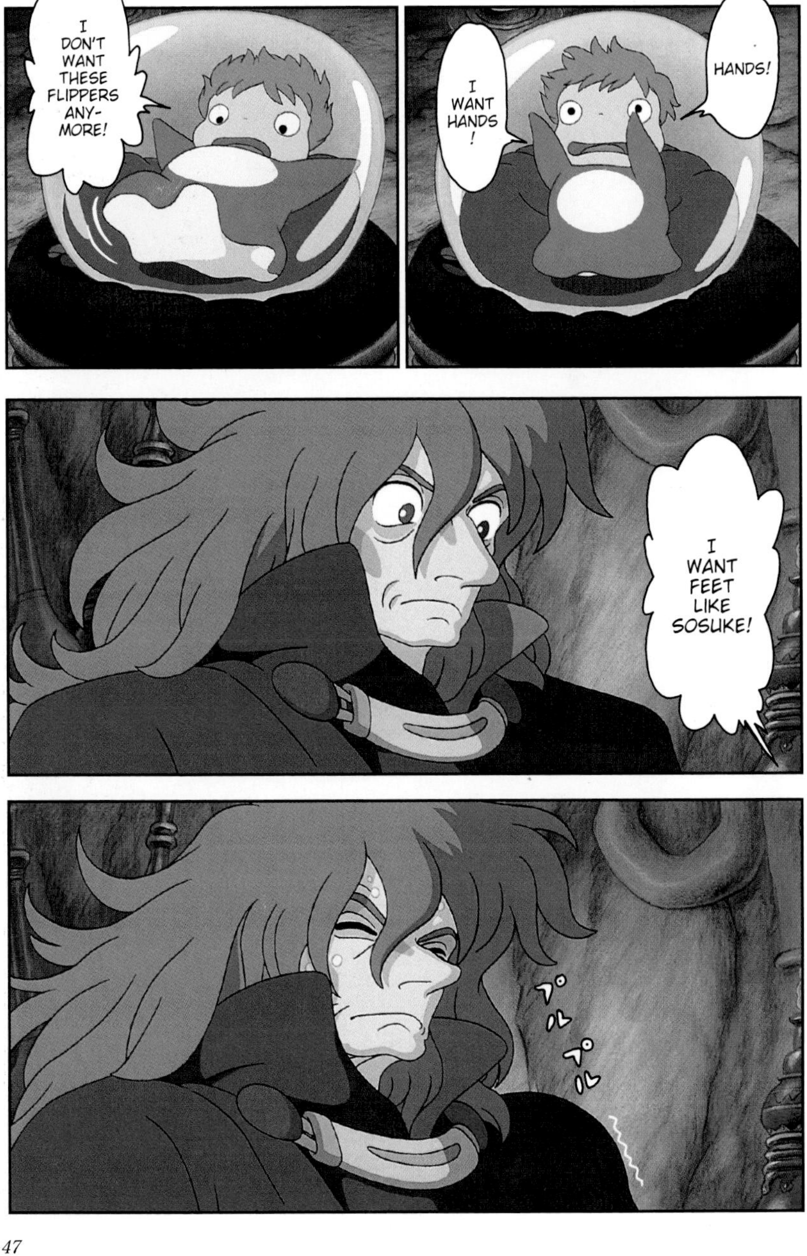
HANDS!
I WANT HANDS!
I DON'T WANT THESE FLIPPERS ANYMORE!
I WANT FEET LIKE SOSUKE!
プルプル

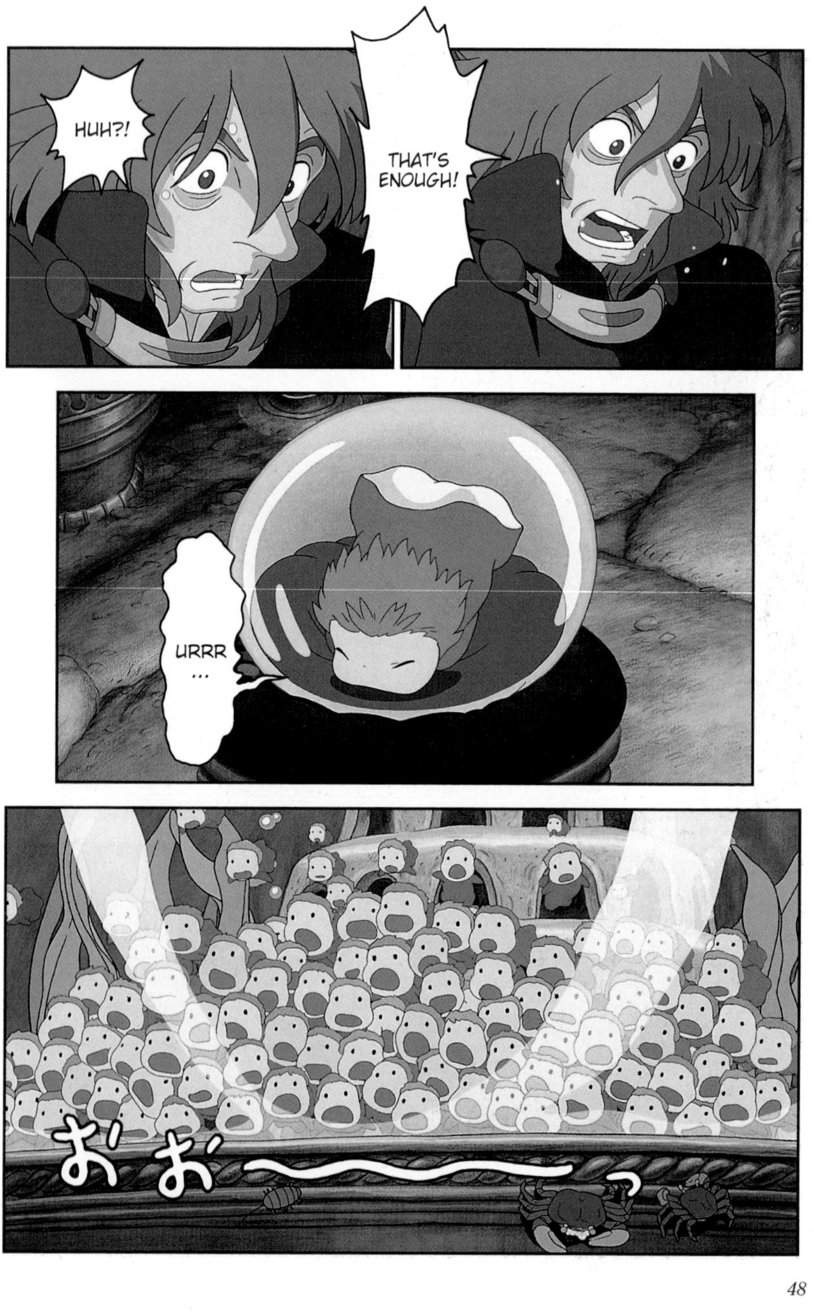
THAT'S ENOUGH!
HUH?!
URRR ...
おお〜〜〜っ

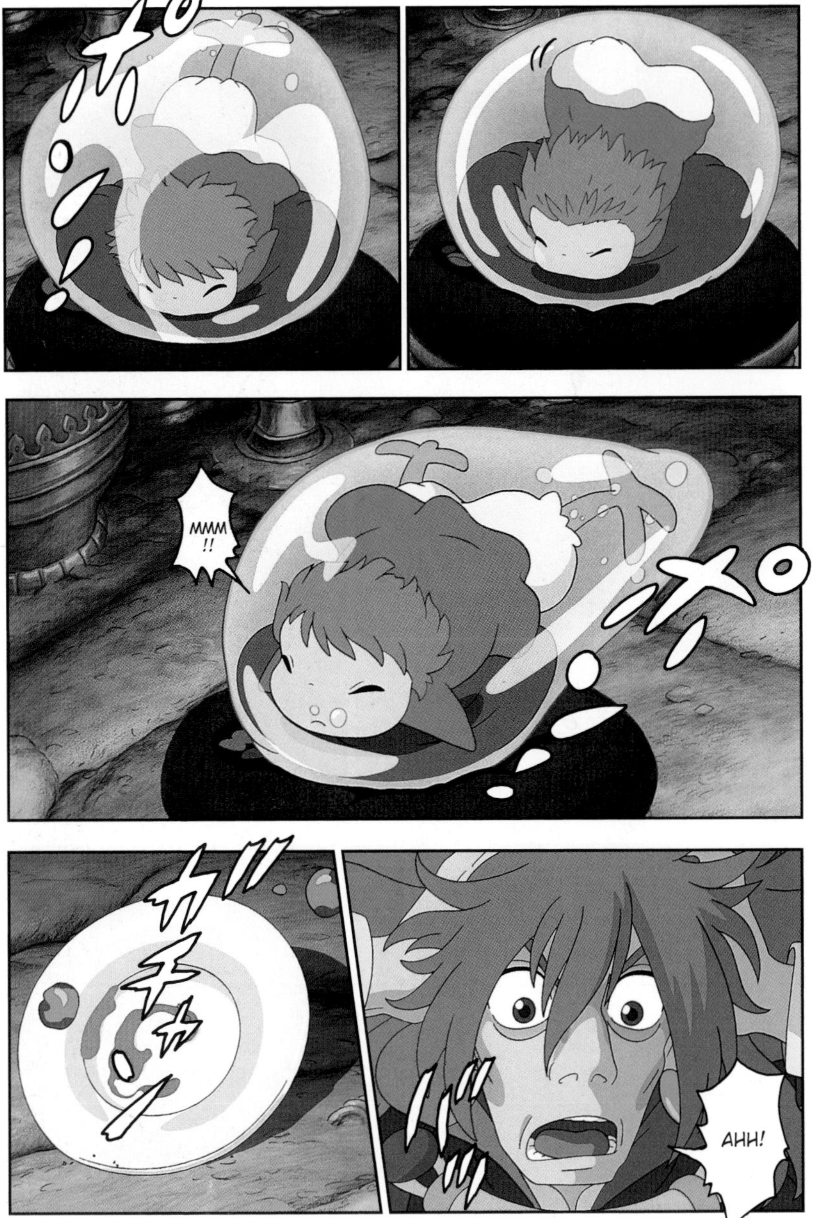
MMM !!
AHH!

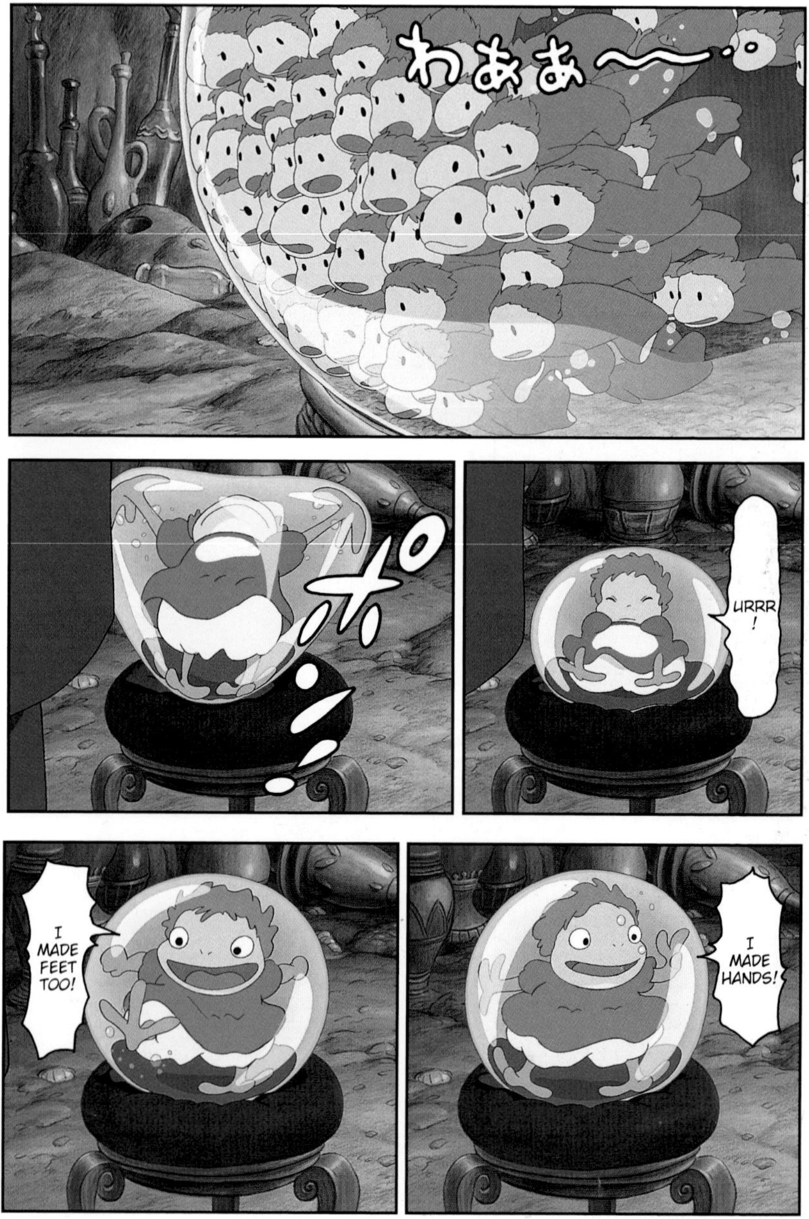
わぁぁ〜〜。
URRR!
ポ
I MADE HANDS!
I MADE FEET TOO!

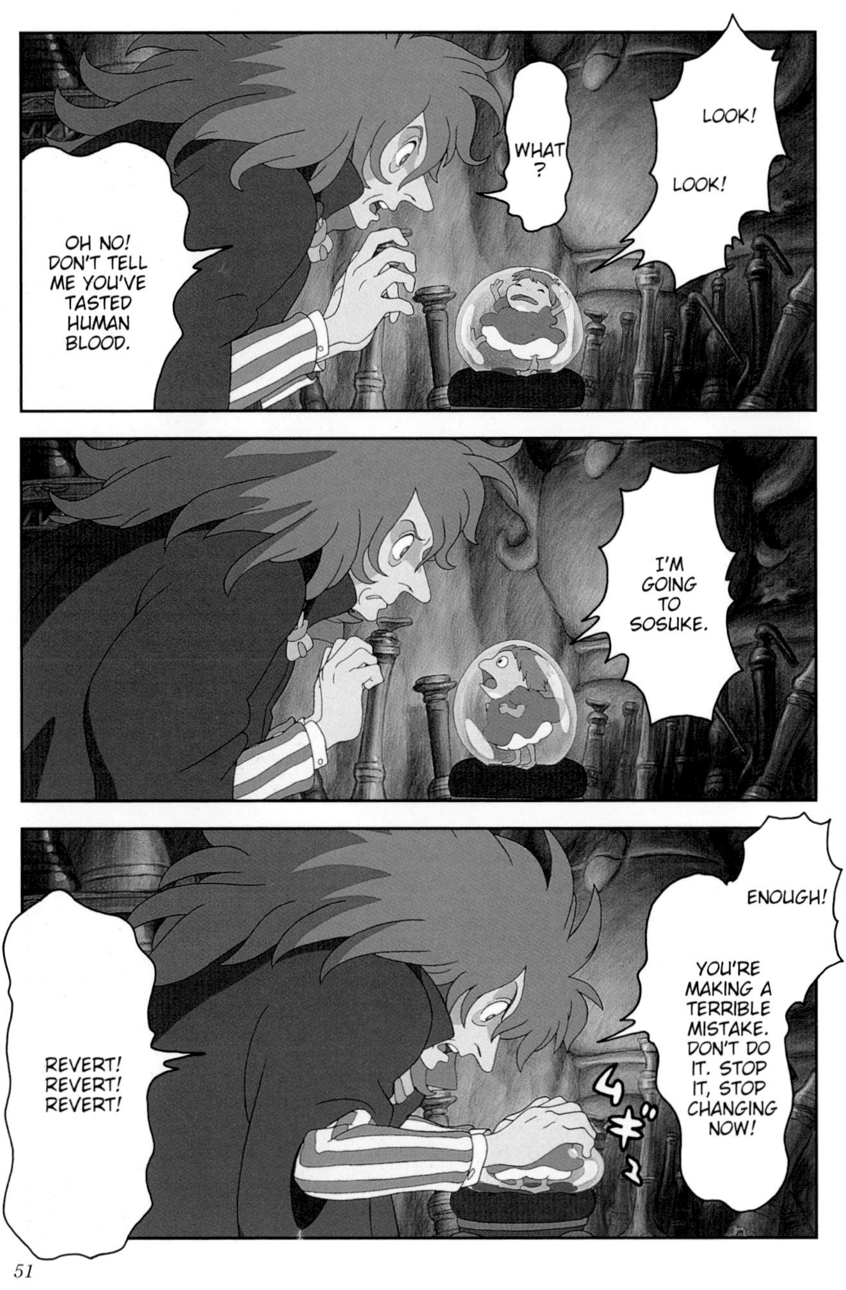
LOOK! LOOK!
WHAT?
OH NO! DON'T TELL ME YOU'VE TASTED HUMAN BLOOD.
I'M GOING TO SOSUKE.
ENOUGH!
YOU'RE MAKING A TERRIBLE MISTAKE. DON'T DO IT. STOP IT, STOP CHANGING NOW!
ムギュ
REVERT! REVERT! REVERT!

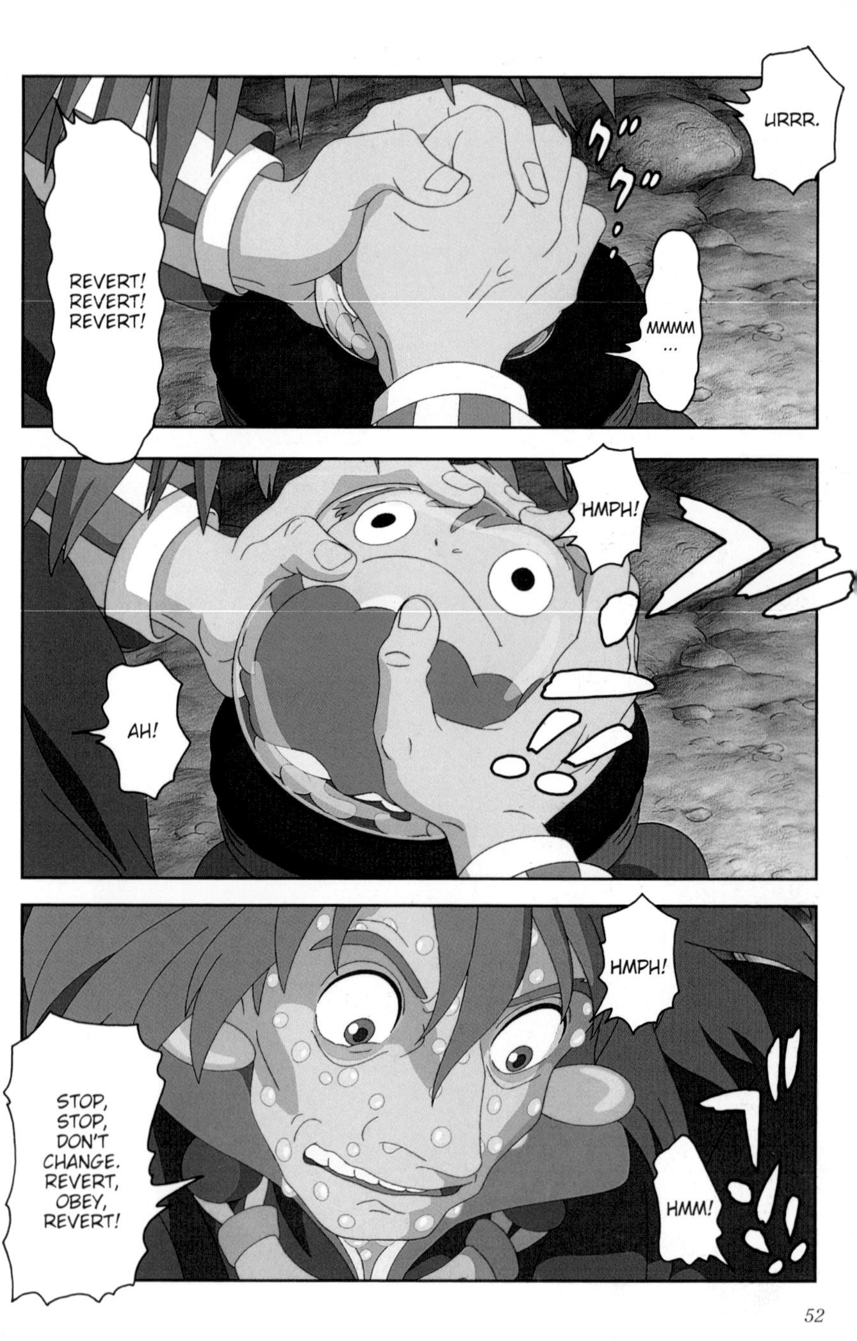
URRR.
MMMM...
REVERT! REVERT! REVERT!
HMPH!
AH!
HMPH!
HMM!
STOP, STOP, DON'T CHANGE. REVERT, OBEY, REVERT!

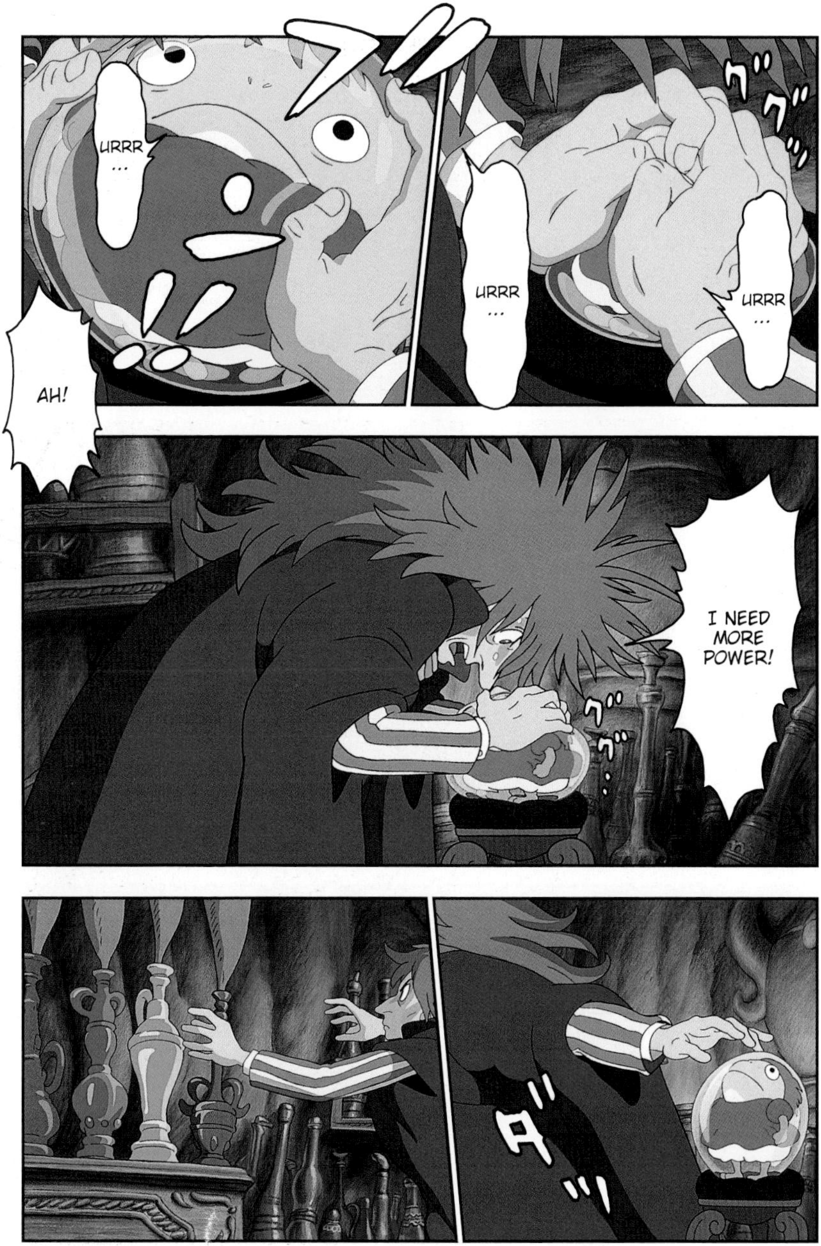
URRR ...
URRR ...
URRR ...
AH!
I NEED MORE POWER!

ゴクゴク
I WANT TO SEE SO-SUKE! LET ME GO! LET ME OUT, LET ME GO.
グイ
ゴクゴク

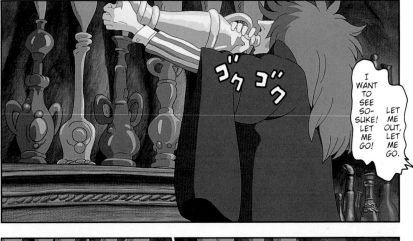

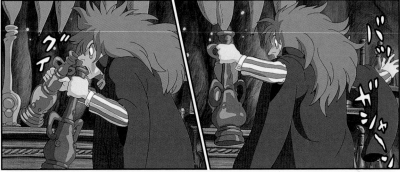

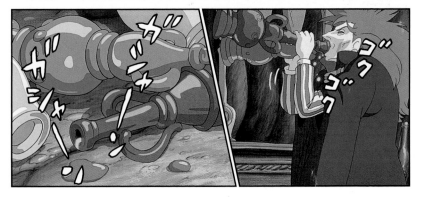

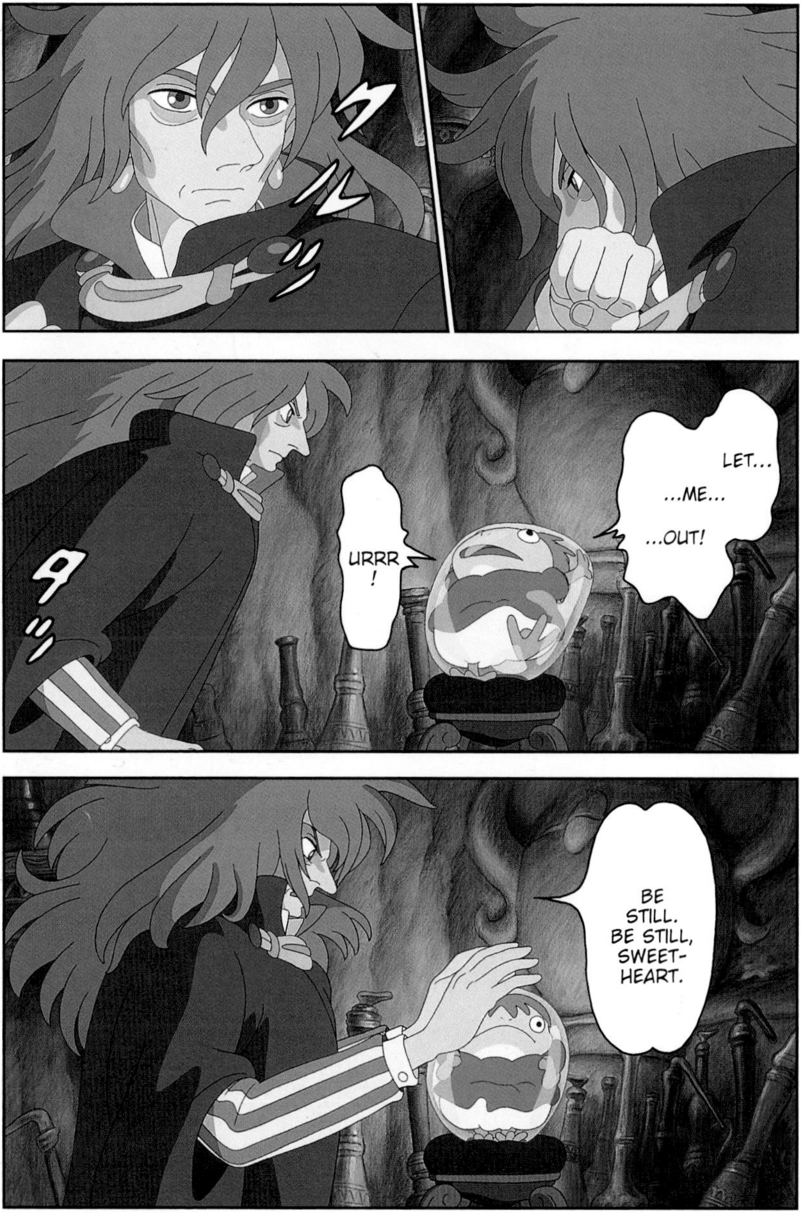
LET... ...ME... ...OUT!
URRR!
BE STILL. BE STILL, SWEET-HEART.

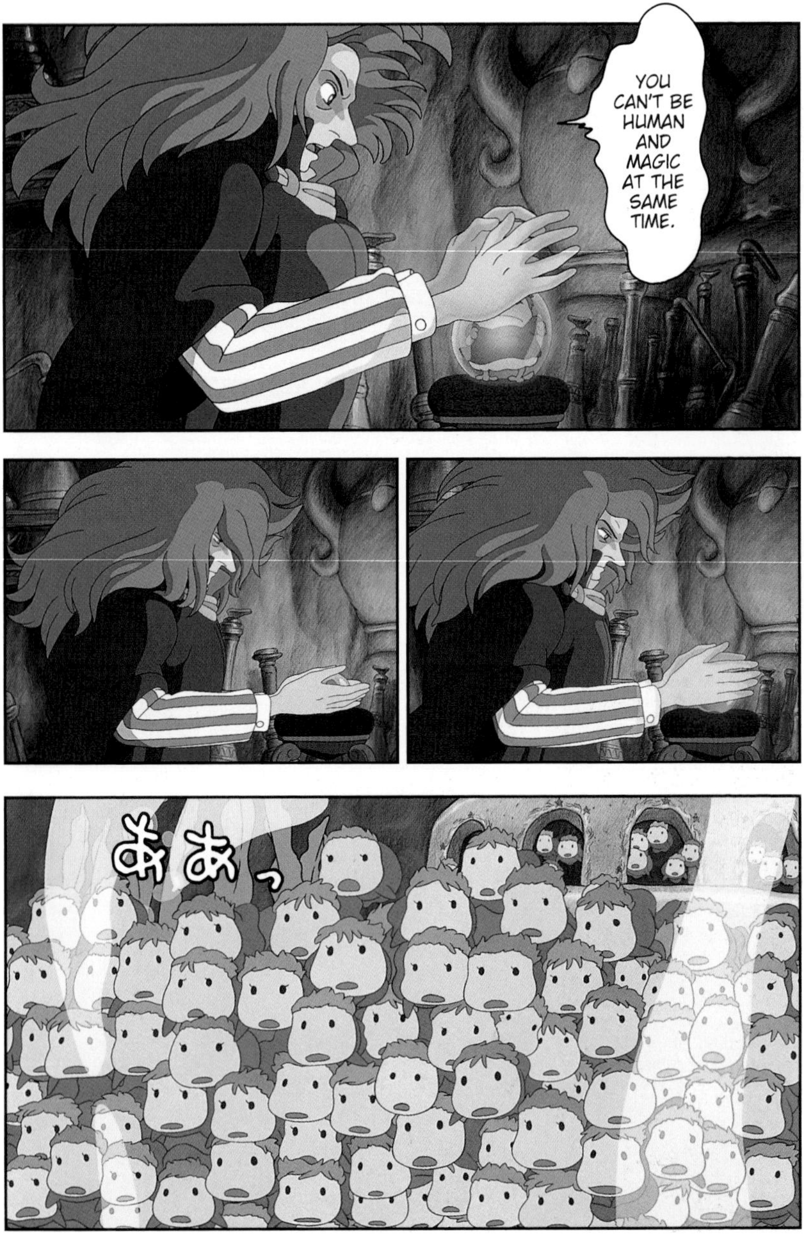
YOU CAN'T BE HUMAN AND MAGIC AT THE SAME TIME.
ああっ

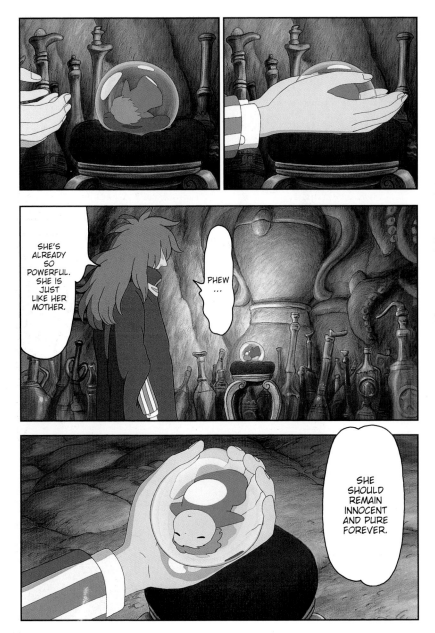

SHE'S ALREADY SO POWERFUL. SHE IS JUST LIKE HER MOTHER.

PHEW ...

SHE SHOULD REMAIN INNOCENT AND PURE FOREVER.

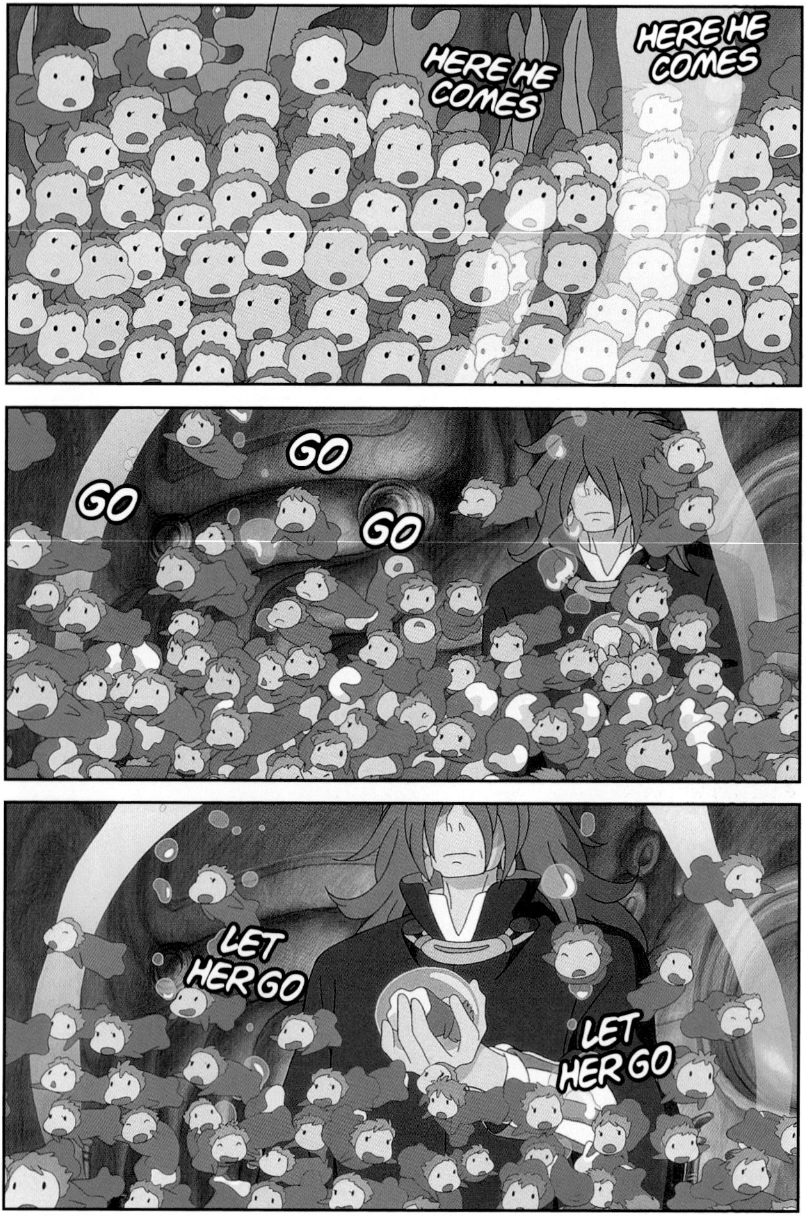
HERE HE COMES
HERE HE COMES
GO
GO
GO
LET HER GO
LET HER GO

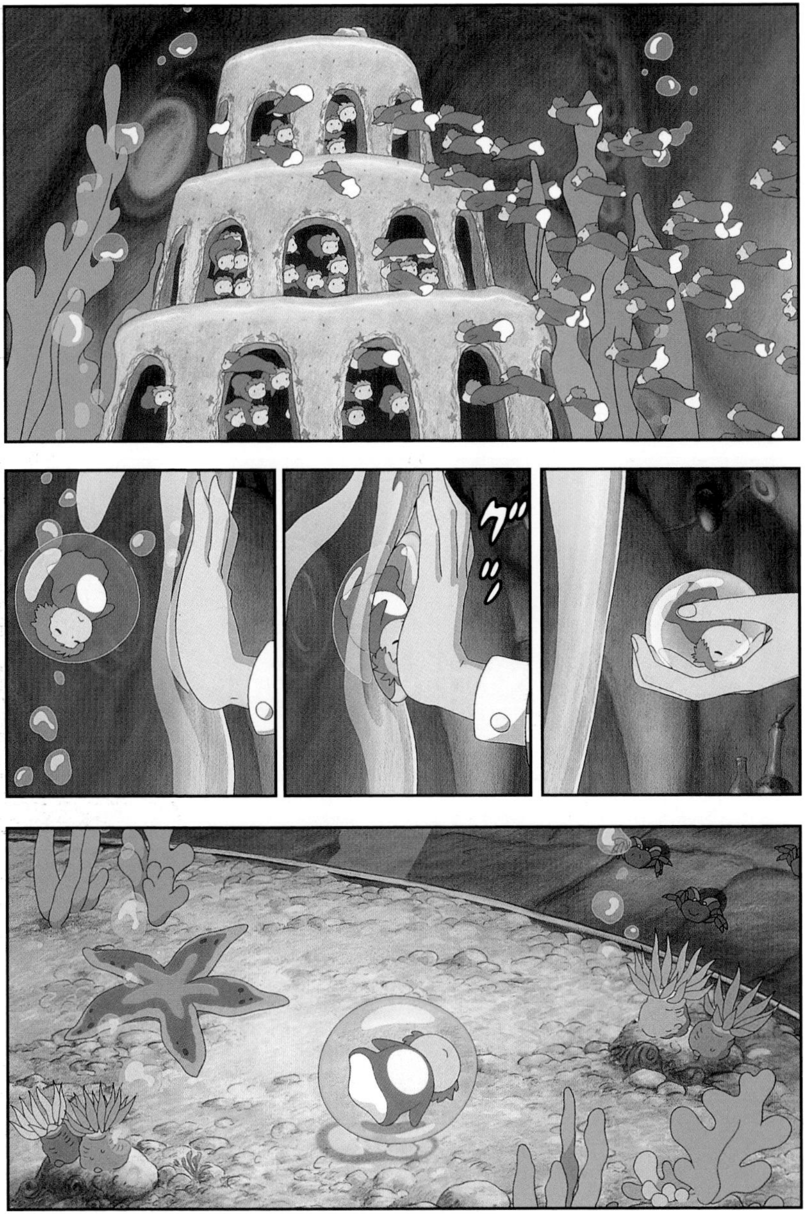
グッ

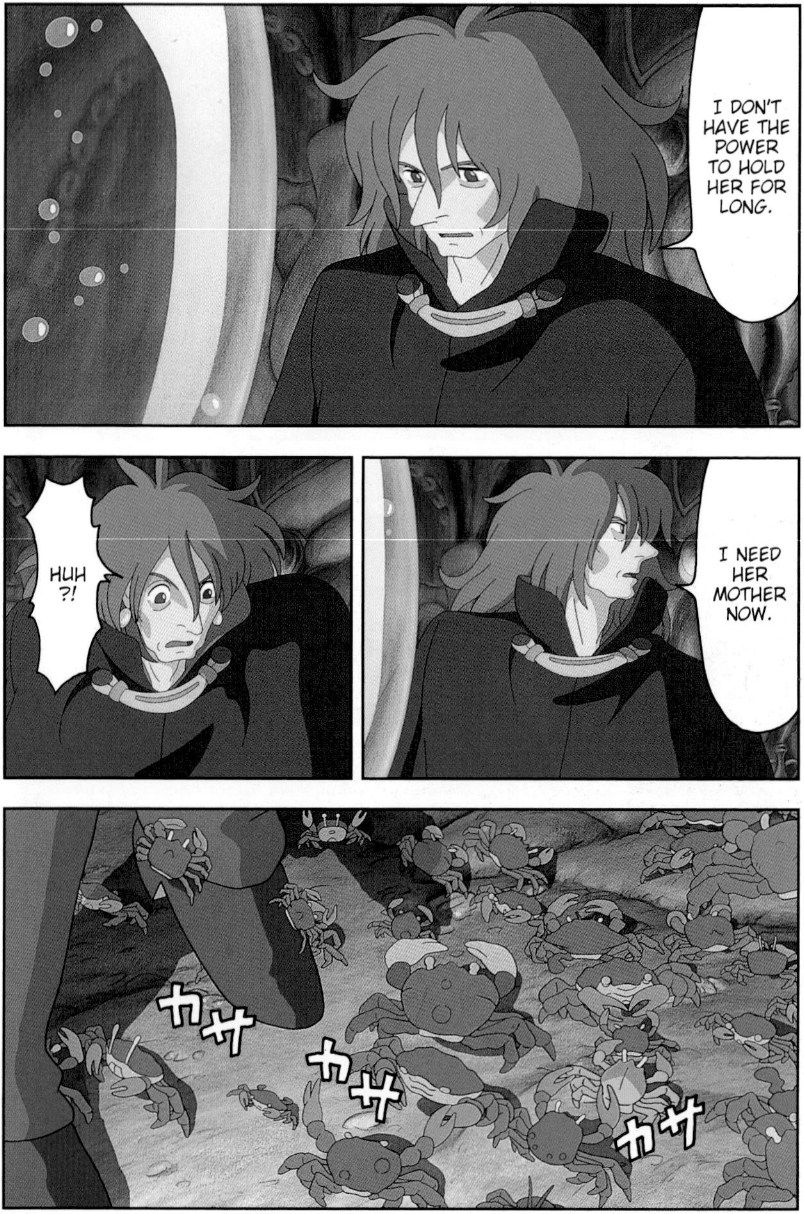
I DON'T HAVE THE POWER TO HOLD HER FOR LONG.
I NEED HER MOTHER NOW.
HUH ?!
カサ
カサ
カサ

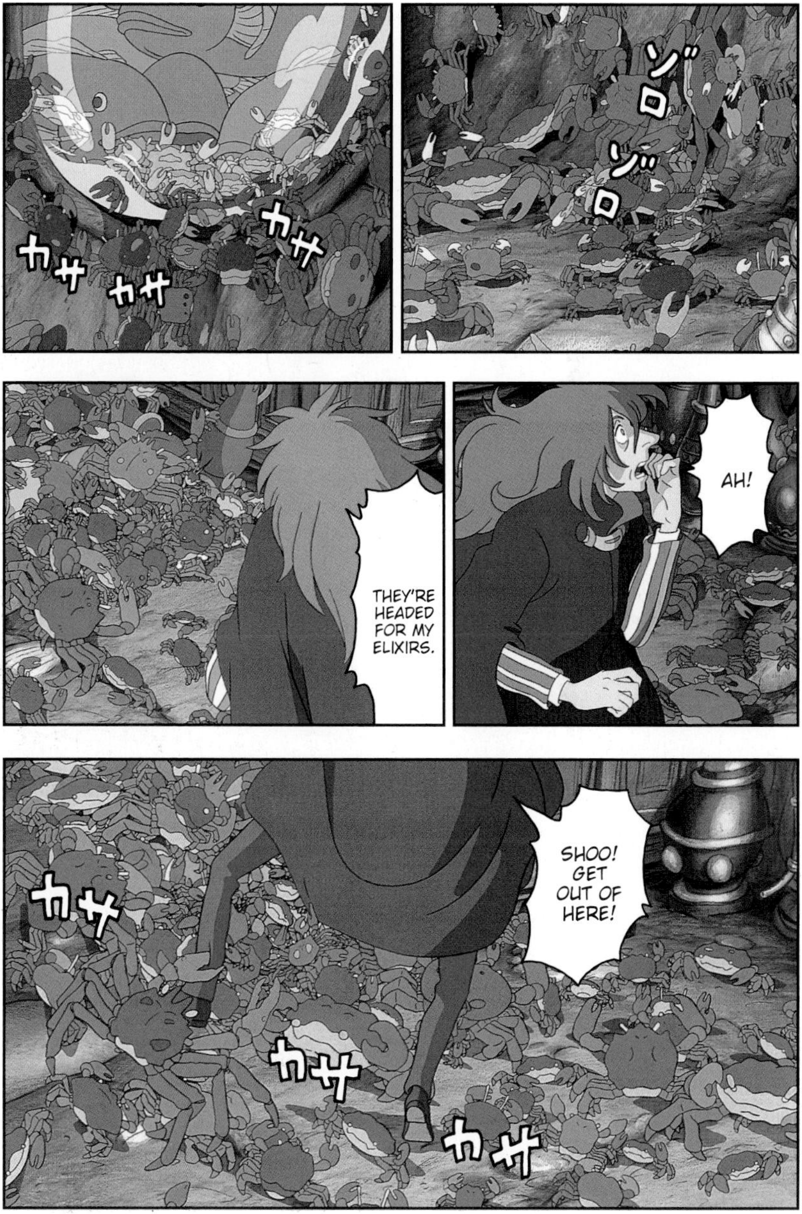
ゾロ
ゾロ
カサ
カサ
カサ
AH!
THEY'RE HEADED FOR MY ELIXIRS.
SHOO! GET OUT OF HERE!
カサ
カサ
カサ

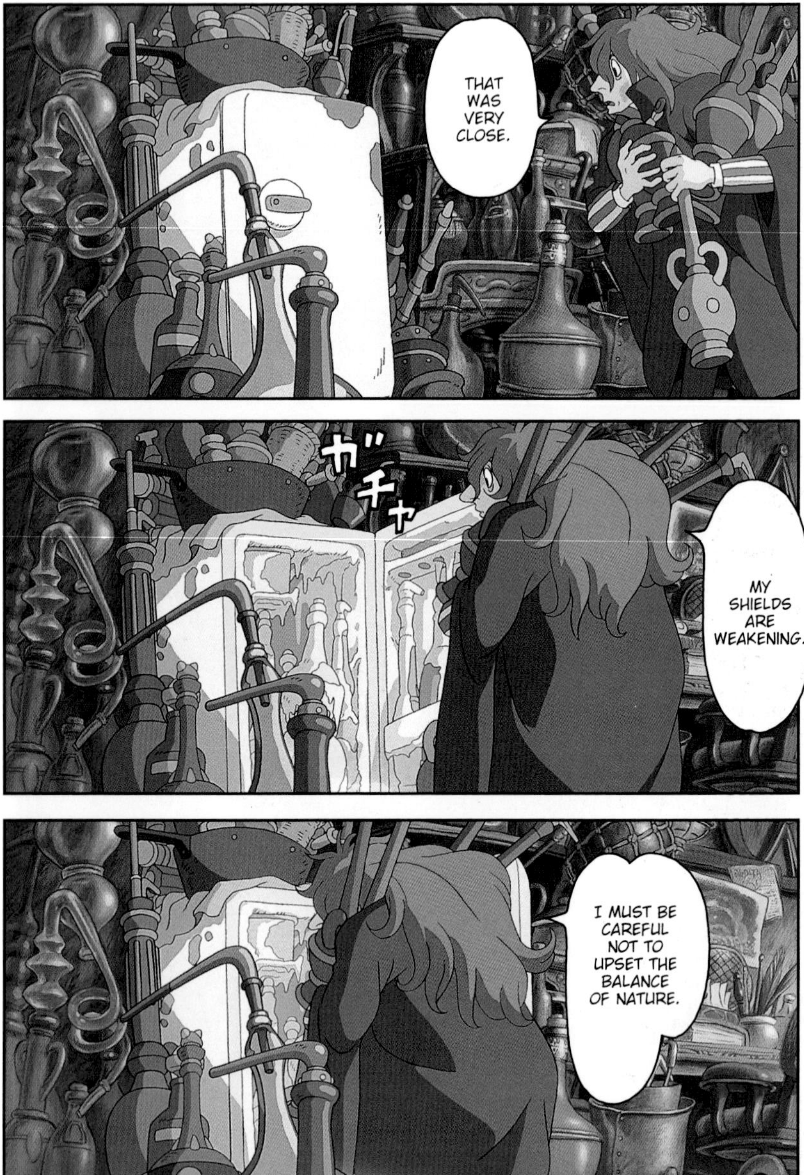
THAT WAS VERY CLOSE.
ガチャ
MY SHIELDS ARE WEAKENING.
I MUST BE CAREFUL NOT TO UPSET THE BALANCE OF NATURE.

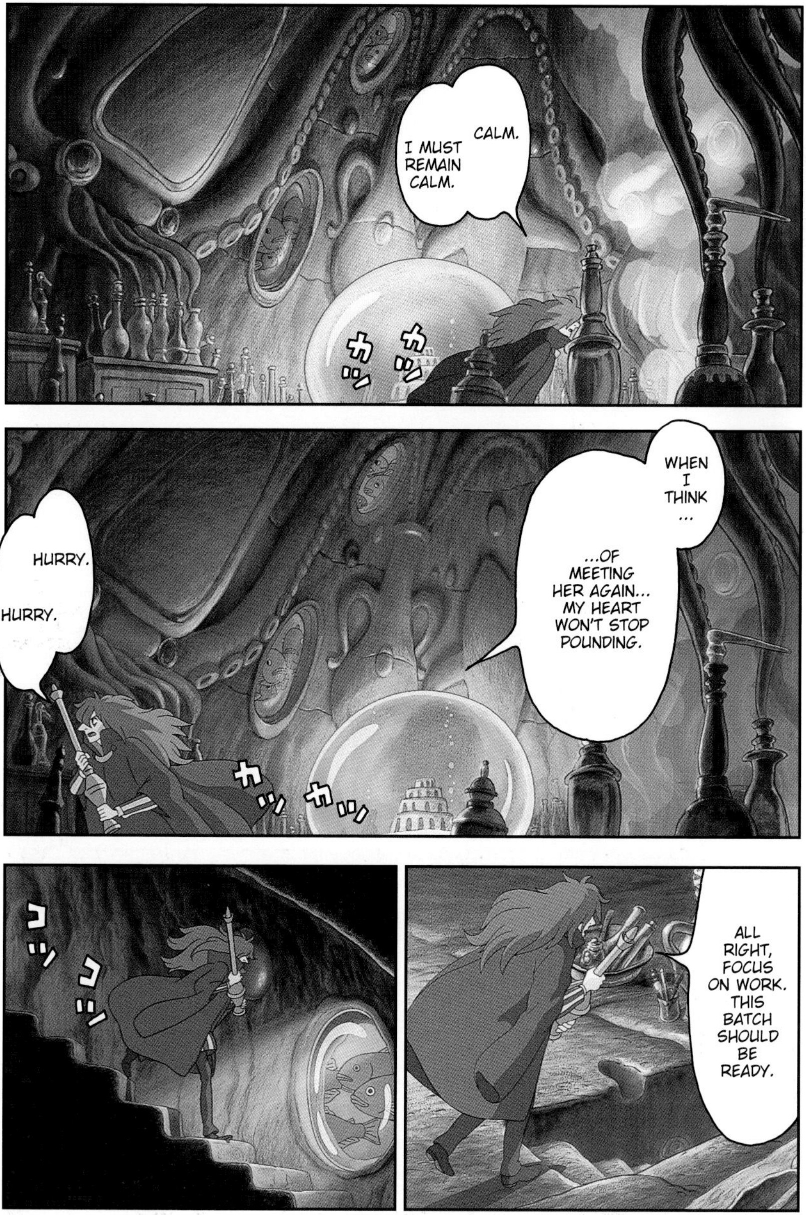
CALM. I MUST REMAIN CALM.
WHEN I THINK...
...OF MEETING HER AGAIN... MY HEART WON'T STOP POUNDING.
HURRY.
HURRY.
ALL RIGHT, FOCUS ON WORK. THIS BATCH SHOULD BE READY.

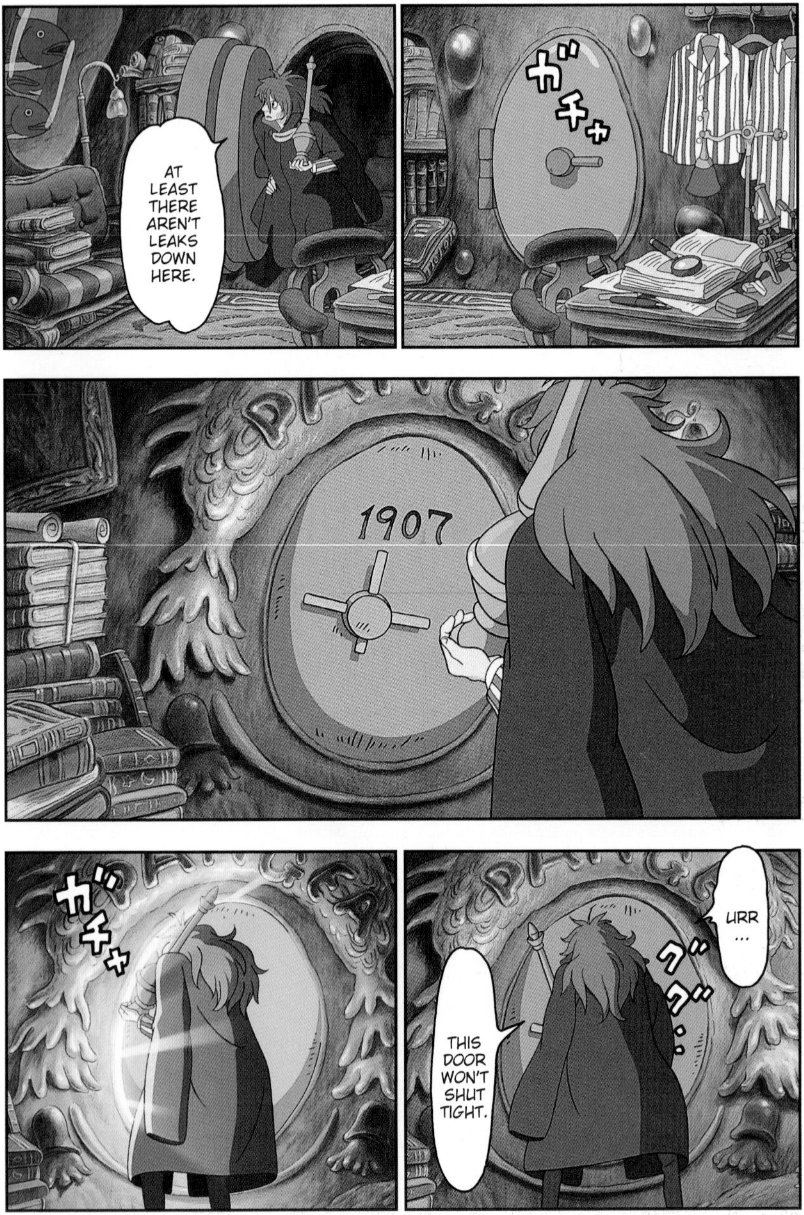
ガチャ
AT LEAST THERE AREN'T LEAKS DOWN HERE.
1907
URR ...
ググ...
THIS DOOR WON'T SHUT TIGHT.
ガチャ

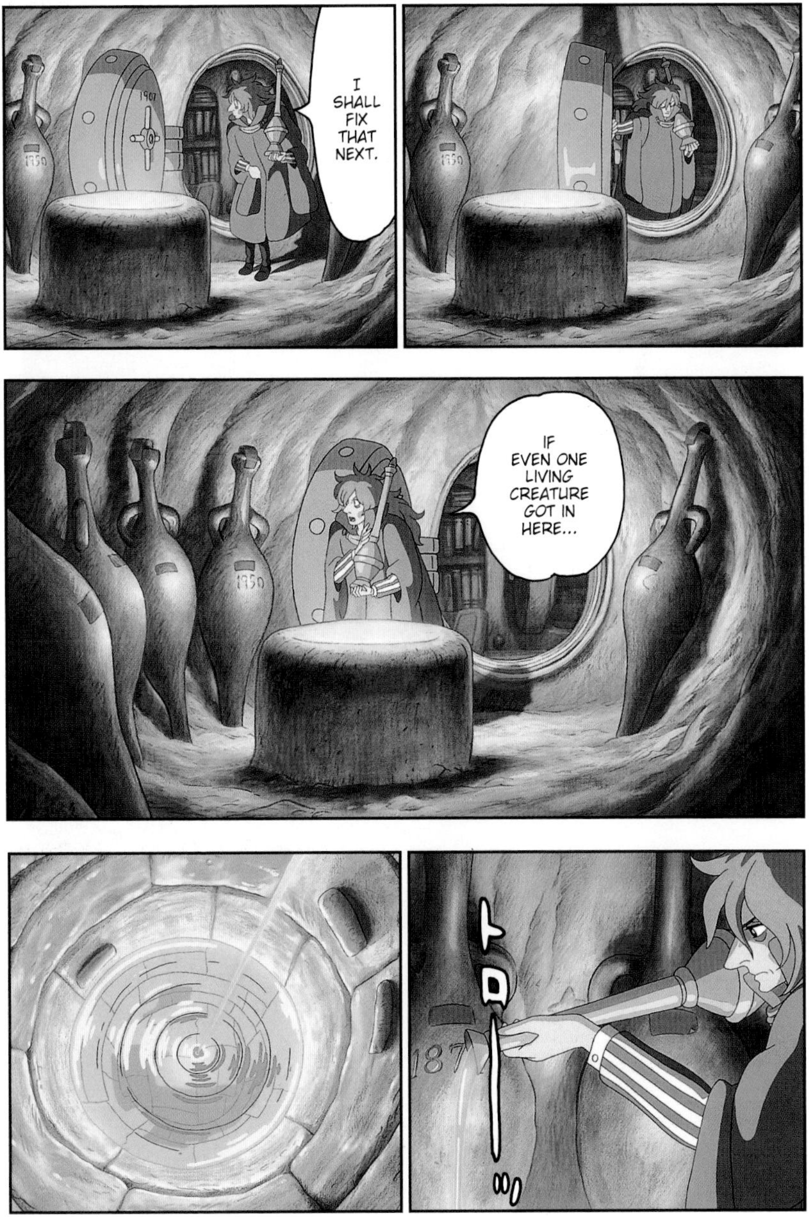
I SHALL FIX THAT NEXT.
IF EVEN ONE LIVING CREATURE GOT IN HERE...
トロー

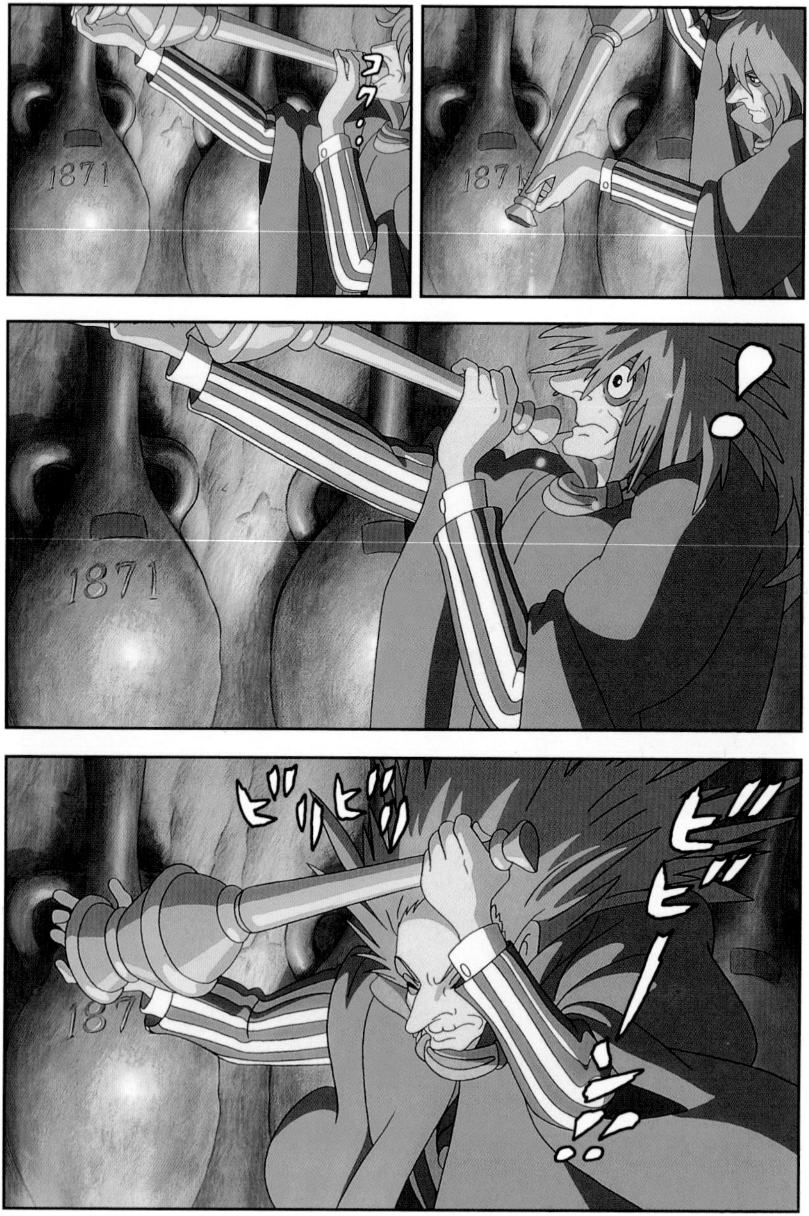
1871
コク・・
1871
!
!
ビビー
ビリビリ
!!

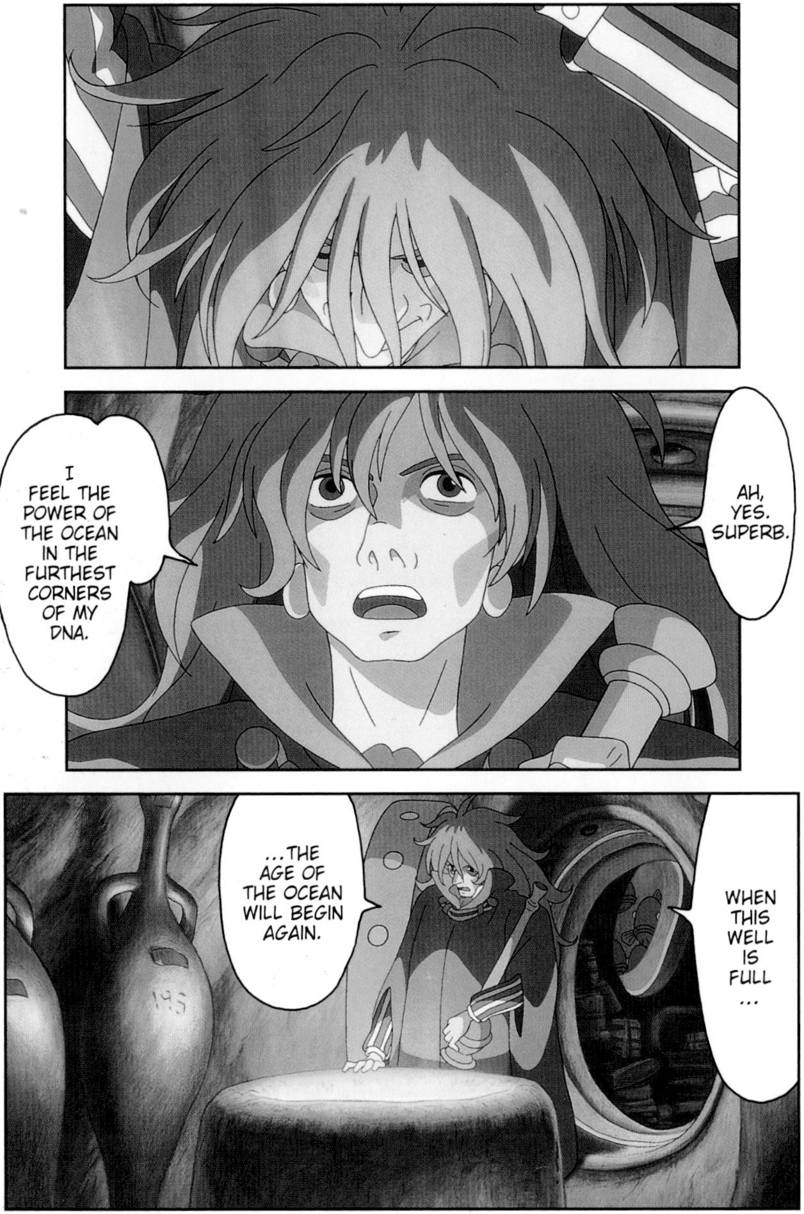
AH, YES. SUPERB.
I FEEL THE POWER OF THE OCEAN IN THE FURTHEST CORNERS OF MY DNA.
WHEN THIS WELL IS FULL ...
...THE AGE OF THE OCEAN WILL BEGIN AGAIN.

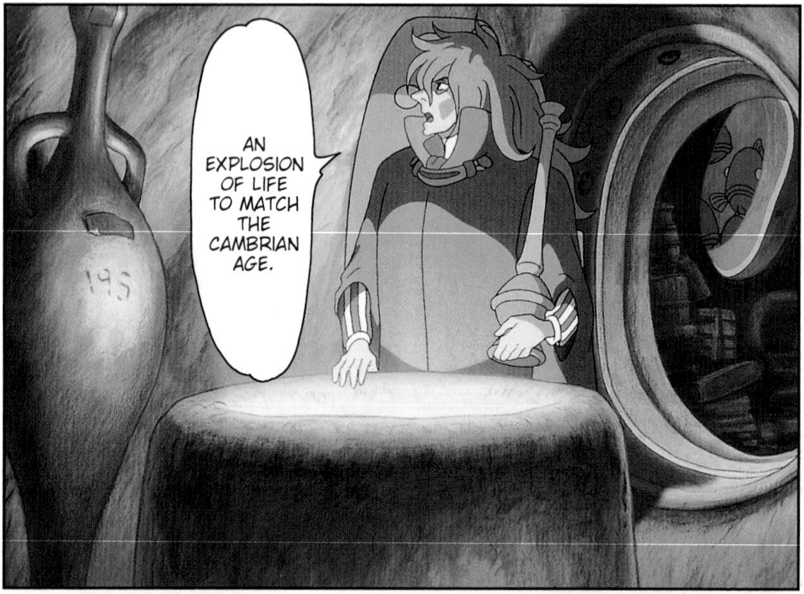
AN EXPLOSION OF LIFE TO MATCH THE CAMBRIAN AGE.

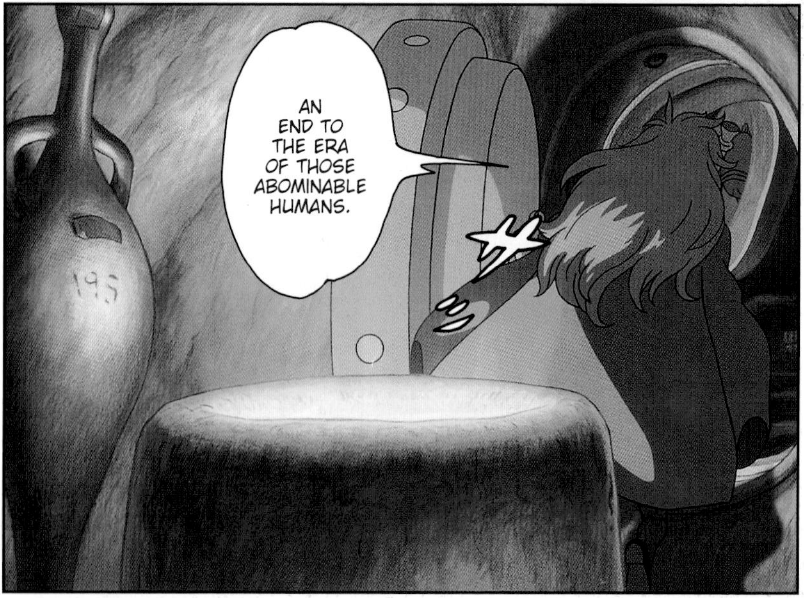
AN END TO THE ERA OF THOSE ABOMINABLE HUMANS.

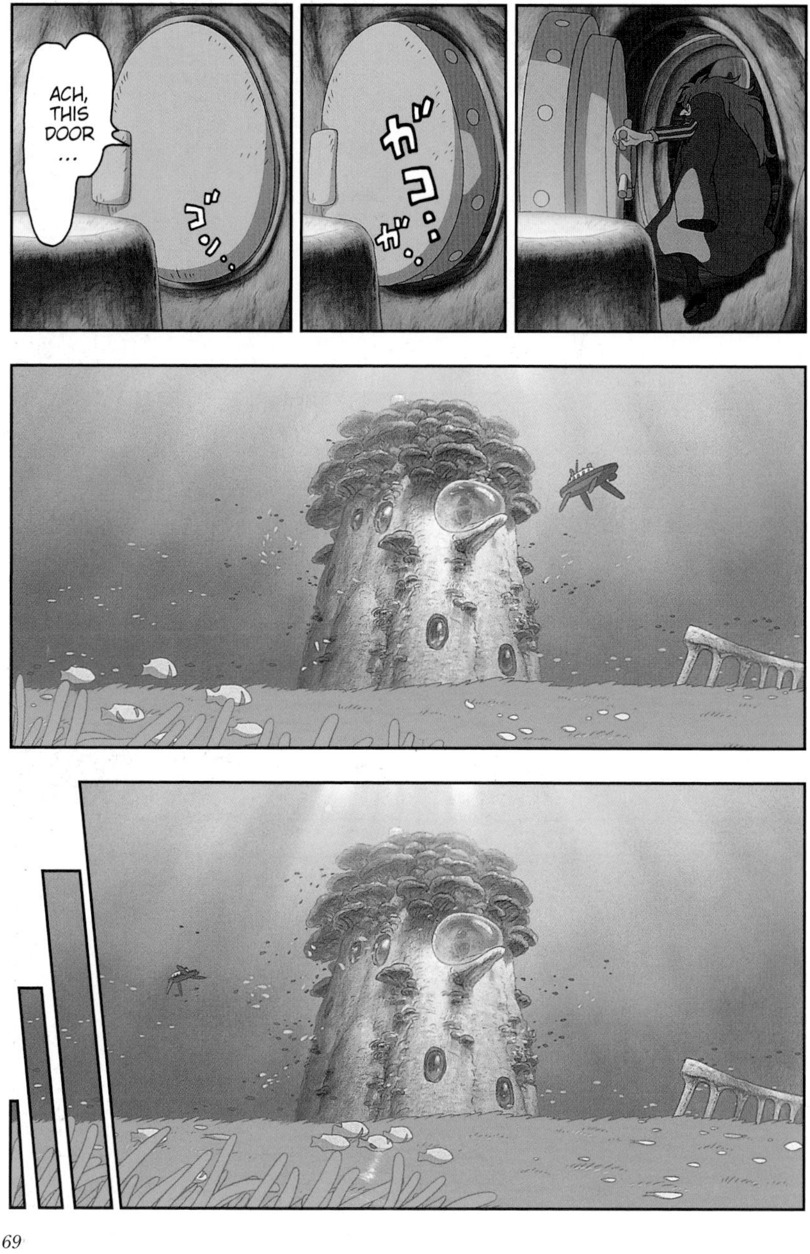
ガコ..
ガ..
ACH, THIS DOOR ...
ゴン..

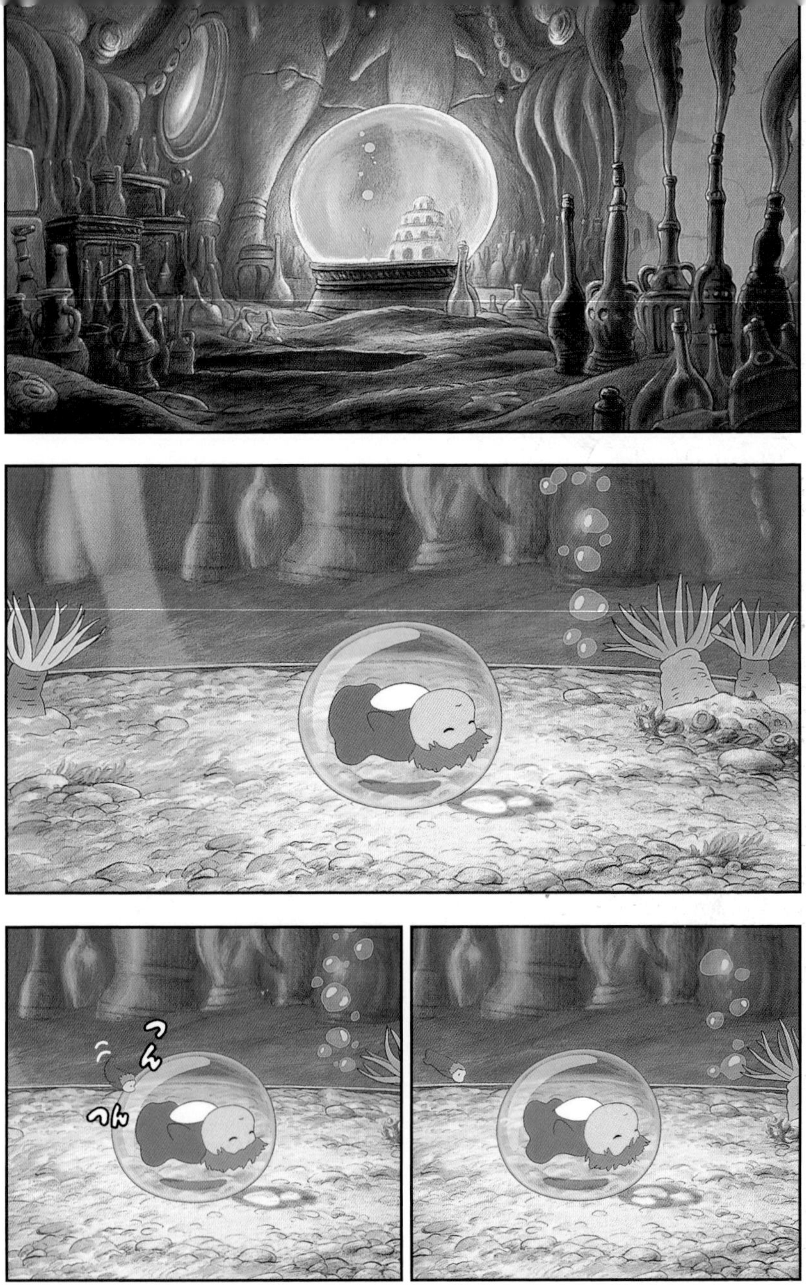
つん
つん

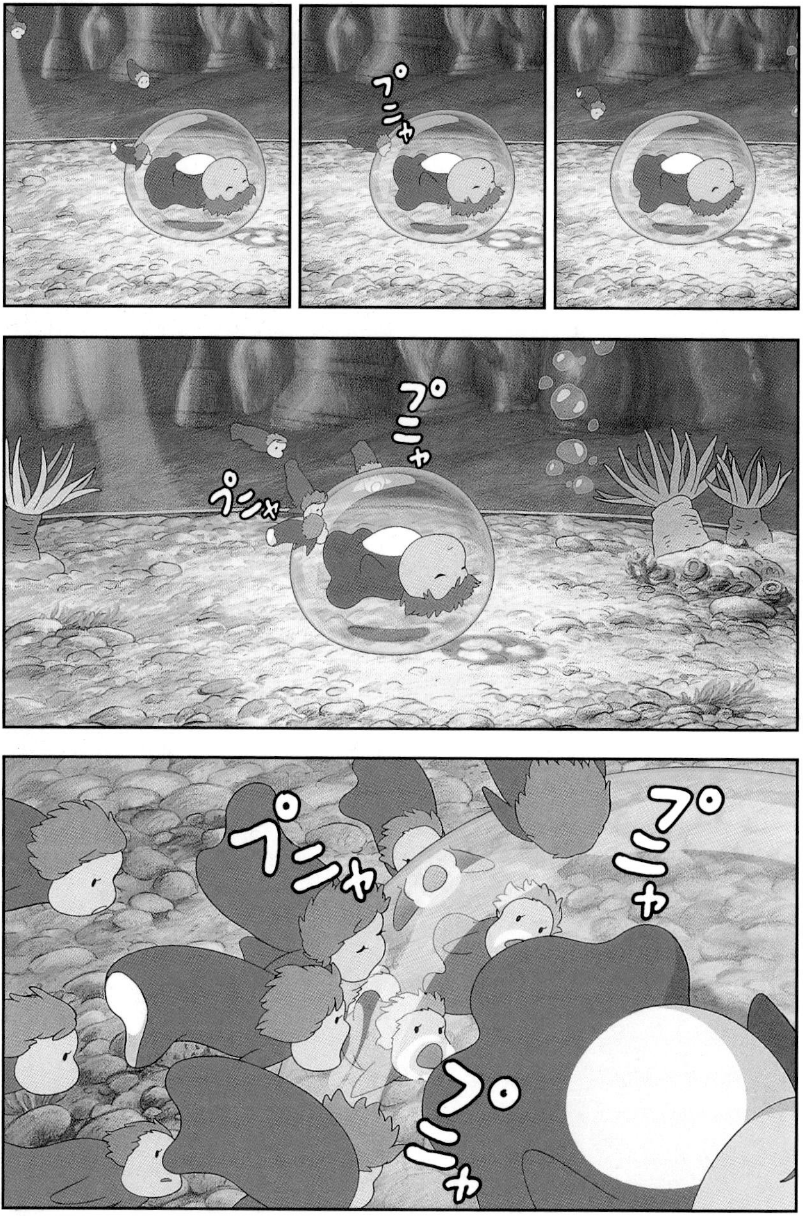
プニャ
プニャ
プニャ
プニャ
プニャ
プニャ

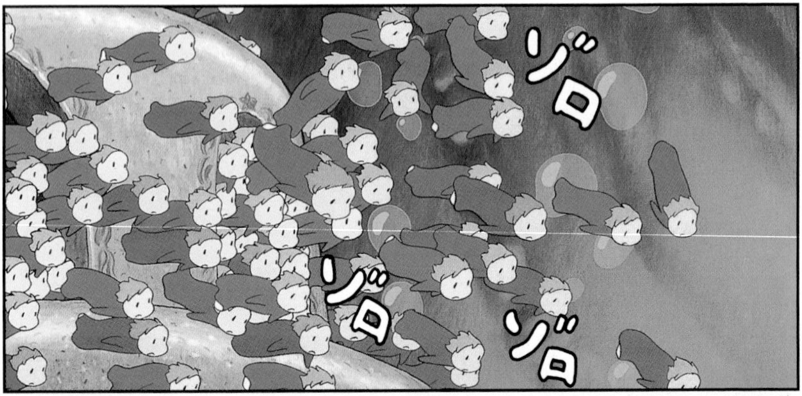
ゾロ
ゾロ
ゾロ
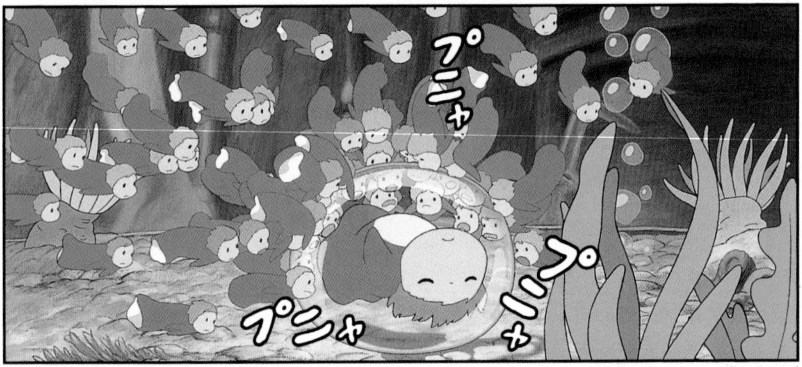
プニャ
プニャ
プニャ
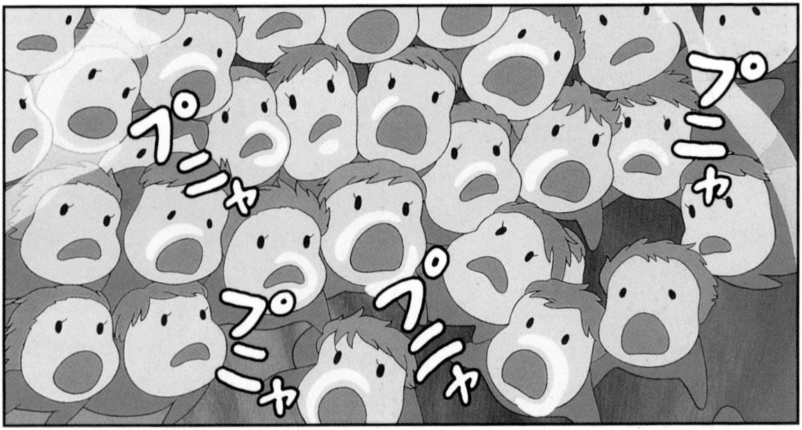
プニャ
プニャ
プニャ
プニャ

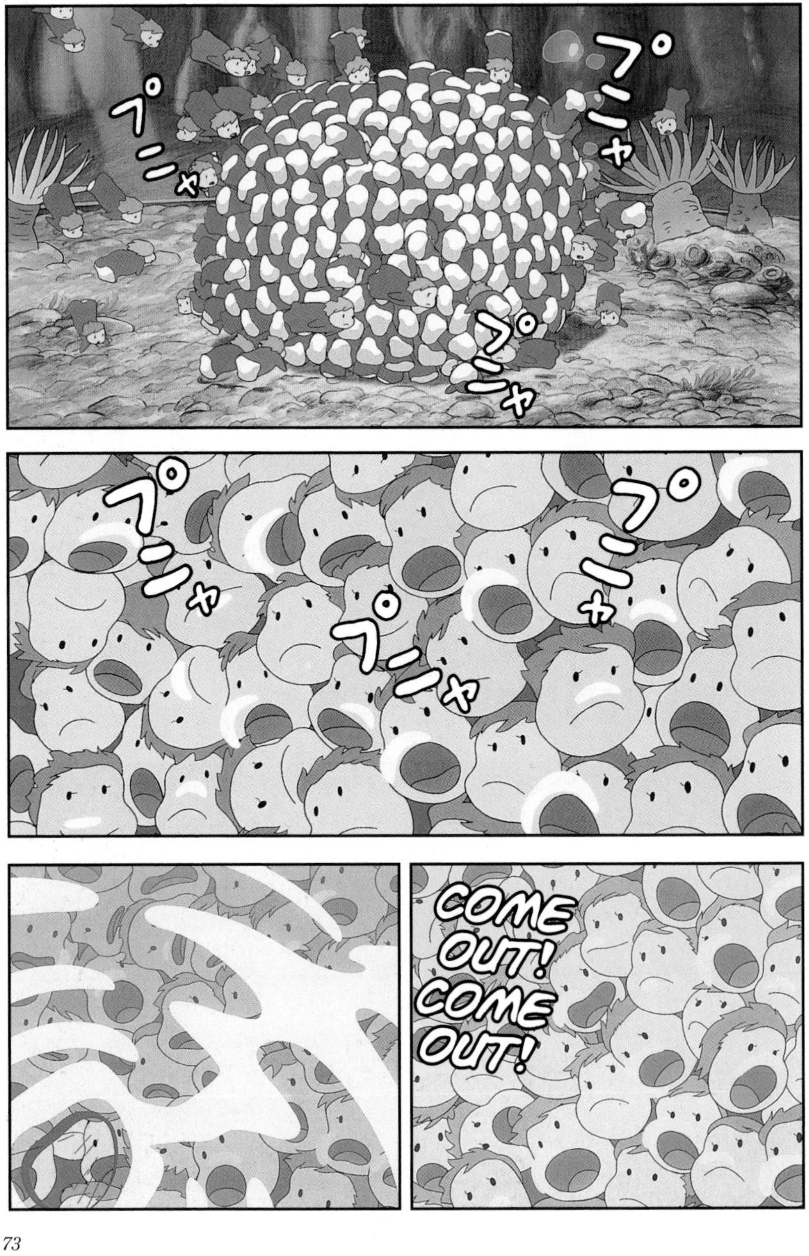
プニャ
プニャ
プニャ
プニャ
プニャ
プニャ
COME OUT! COME OUT!

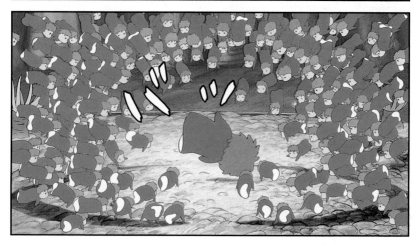

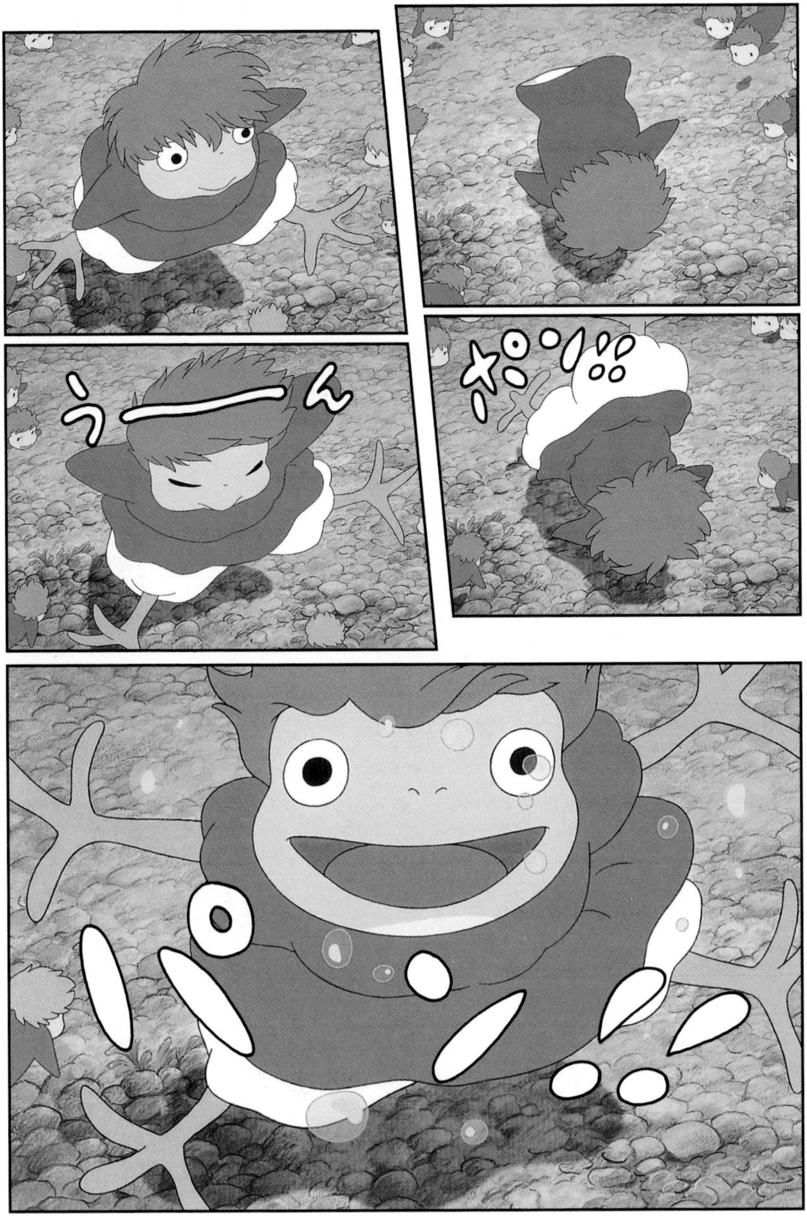
ポン!!
うーーん

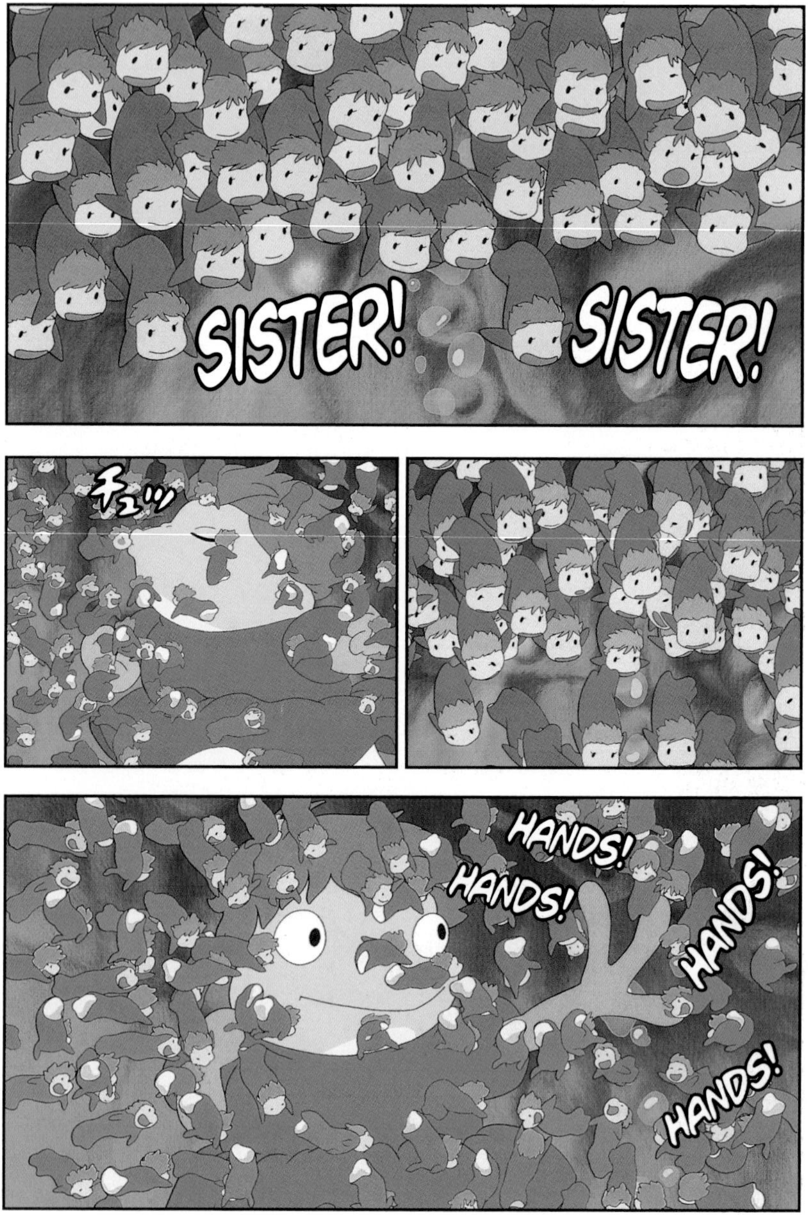
SISTER!
SISTER!
チュッ
HANDS!
HANDS!
HANDS!
HANDS!

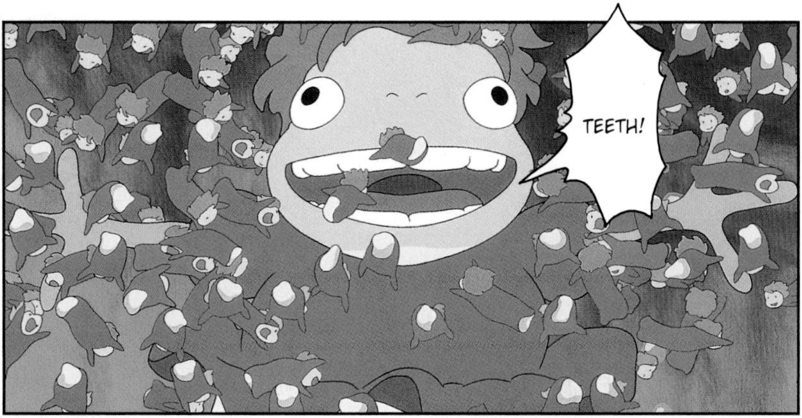
TEETH!

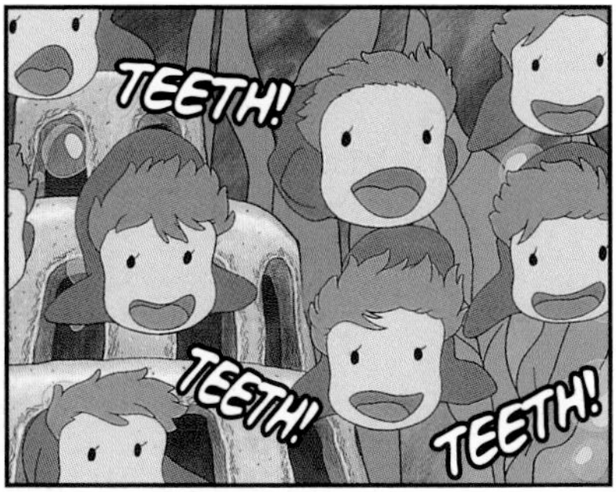
TEETH!
TEETH!
TEETH!

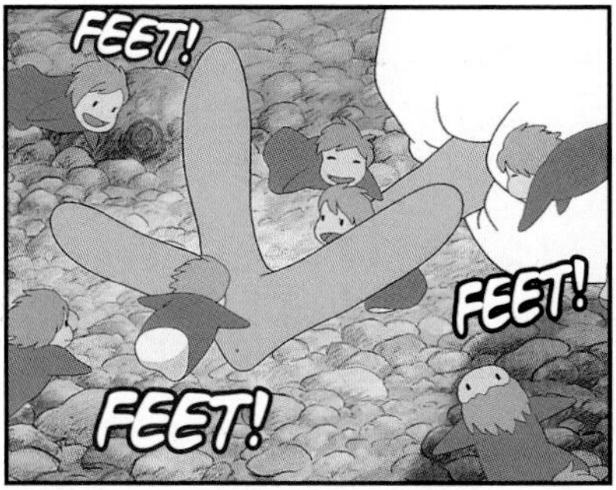
FEET!
FEET!
FEET!

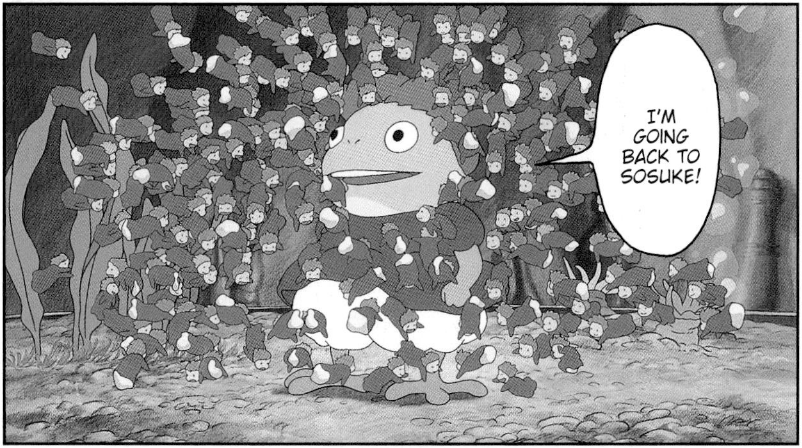
I'M GOING BACK TO SOSUKE!

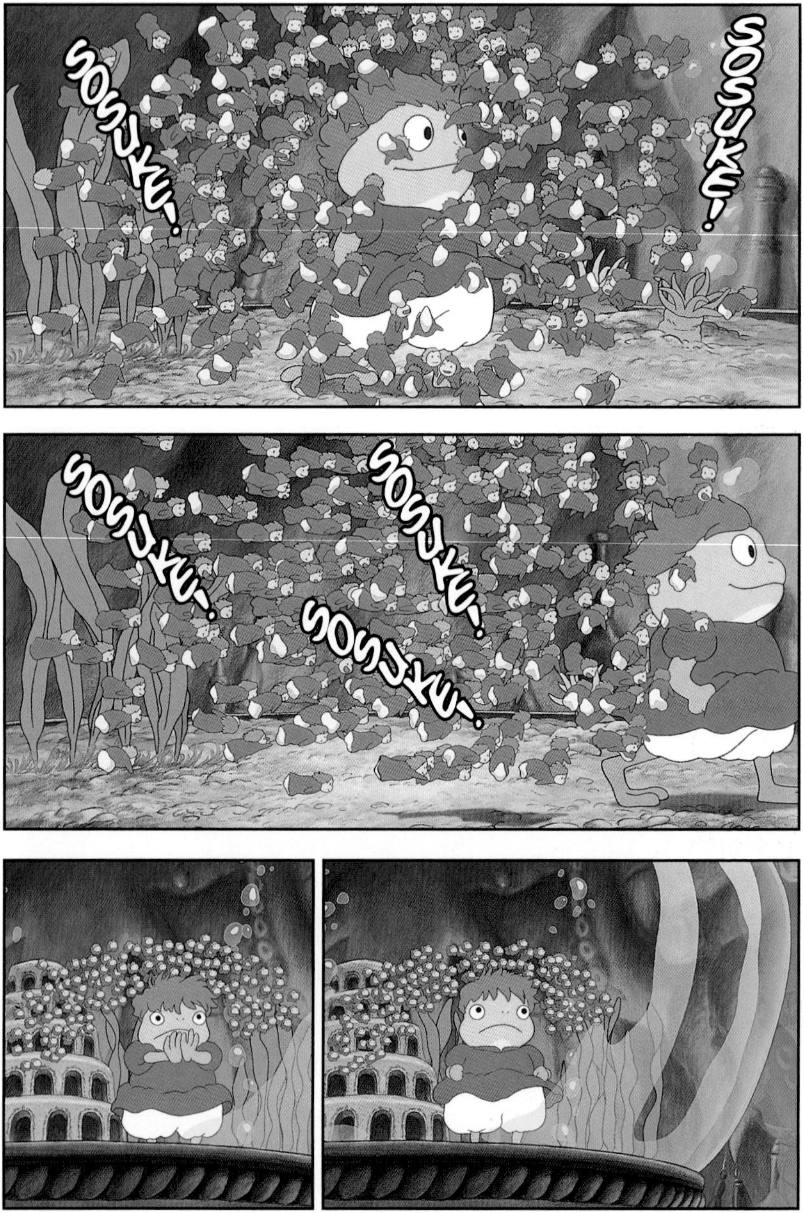
SOSUKE!
SOSUKE!
SOSUKE!
SOSUKE!
SOSUKE!

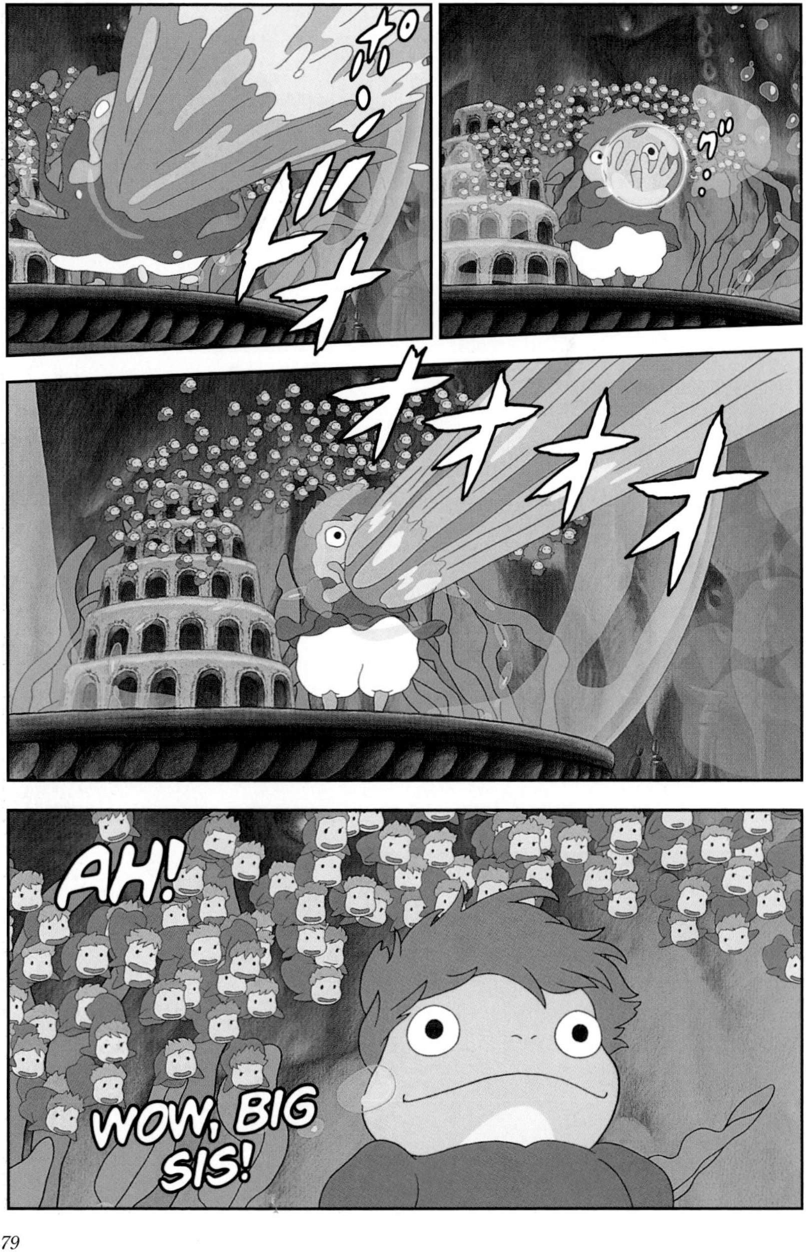
グ
ポ
ドォ
オオオオ
AH!
WOW, BIG SIS!

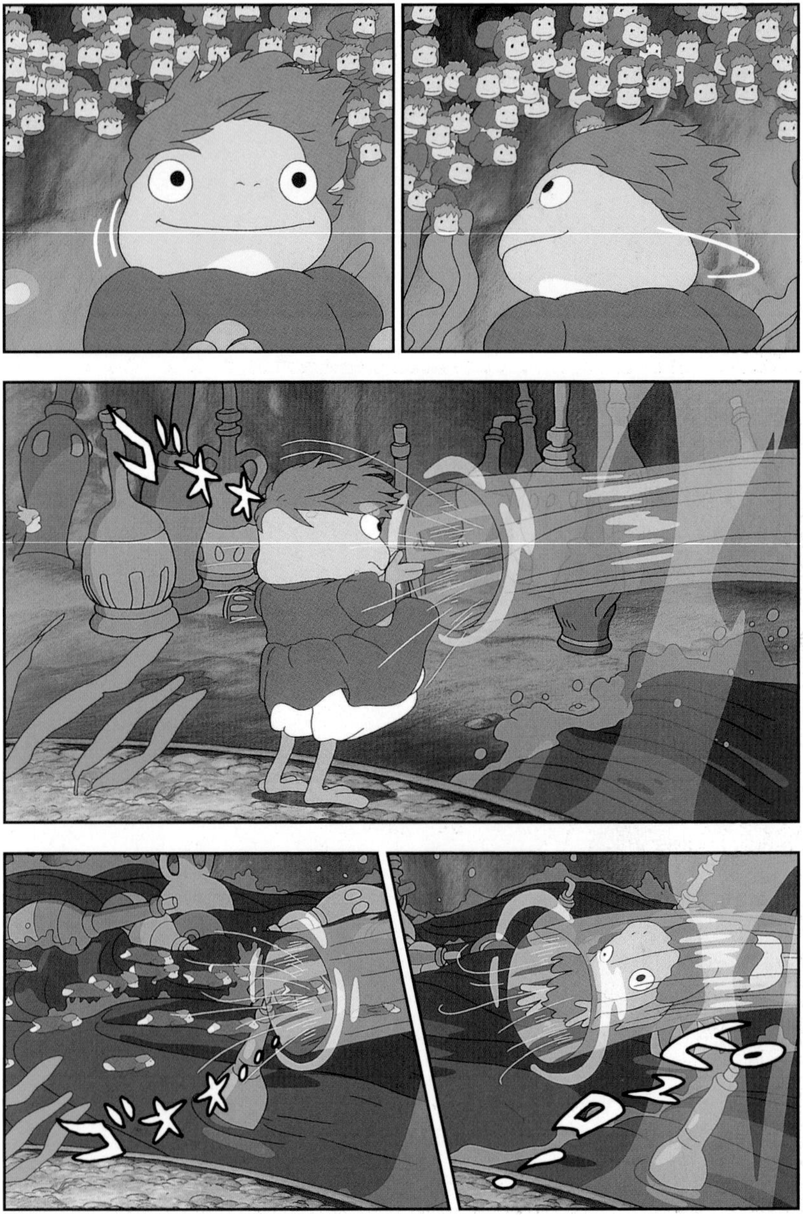
ゴ☆☆
ゴ☆

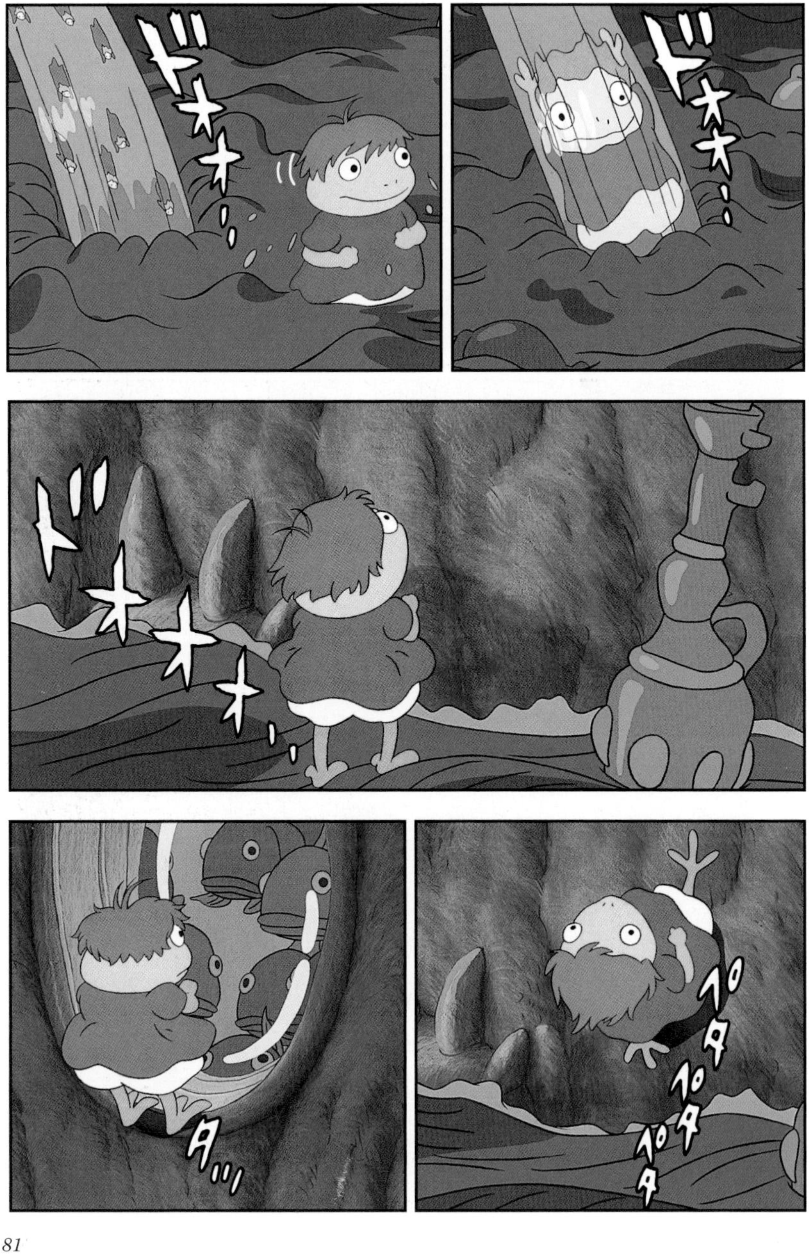
ドォォ・・
ドォォ・・
ドォォォ・・
パタパタパタ
ダッ

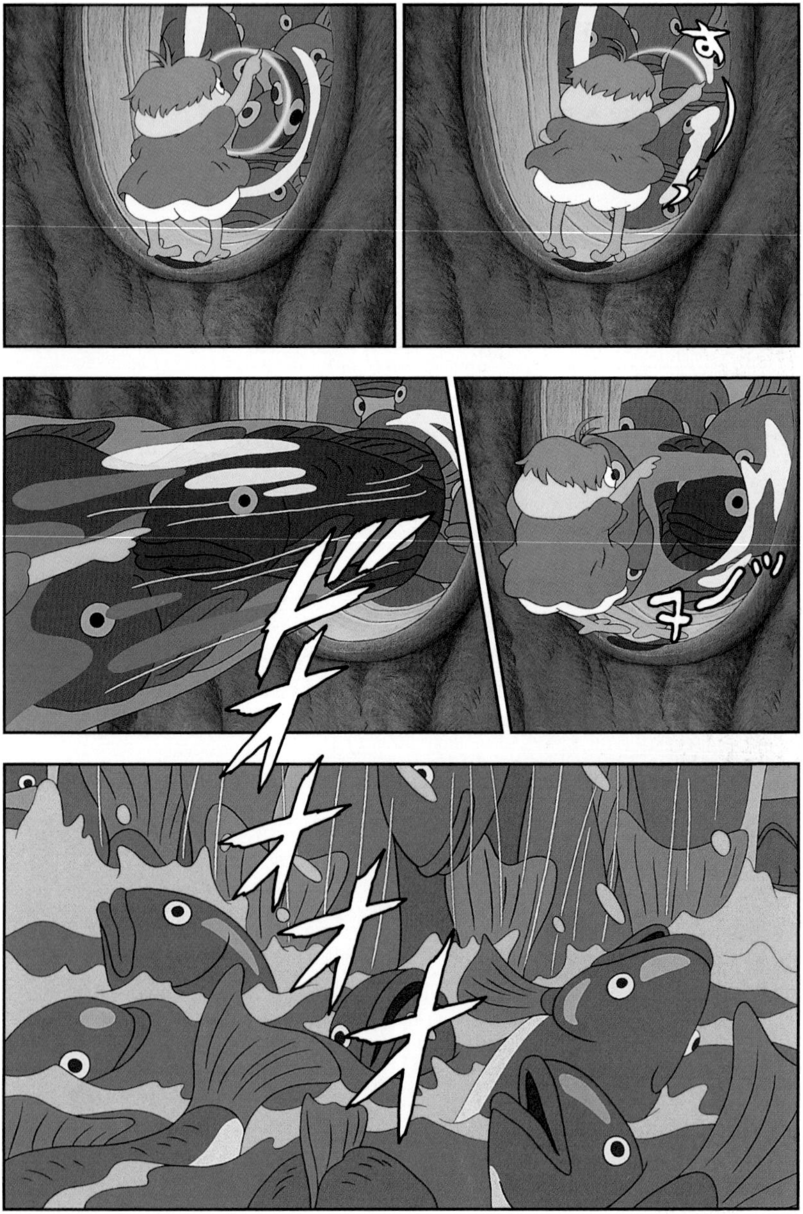
ヌーッ
ドオオオオ

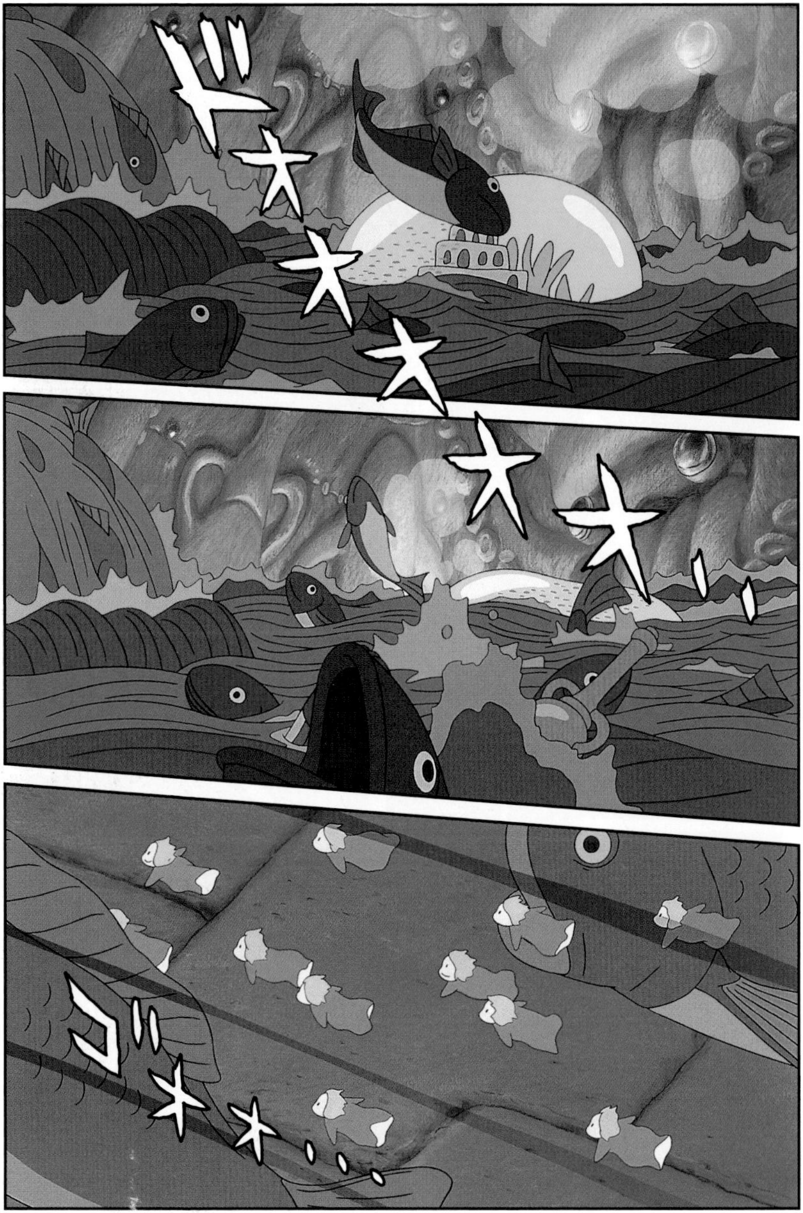
ドォォォォォ…
ゴォォ…

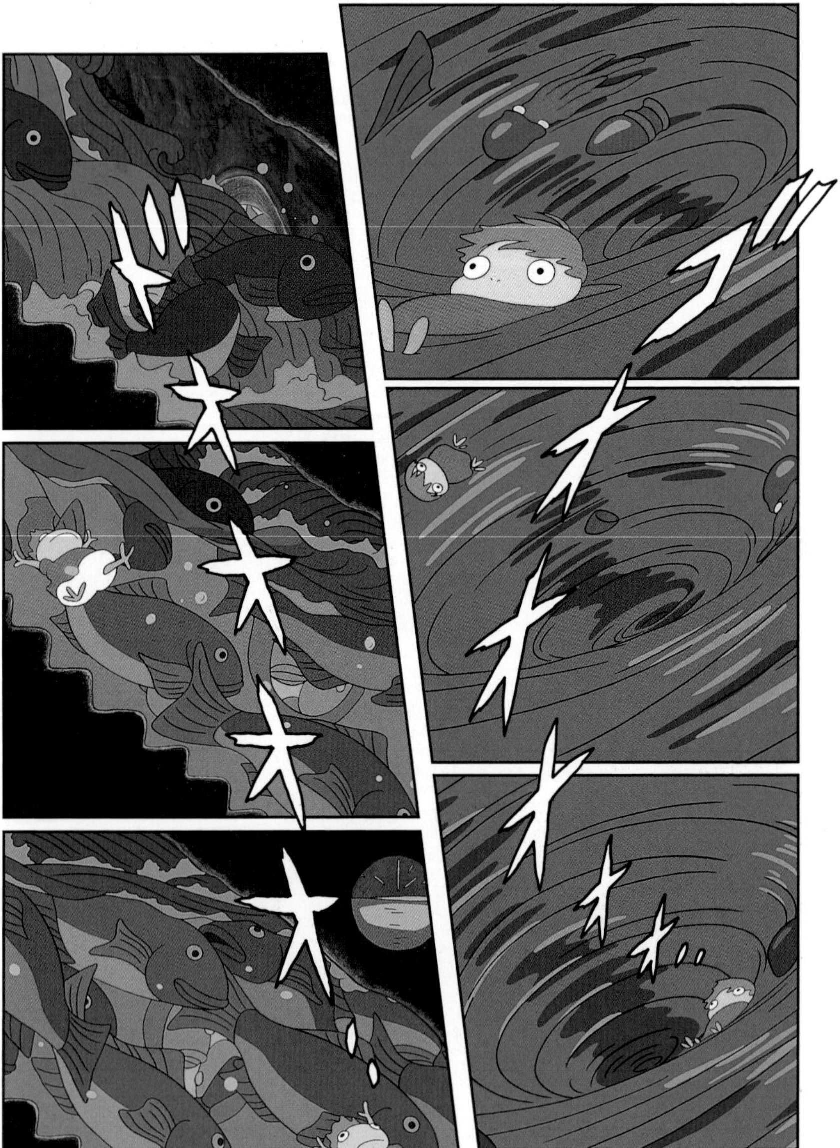
ブオオオォォ…
ドオオオオオ…

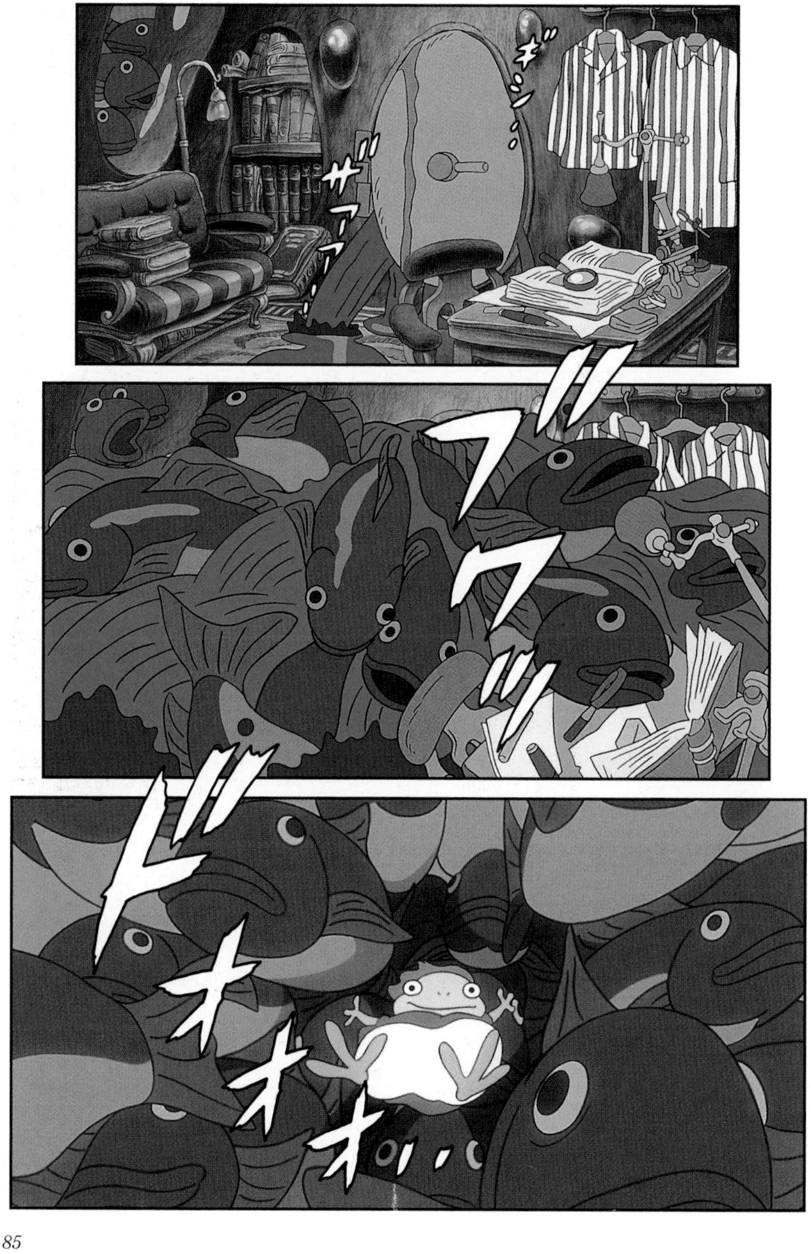
ギシ…
ザァァァ…
ブワッ
ドオオオ…

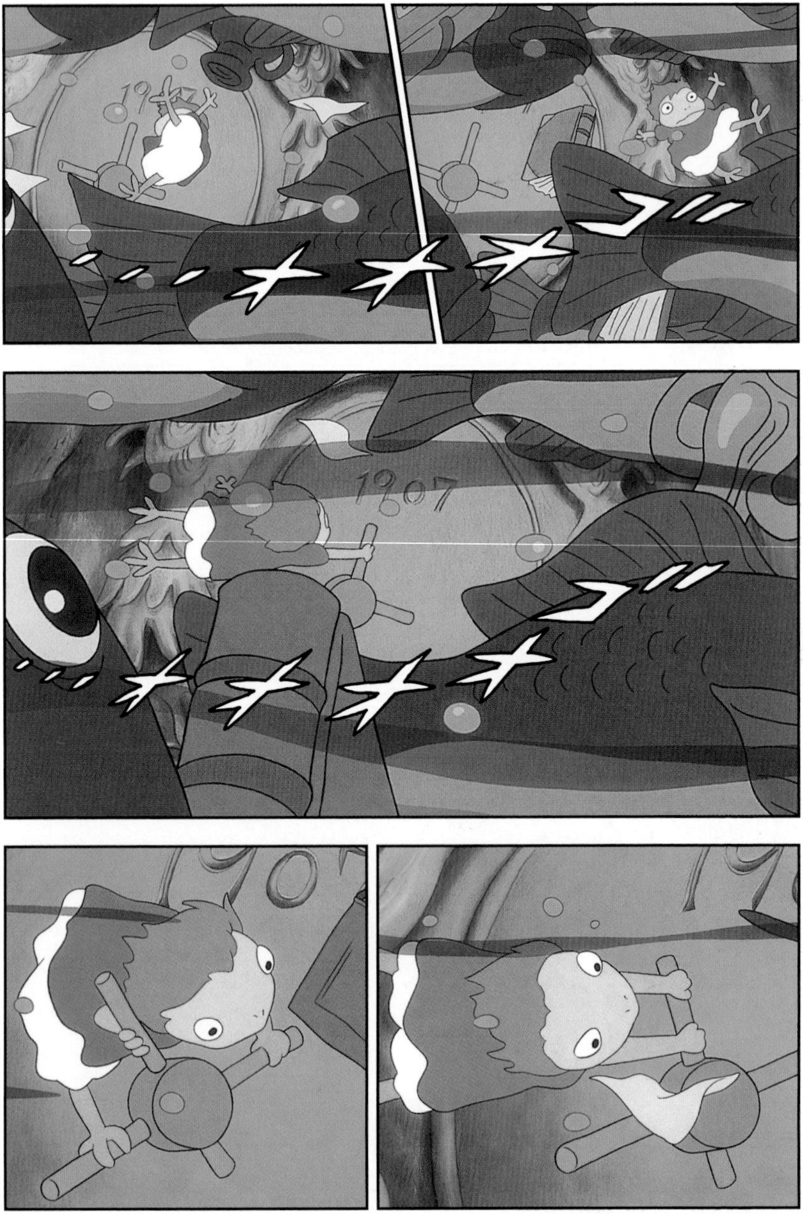
ゴオオオ…
1907
ゴオオオオ…

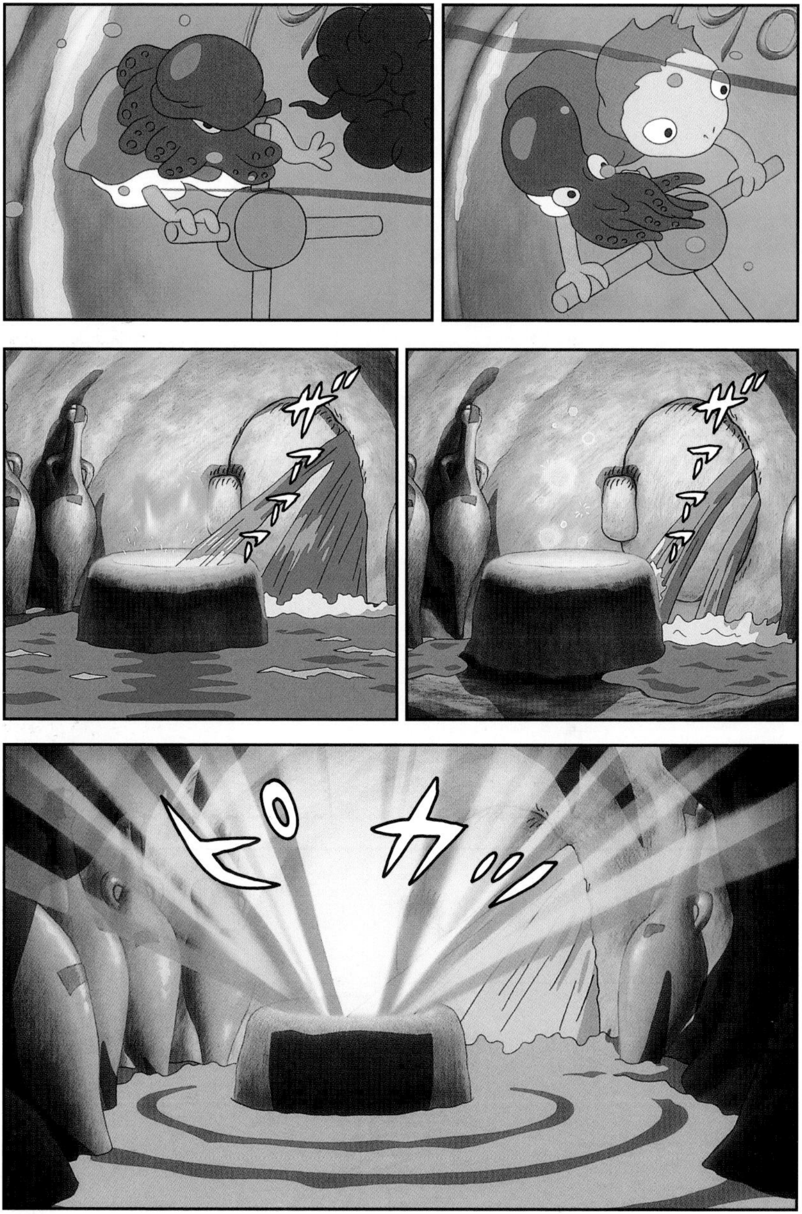
ザァァァ
ザァァァ
ピカッ

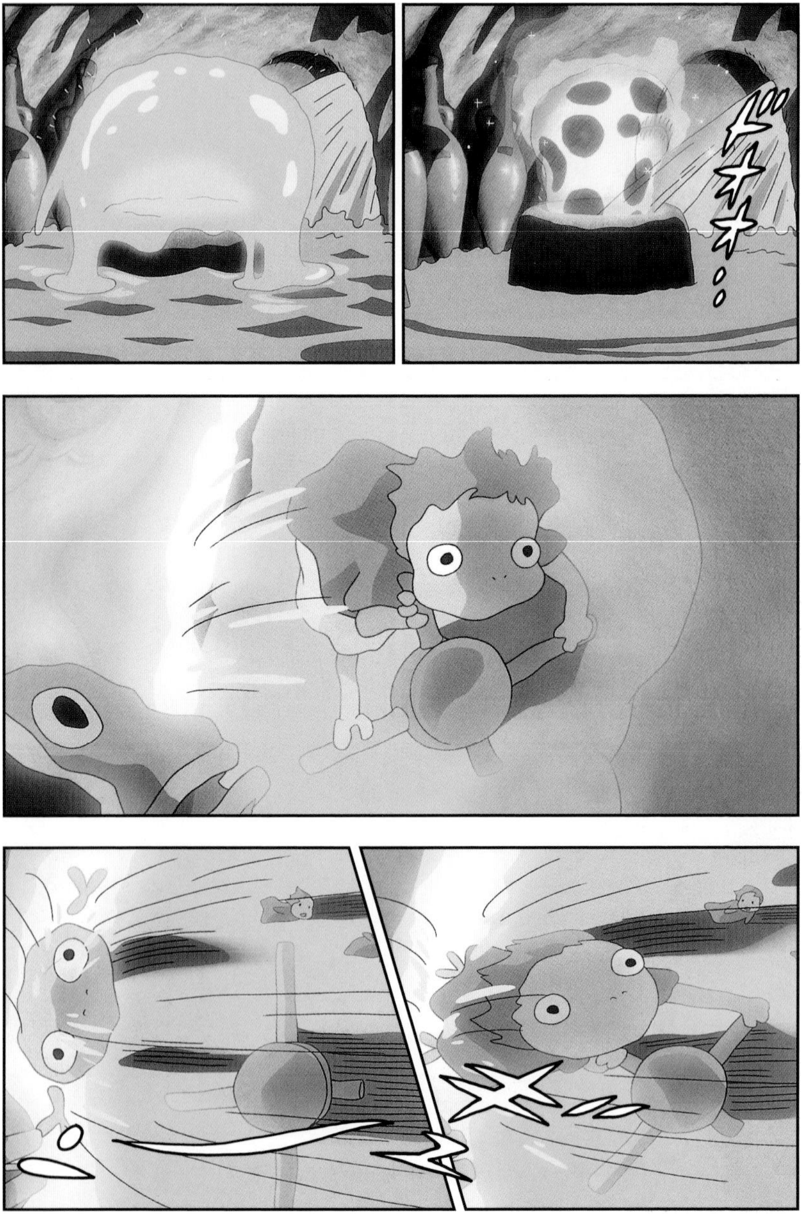
ドオオ。。

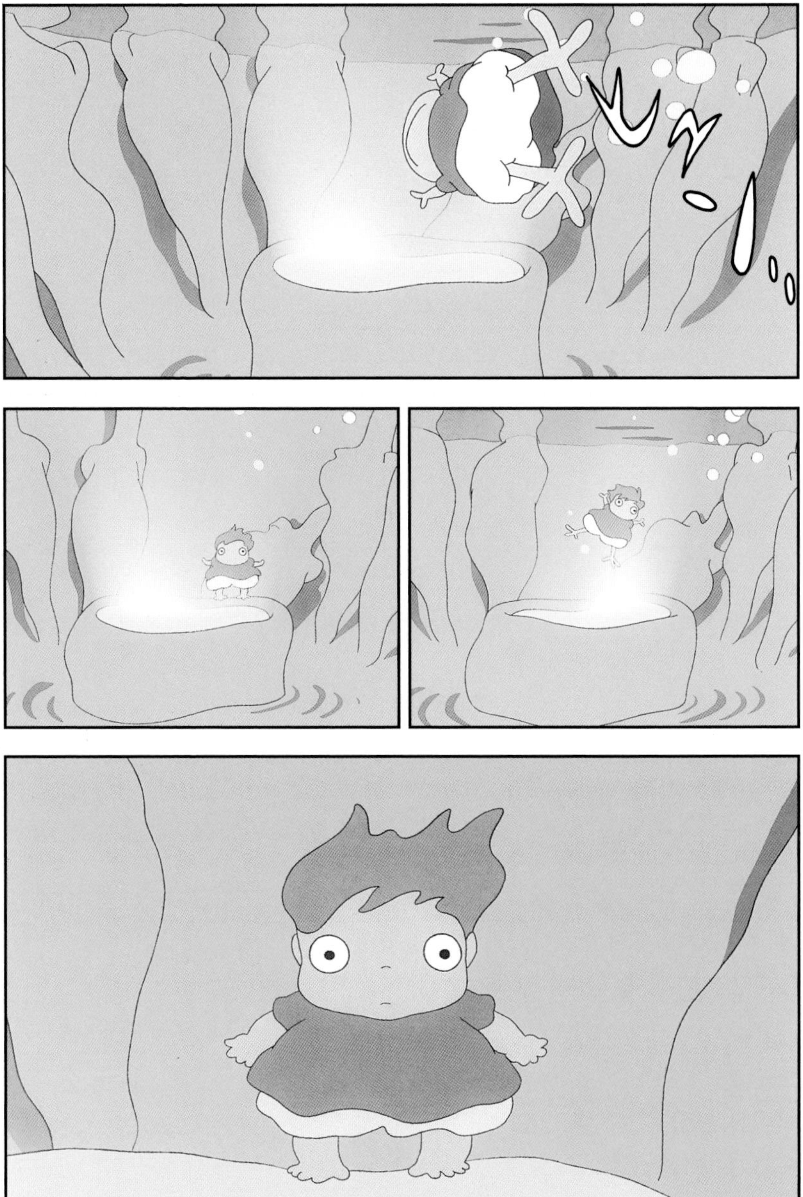

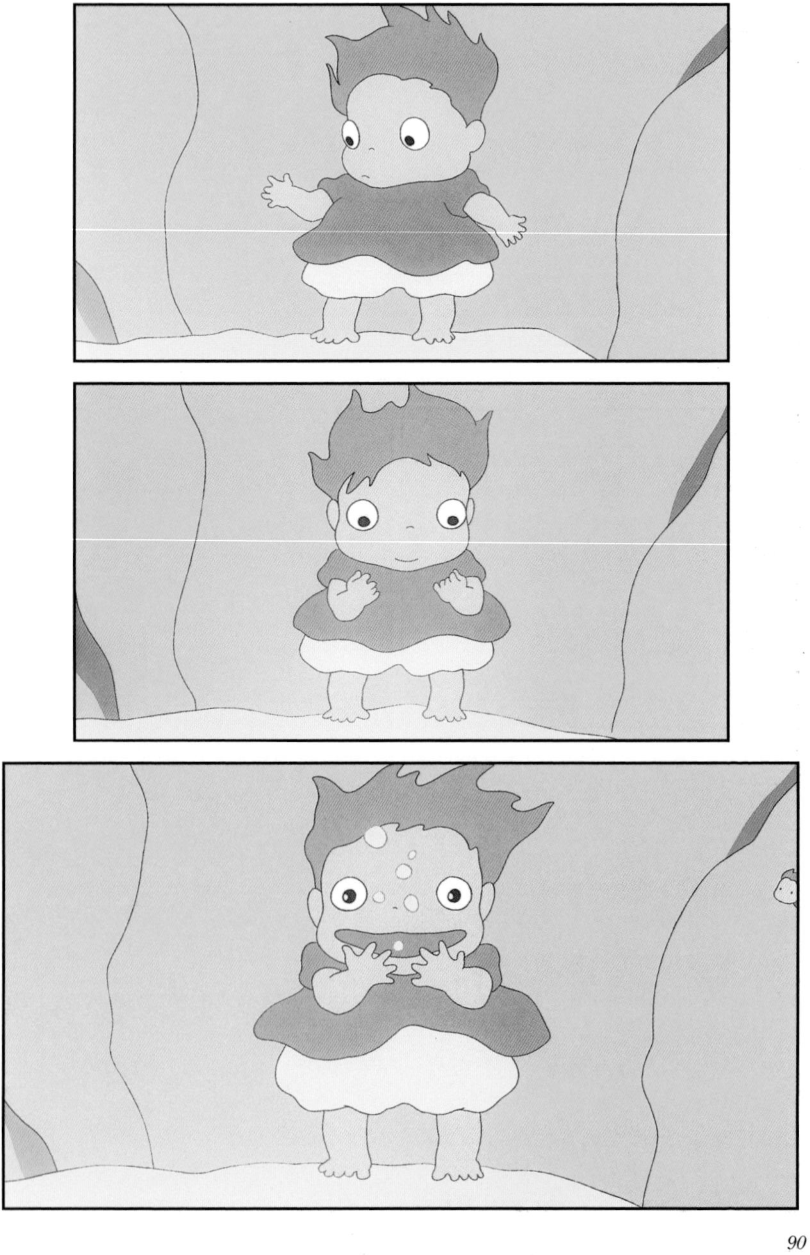

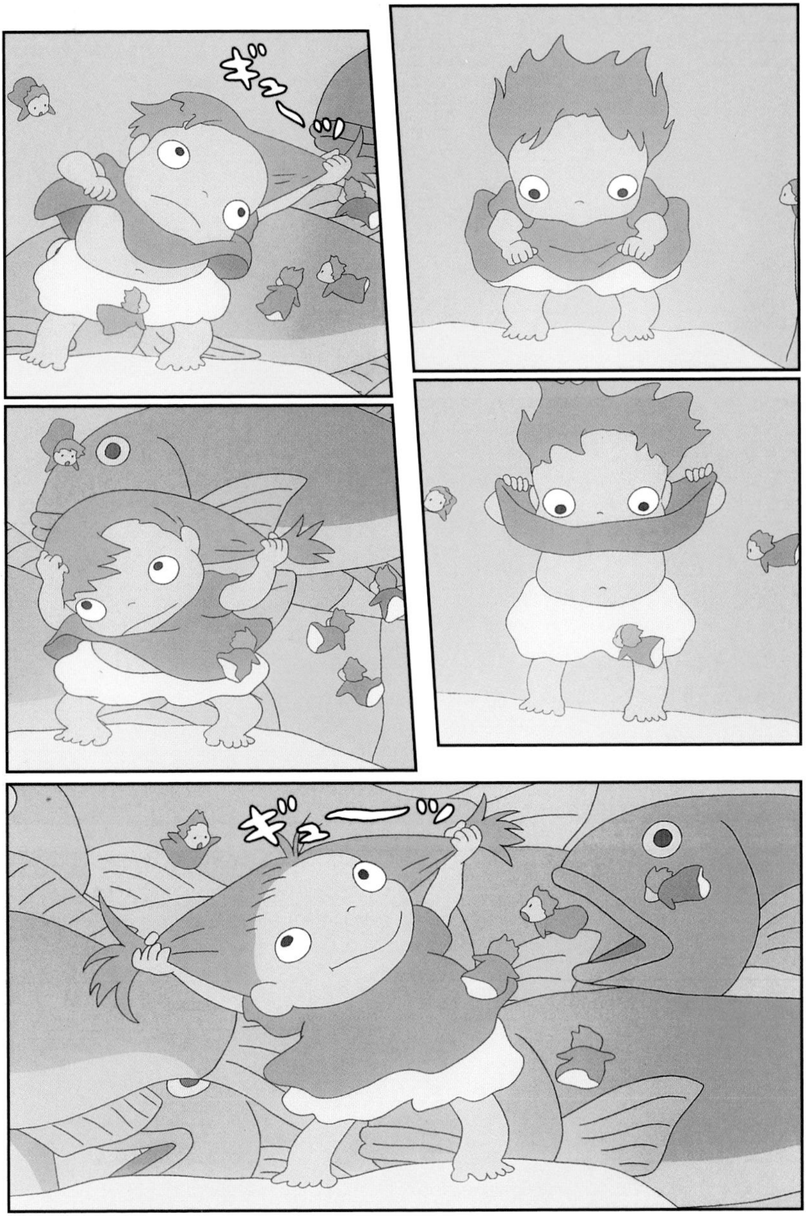
ギューッ
ギューーッ

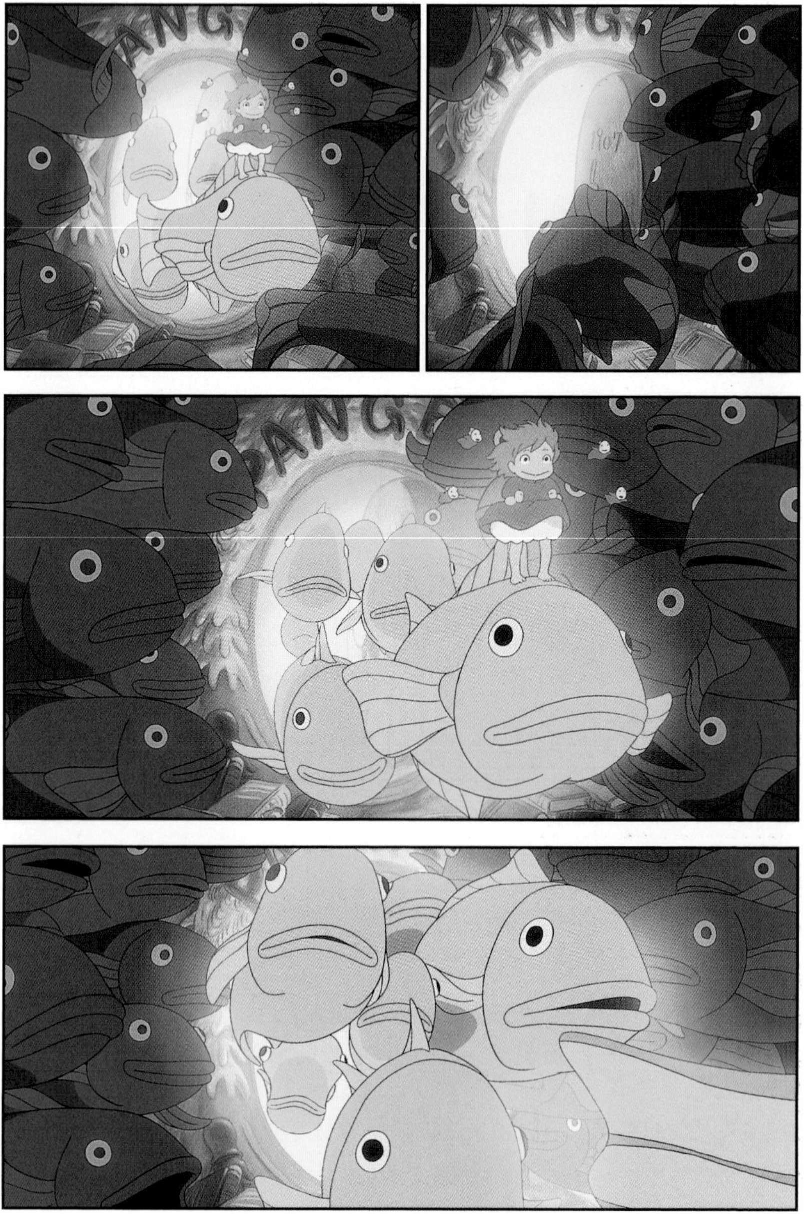

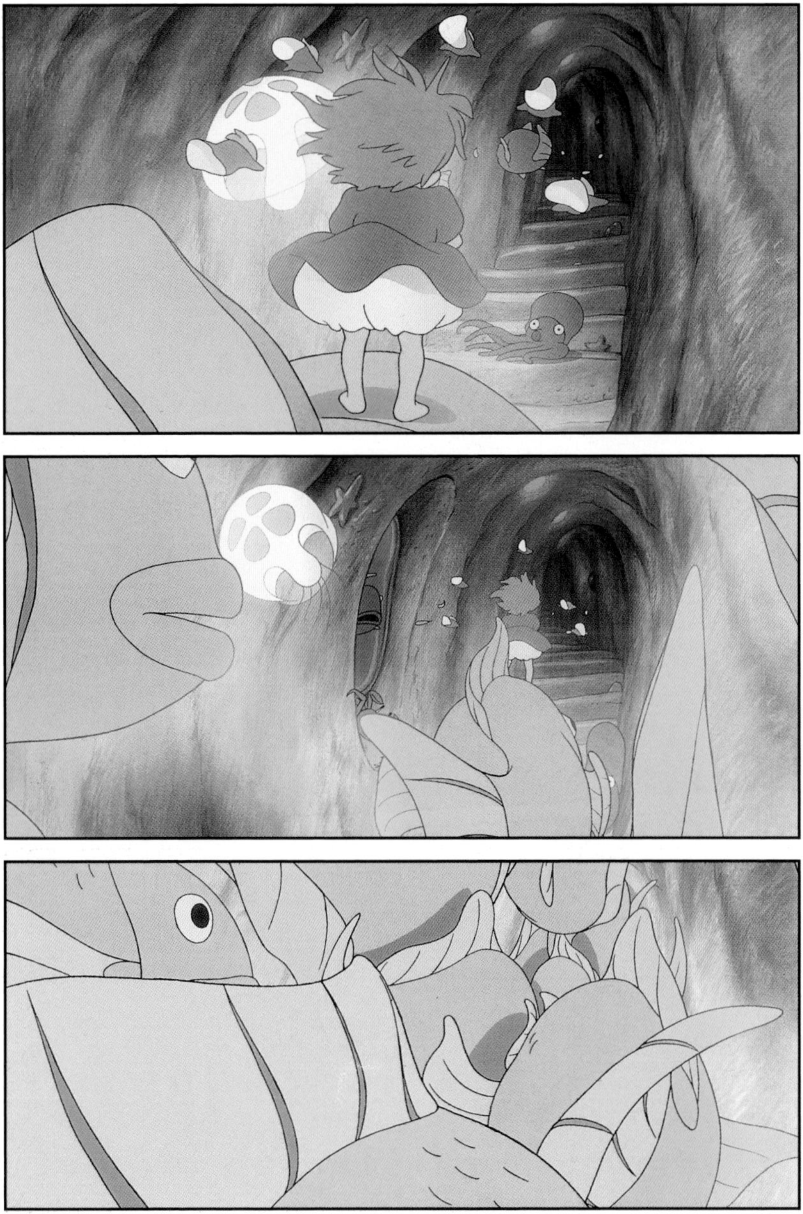

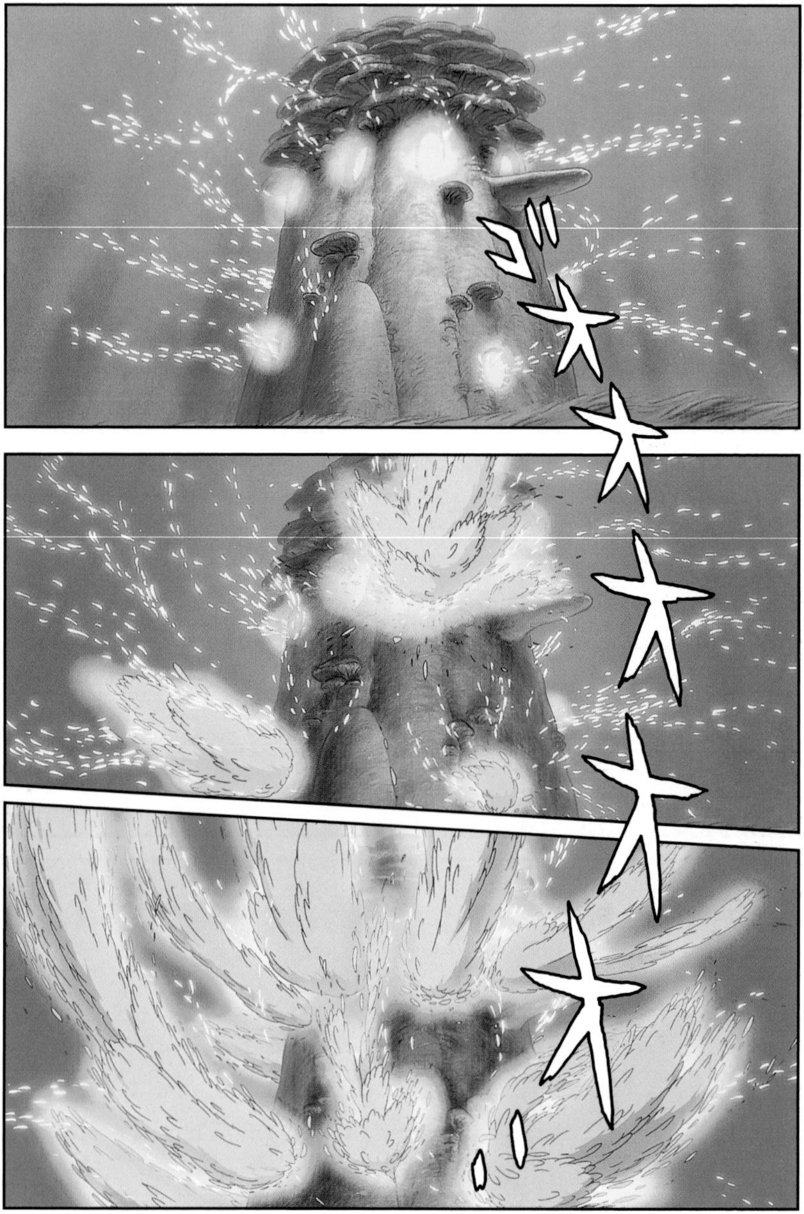
ゴオオオオオオ‥

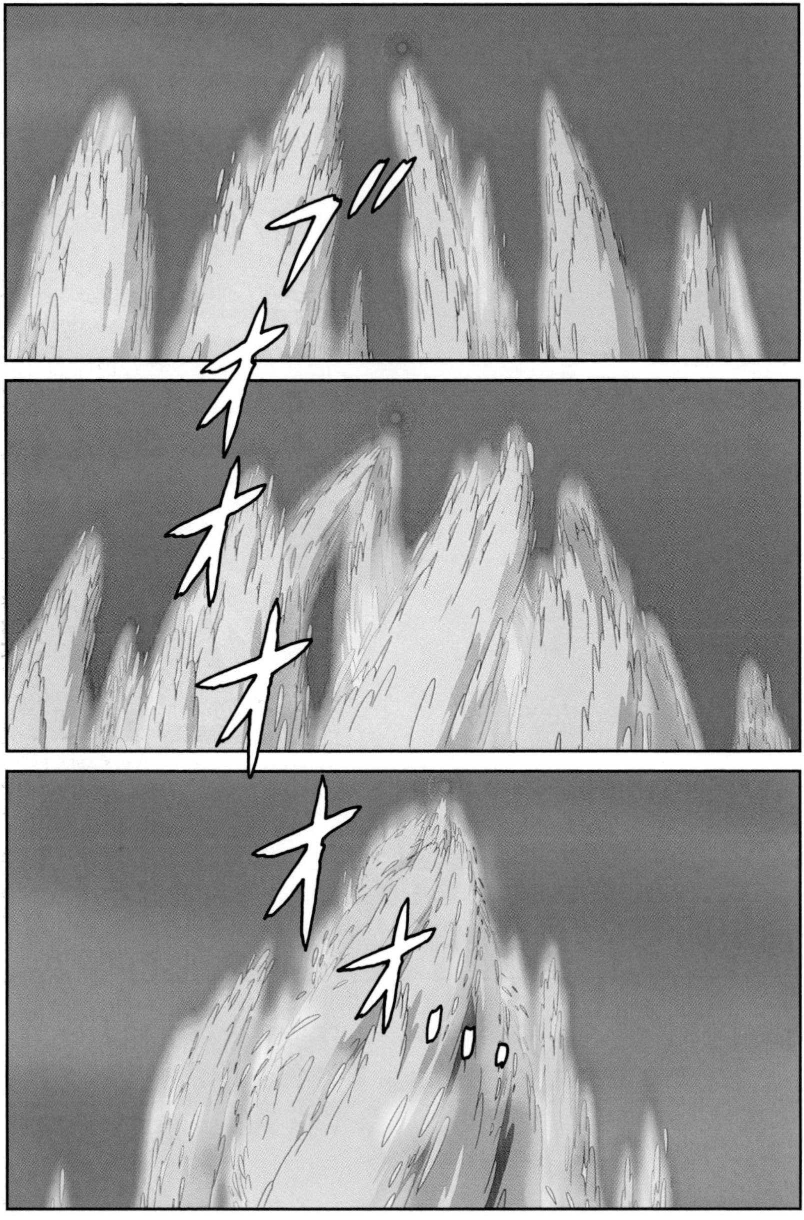
ブォォォォォ...

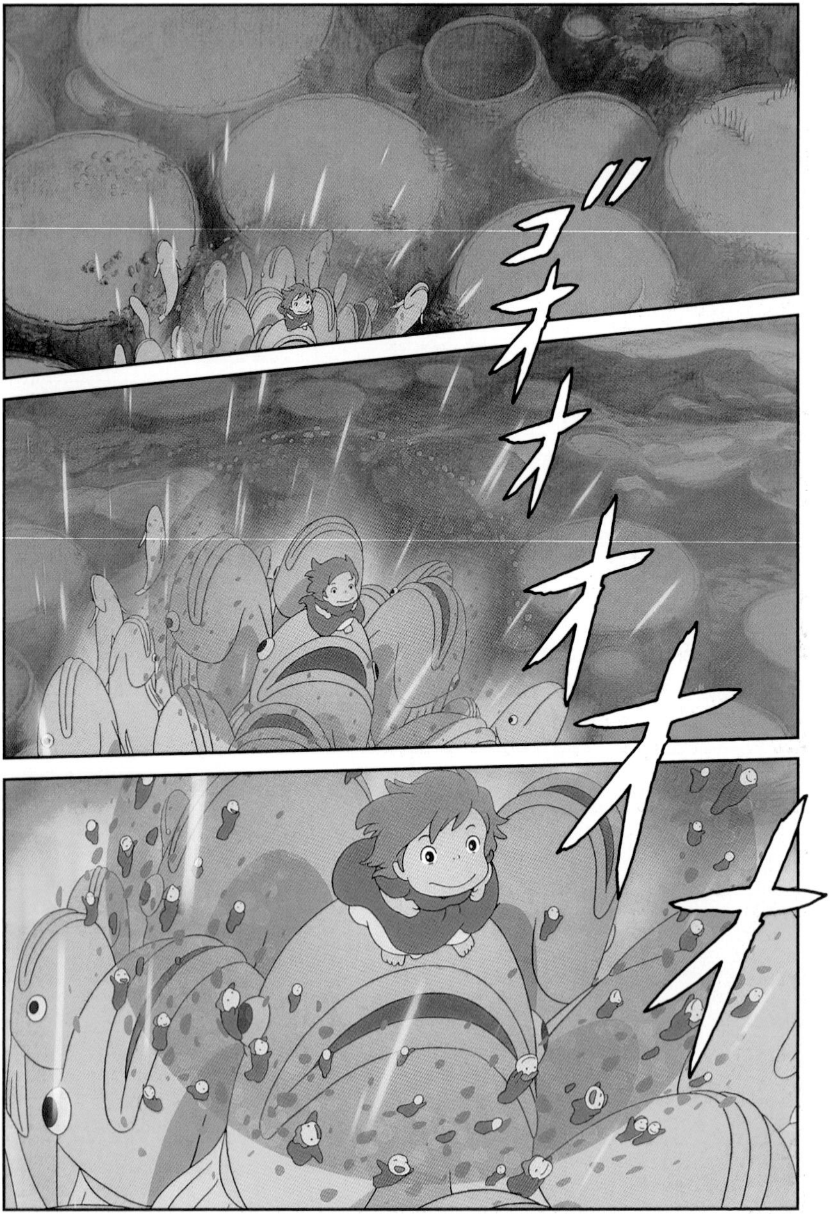
ゴオオオオオ

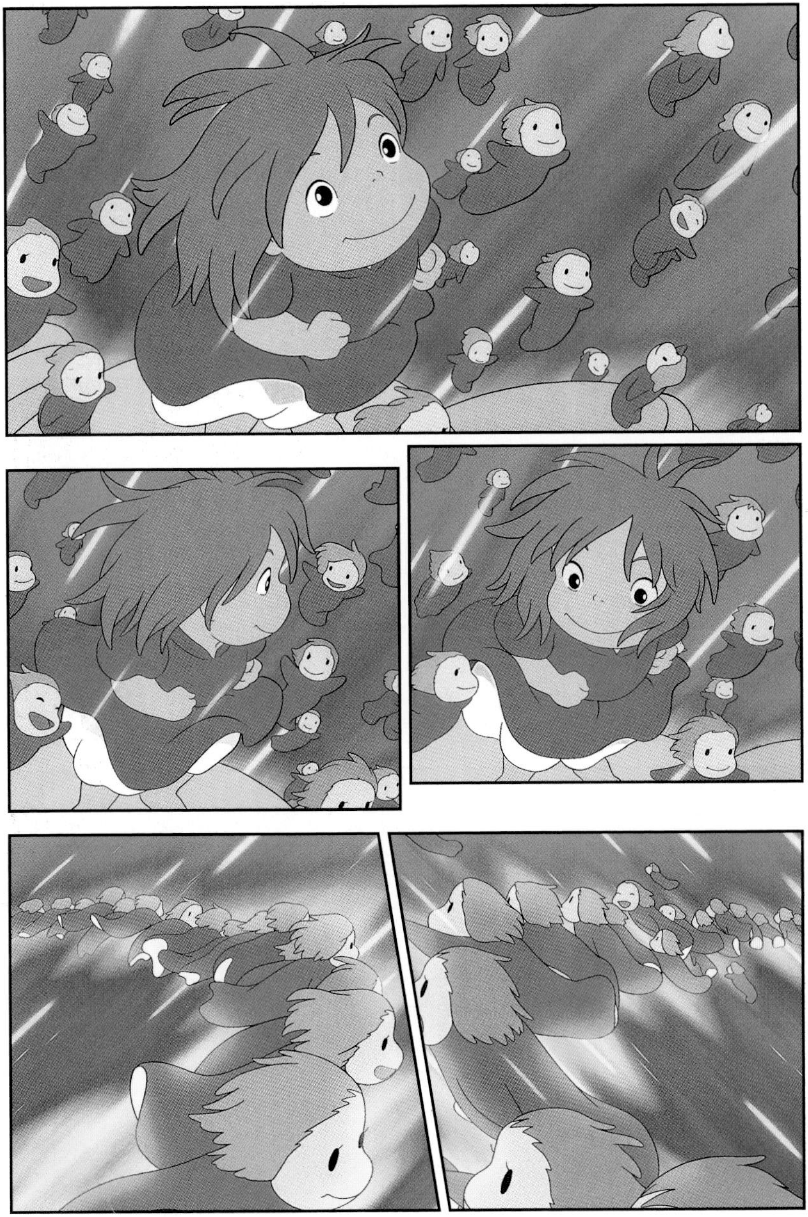

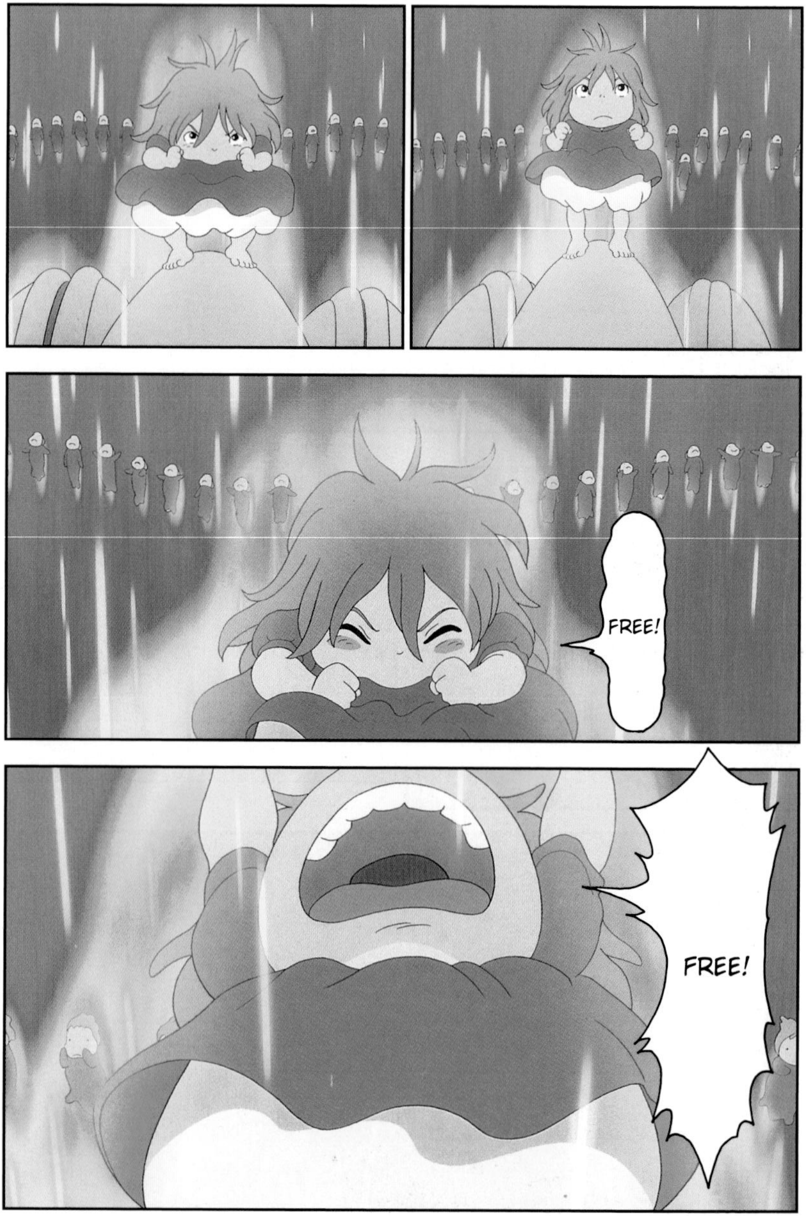
FREE!
FREE!

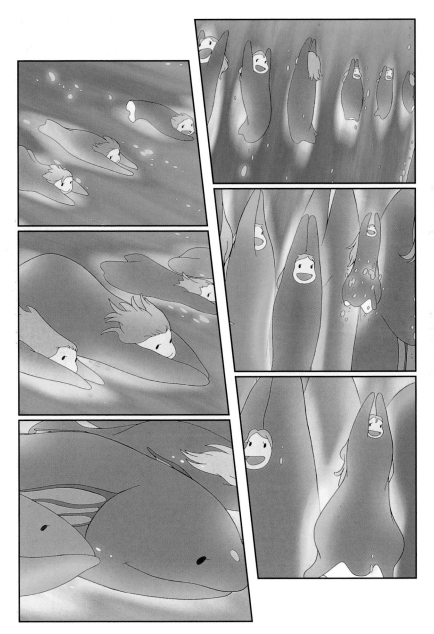

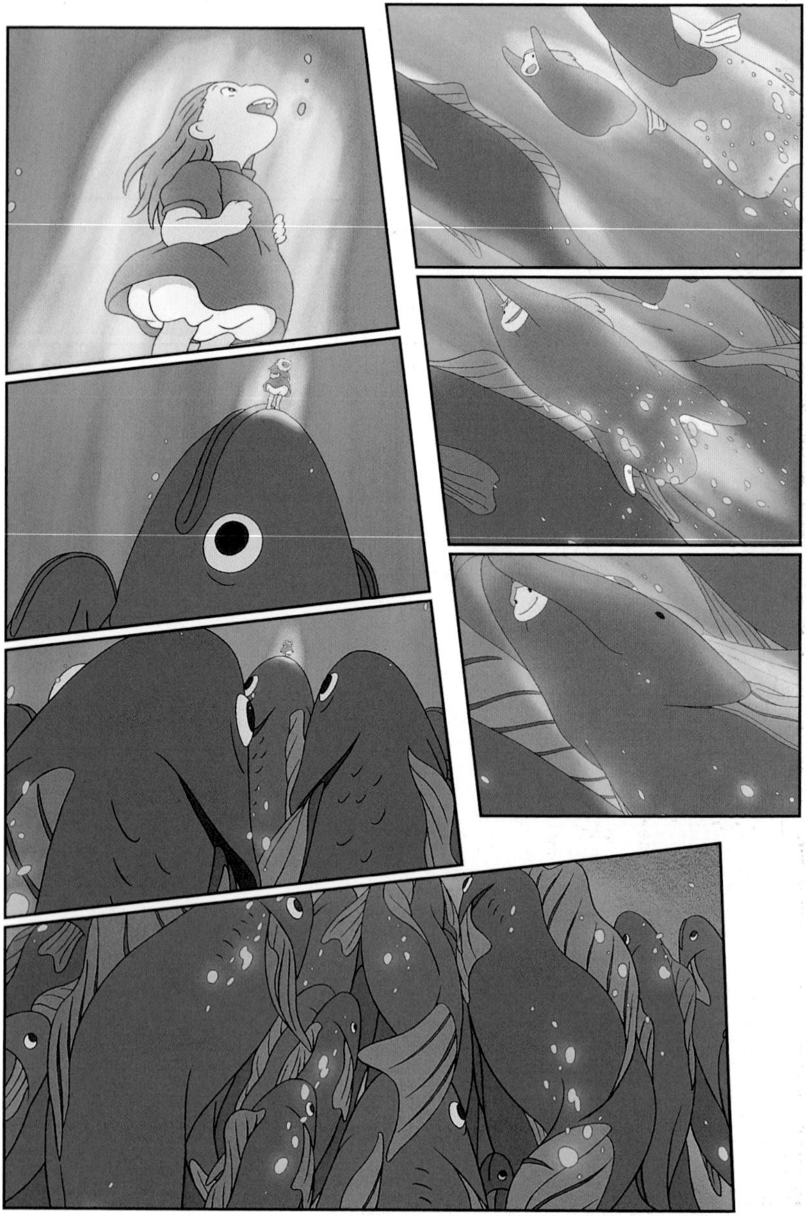

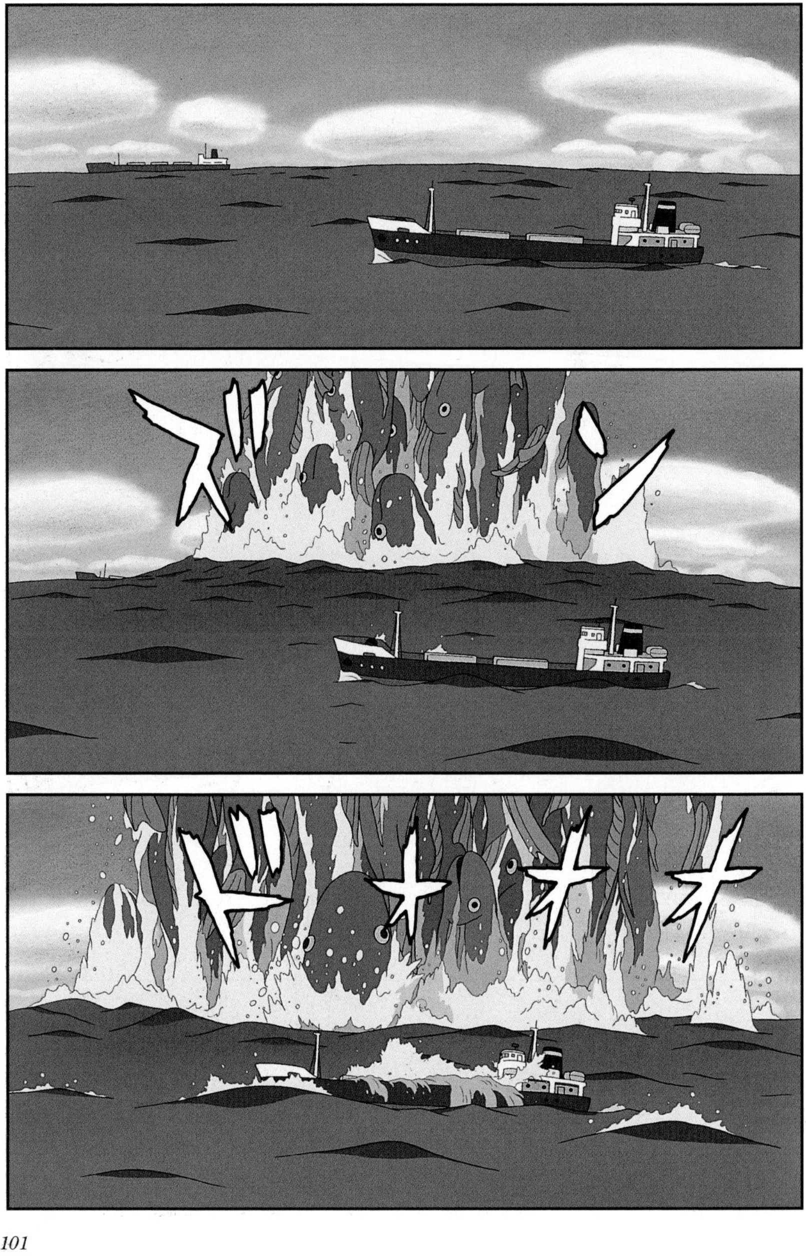
ズン
ドオオオ

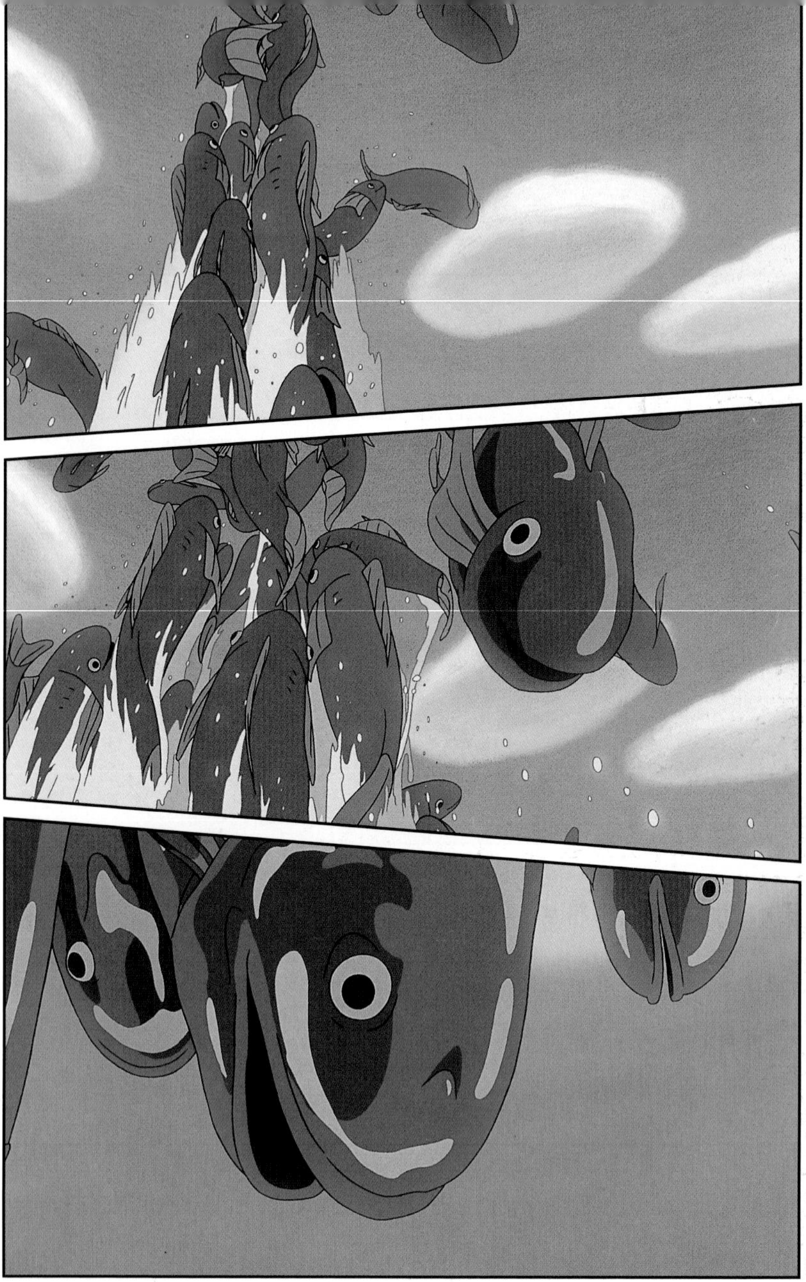

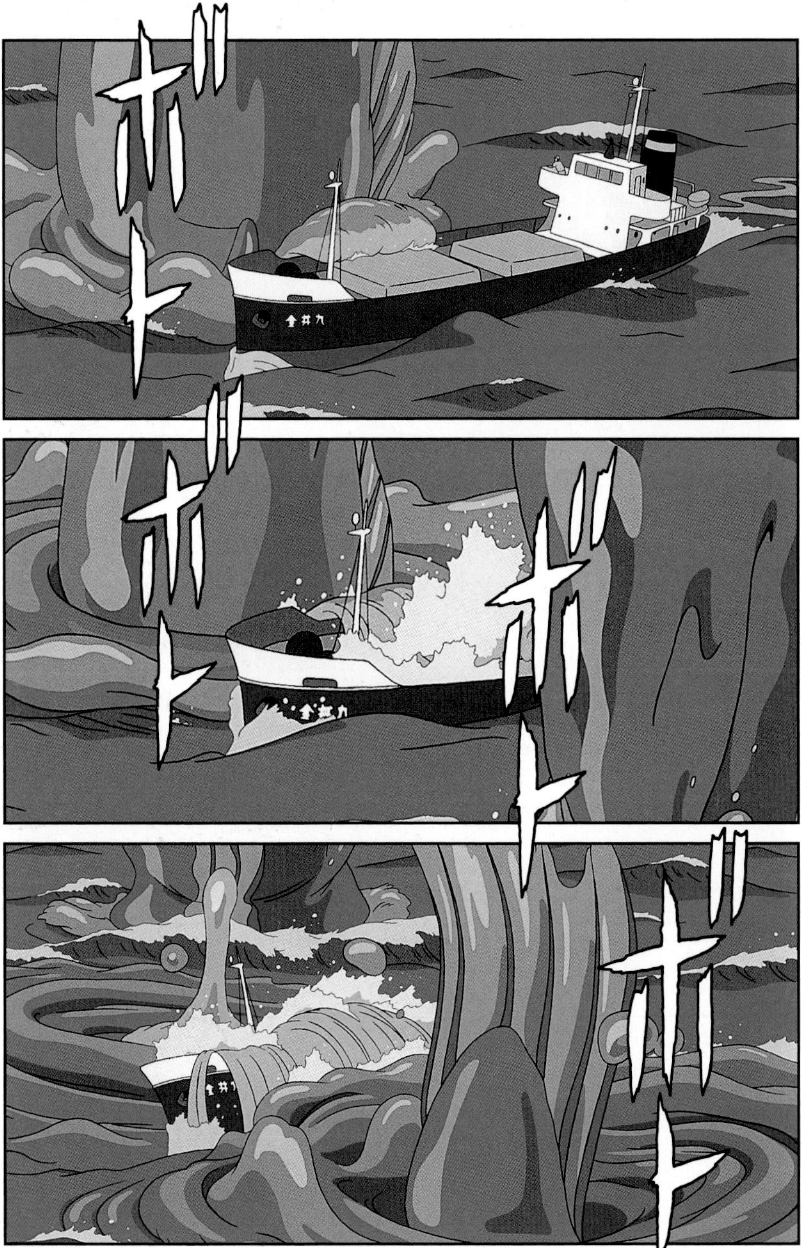
ボト
ボト
ボト
ボト

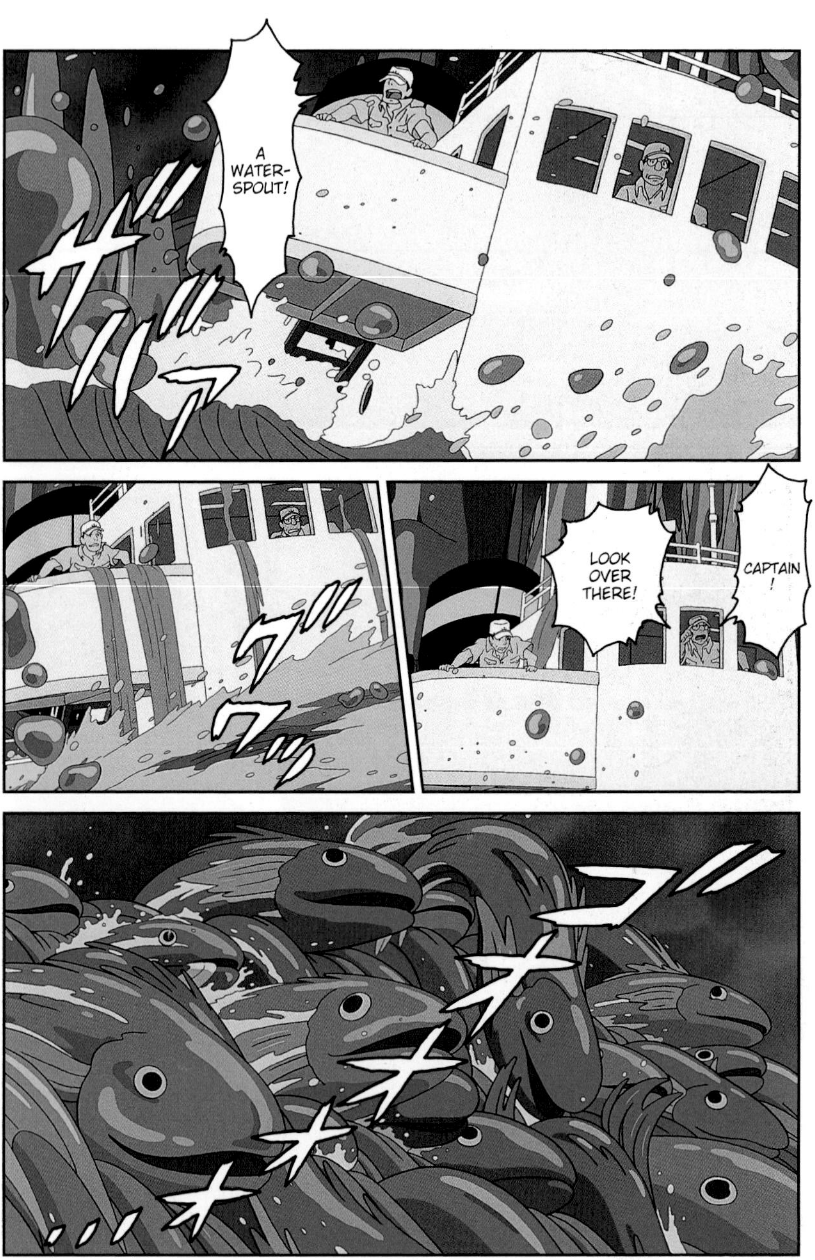
A WATER-SPOUT!
CAPTAIN!
LOOK OVER THERE!

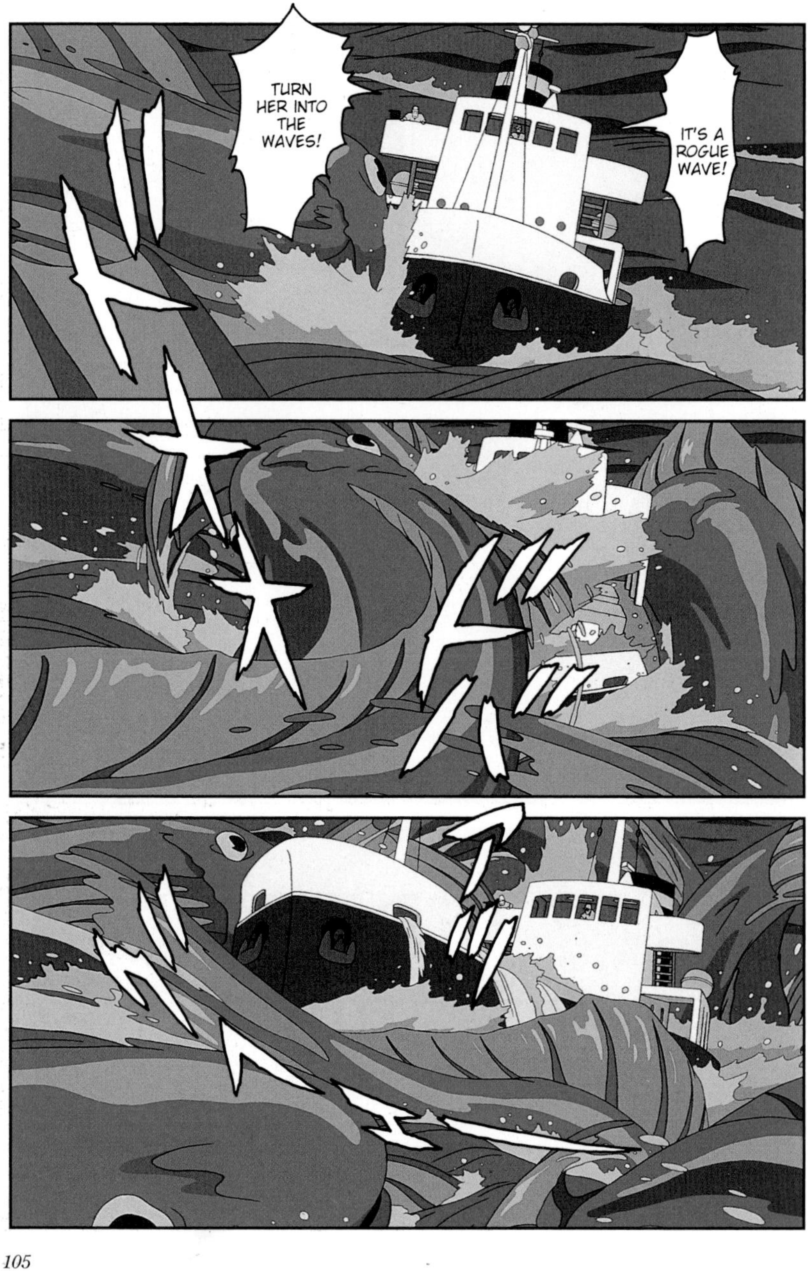
IT'S A ROGUE WAVE!
TURN HER INTO THE WAVES!

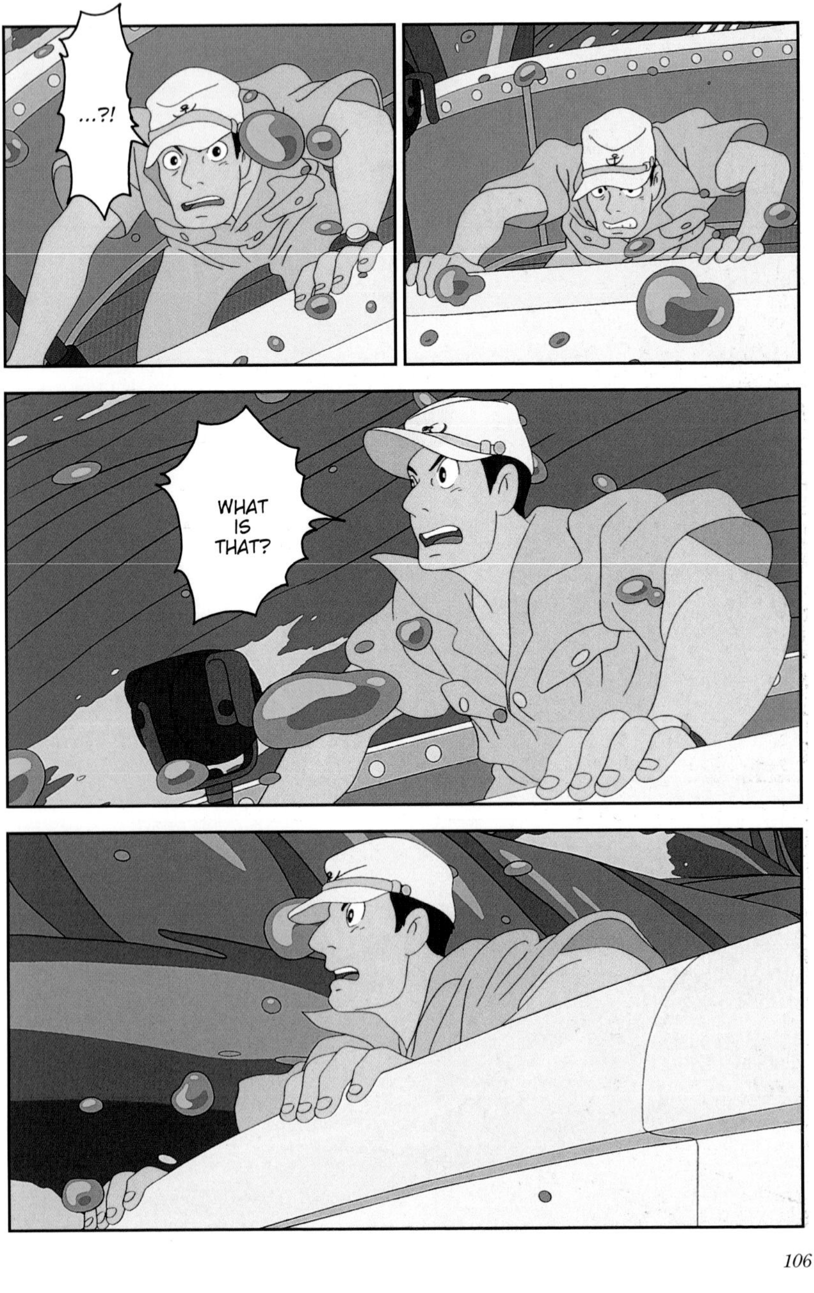
...?!
WHAT IS THAT?

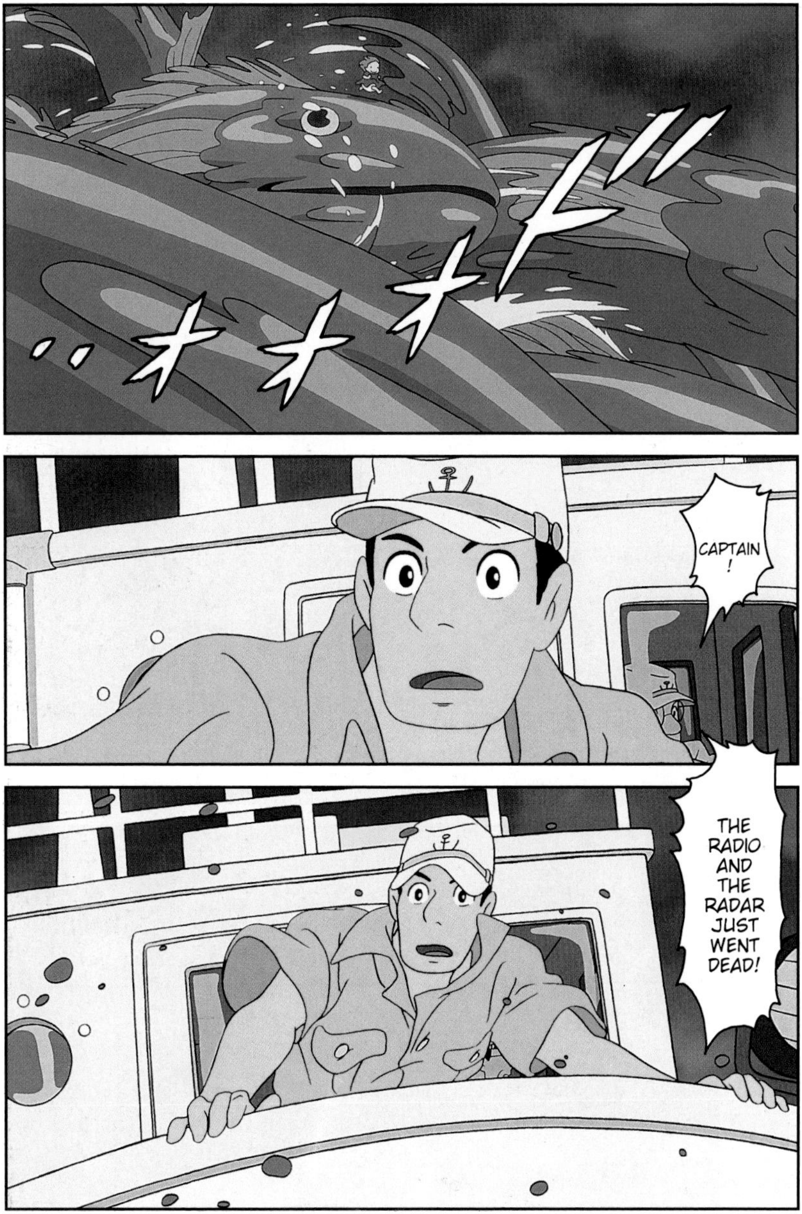
..オオオド
CAPTAIN!
THE RADIO AND THE RADAR JUST WENT DEAD!

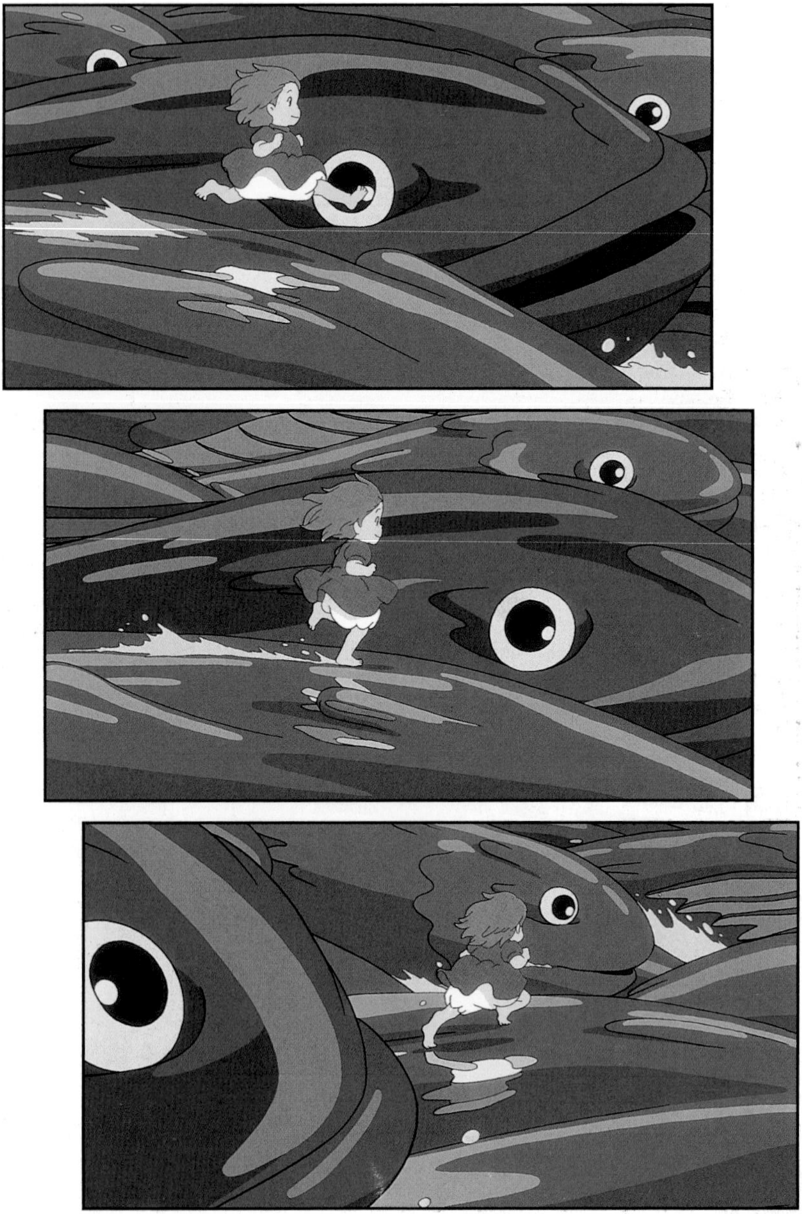

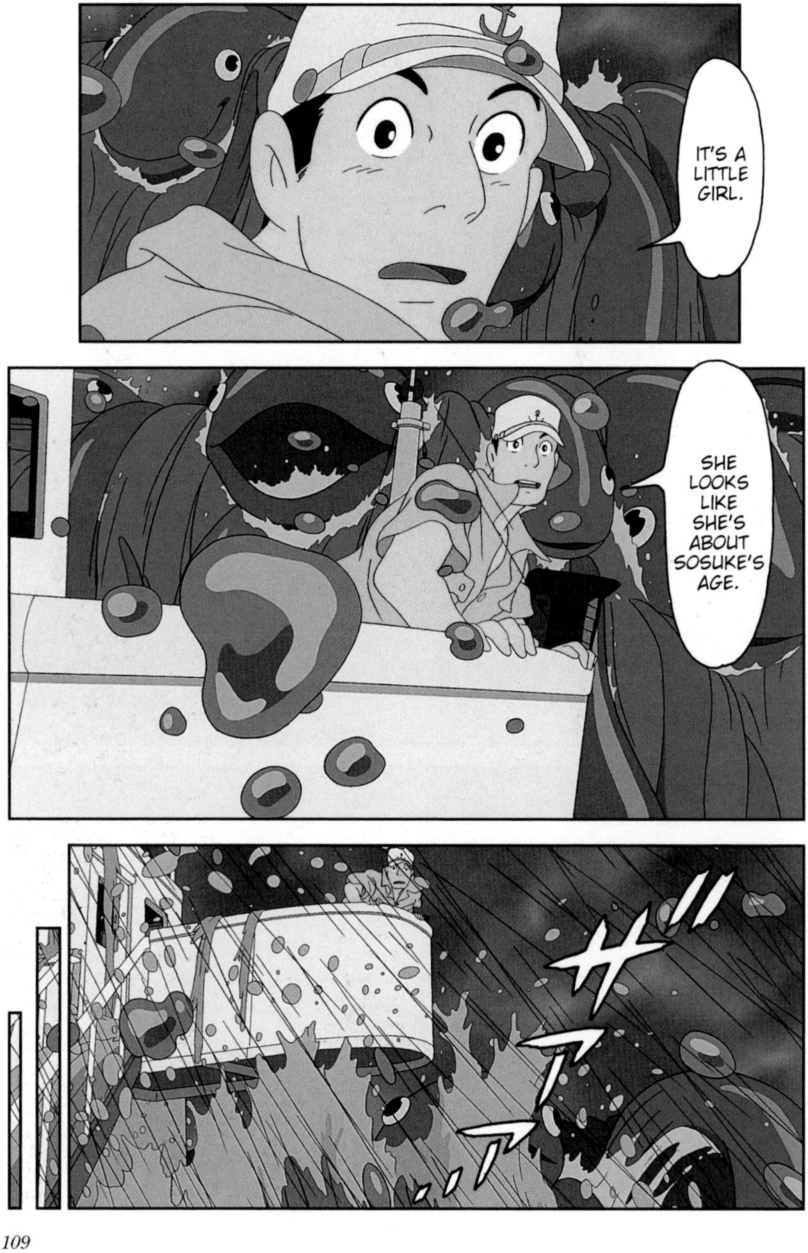
IT'S A LITTLE GIRL.
SHE LOOKS LIKE SHE'S ABOUT SOSUKE'S AGE.
ザ!!
ァァ...

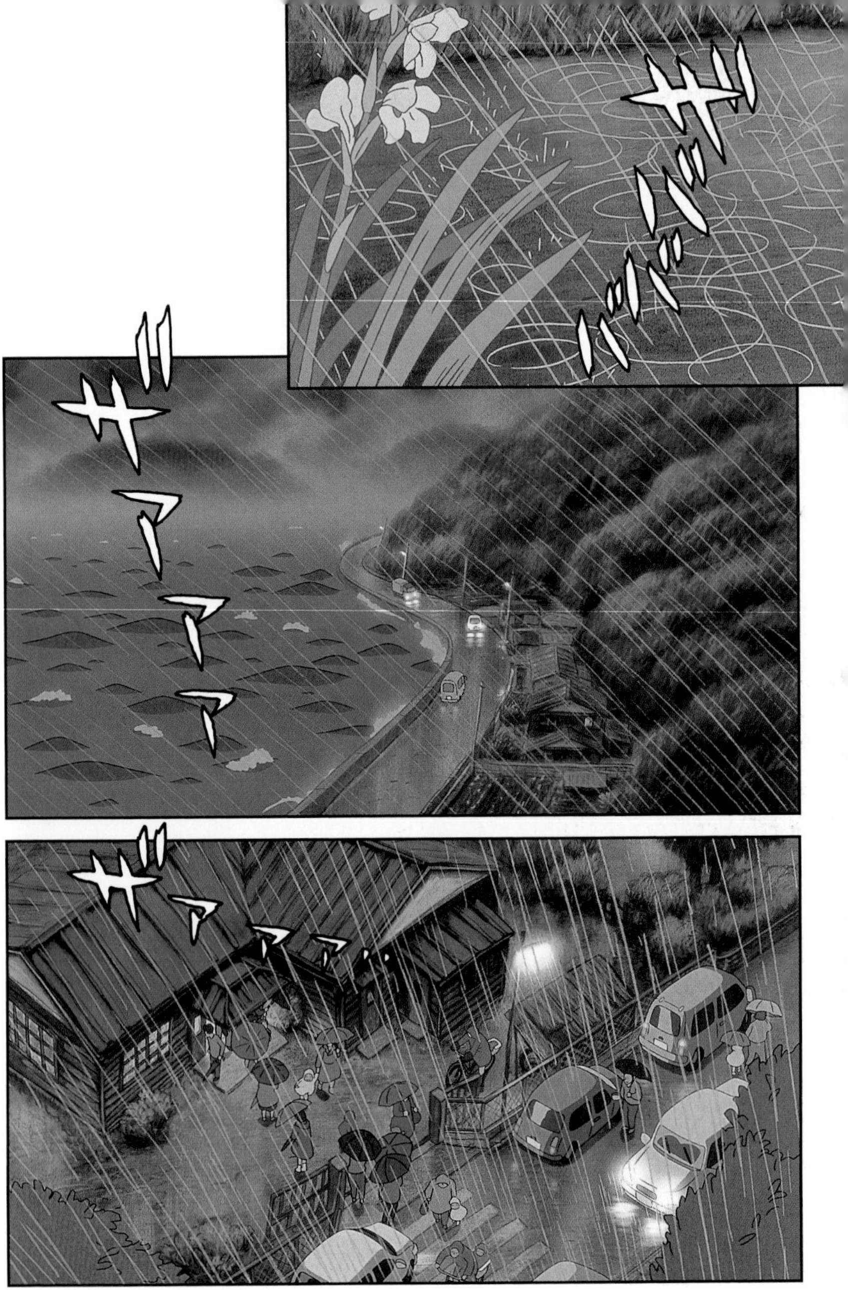
ザバババ
ザアアア
ザアァァ…

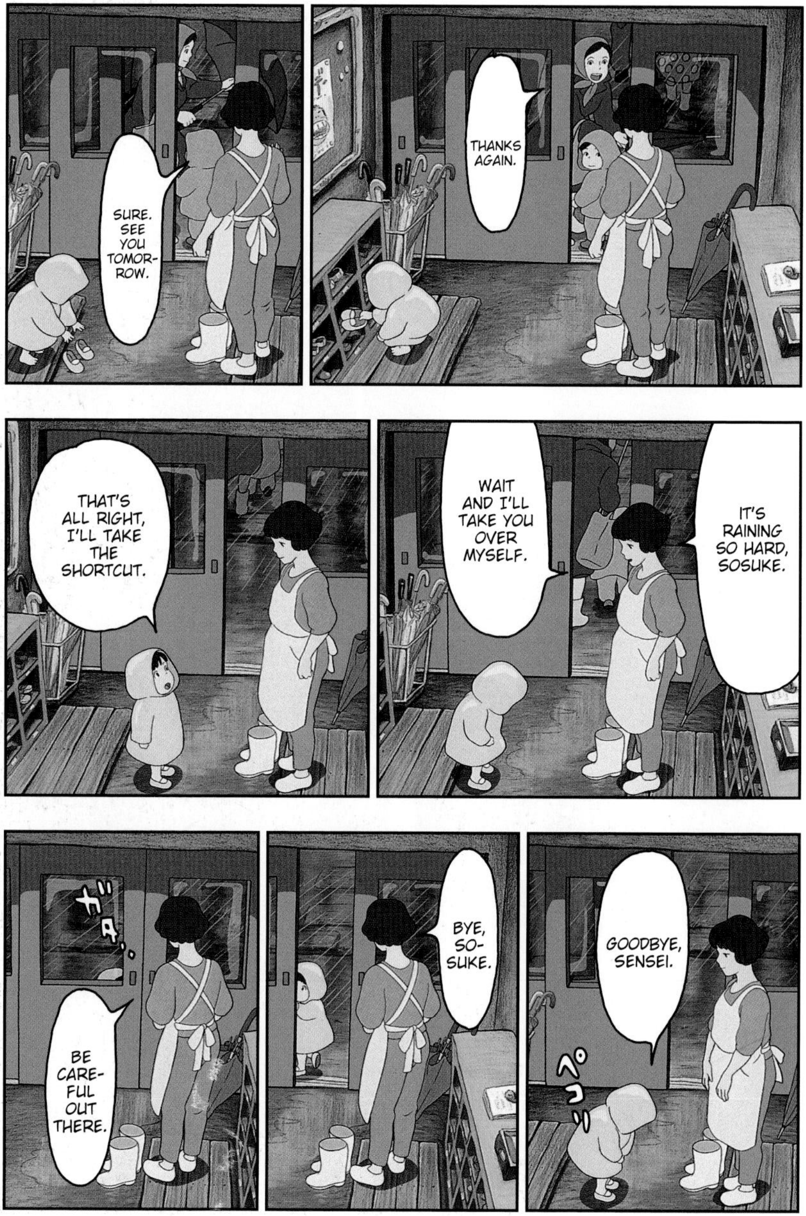
THANKS AGAIN.
SURE. SEE YOU TOMOR-ROW.
IT'S RAINING SO HARD, SOSUKE.
WAIT AND I'LL TAKE YOU OVER MYSELF.
THAT'S ALL RIGHT, I'LL TAKE THE SHORTCUT.
GOODBYE, SENSEI.
ペコ
BYE, SO-SUKE.
ガタ
BE CARE-FUL OUT THERE.

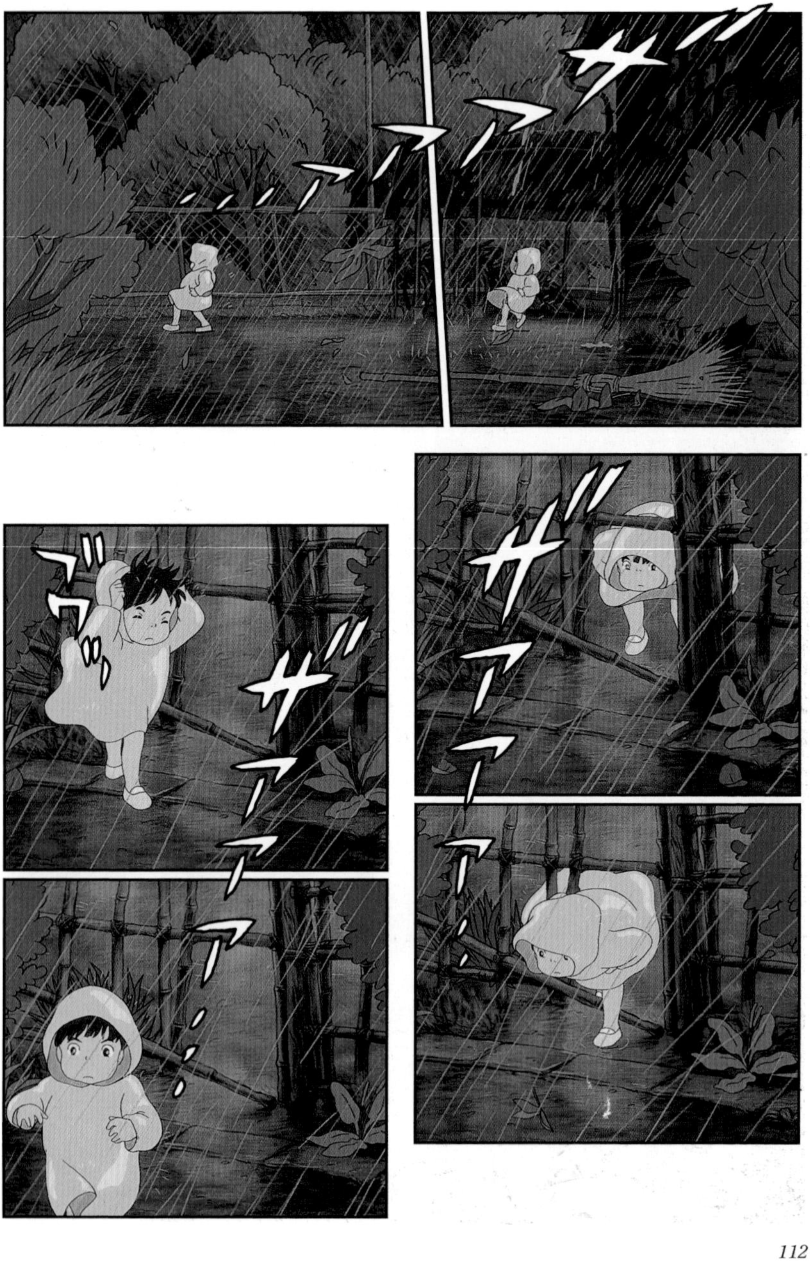

ザアアアア…
ザアアアーアー…
ブワッ
ザアアアア…

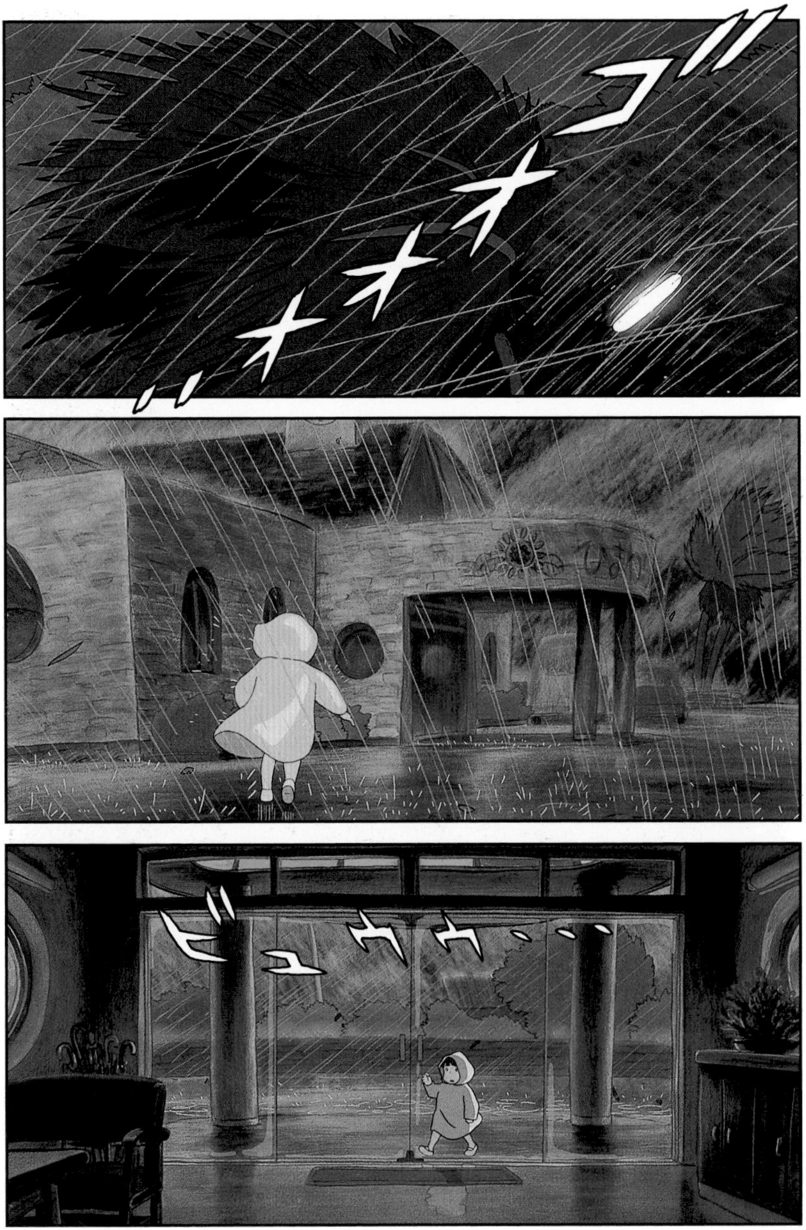
ゴオオオ…
ビュウウ…

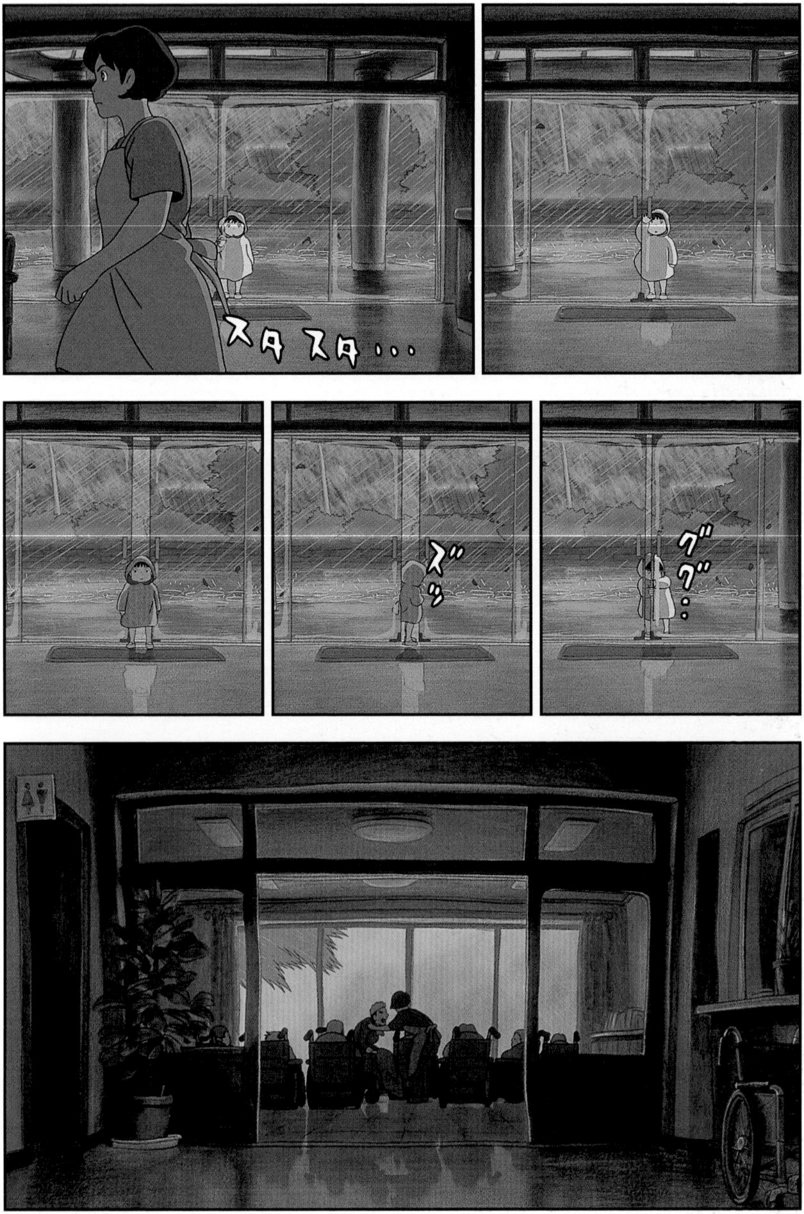
スタスタ…
ググ…
ズッ

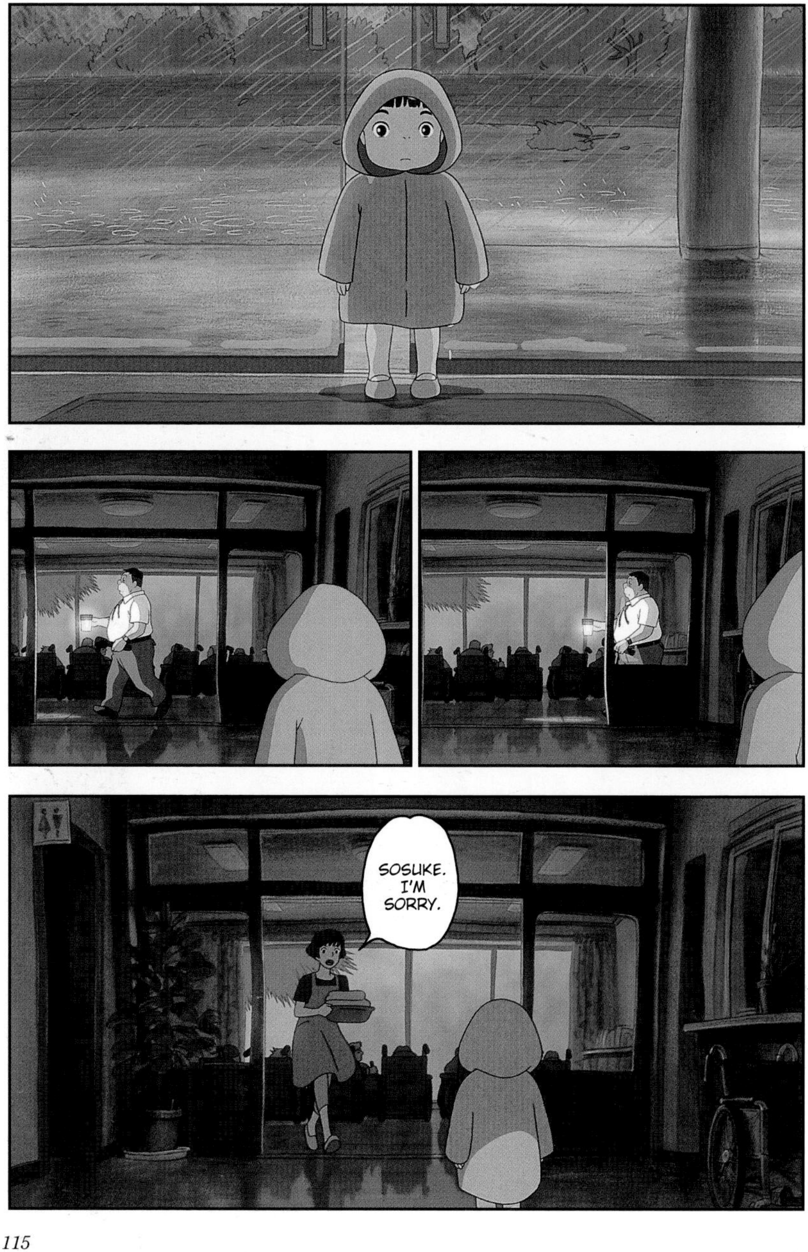
SOSUKE. I'M SORRY.

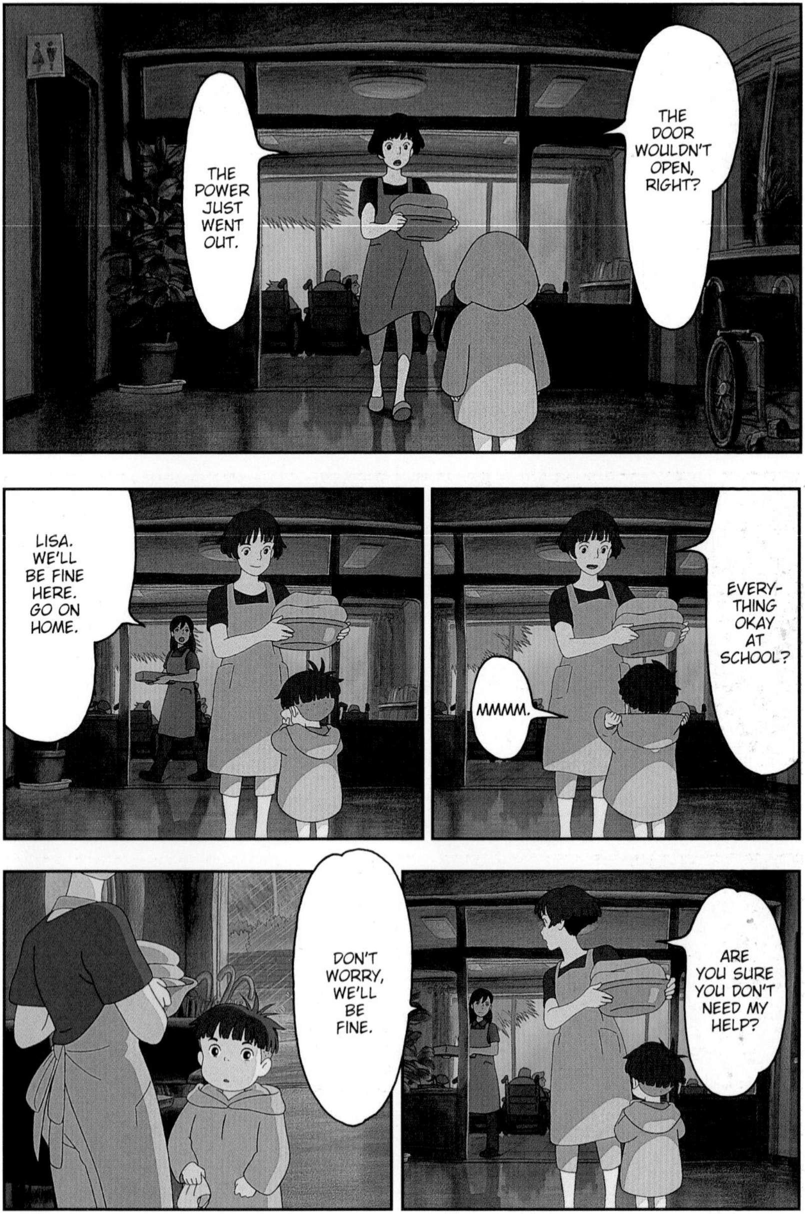
THE DOOR WOULDN'T OPEN, RIGHT?
THE POWER JUST WENT OUT.
EVERY-THING OKAY AT SCHOOL?
MMMM.
LISA. WE'LL BE FINE HERE. GO ON HOME.
ARE YOU SURE YOU DON'T NEED MY HELP?
DON'T WORRY, WE'LL BE FINE.

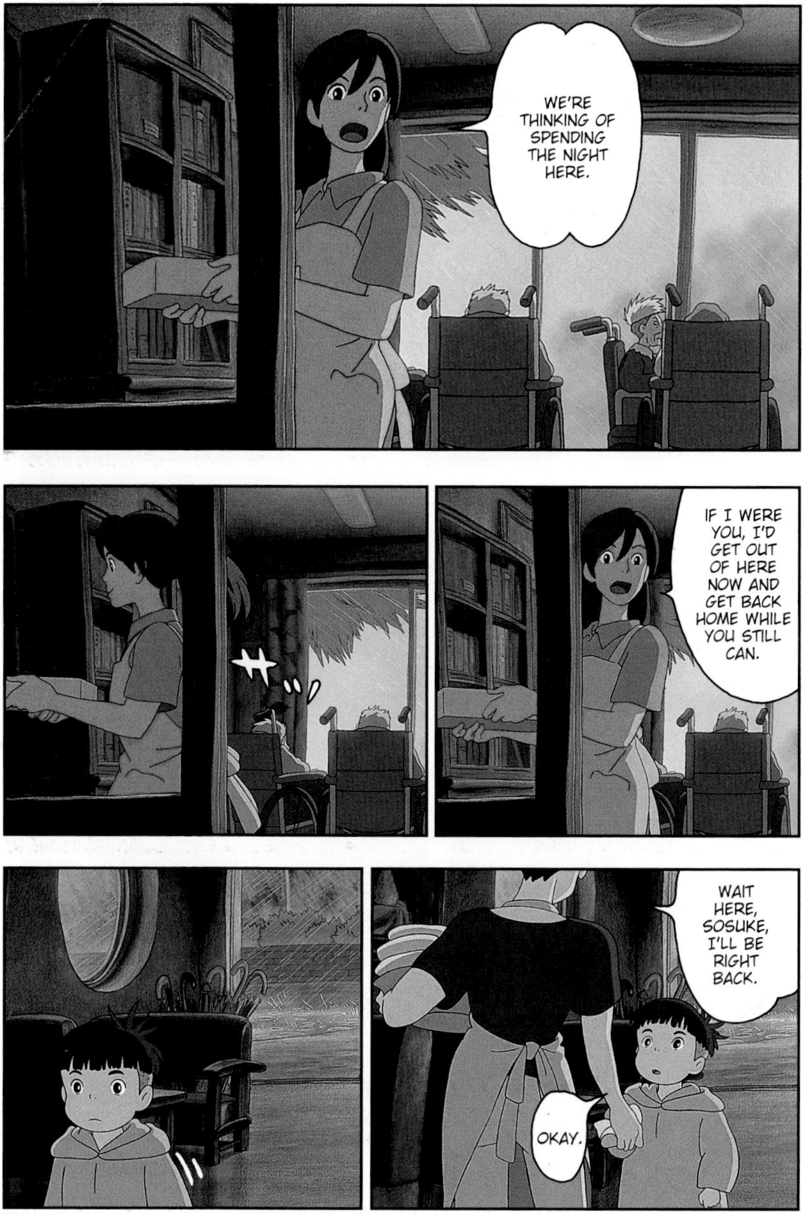
WE'RE THINKING OF SPENDING THE NIGHT HERE.
IF I WERE YOU, I'D GET OUT OF HERE NOW AND GET BACK HOME WHILE YOU STILL CAN.
WAIT HERE, SOSUKE, I'LL BE RIGHT BACK.
OKAY.

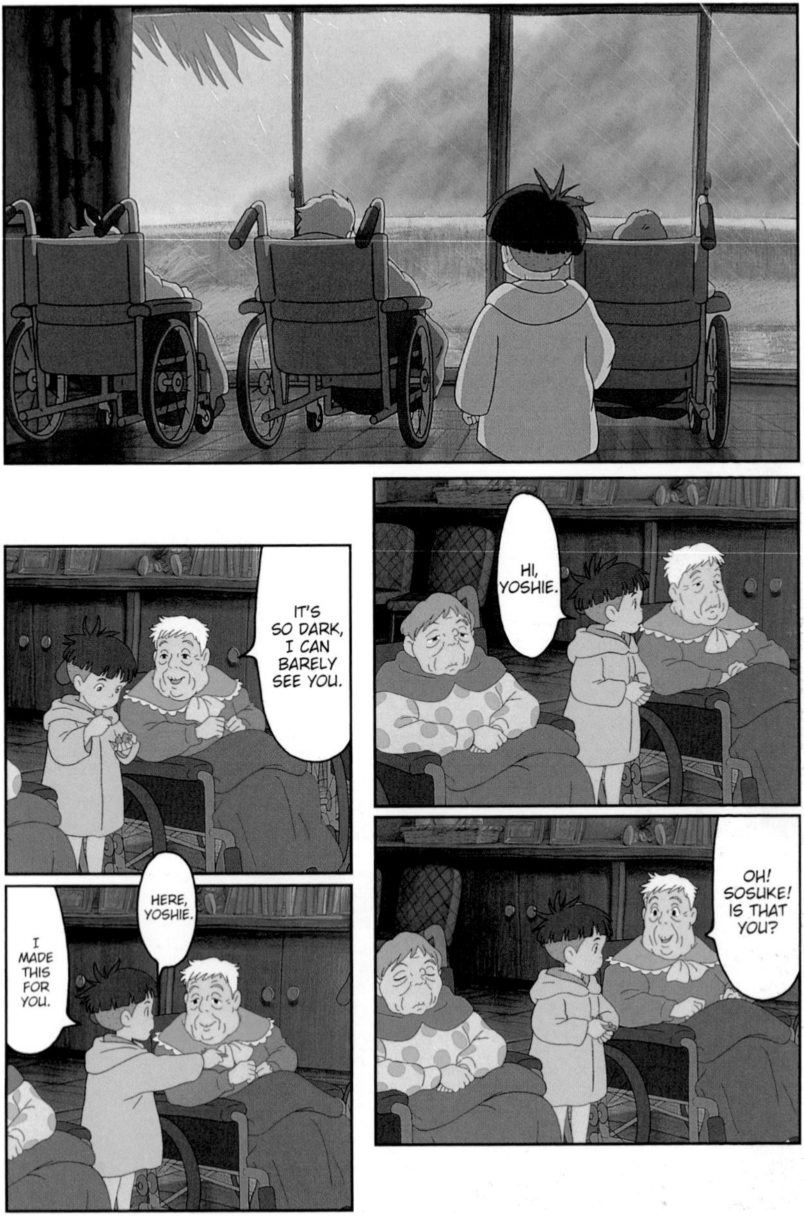
HI, YOSHIE.
IT'S SO DARK, I CAN BARELY SEE YOU.
OH! SOSUKE! IS THAT YOU?
HERE, YOSHIE.
I MADE THIS FOR YOU.

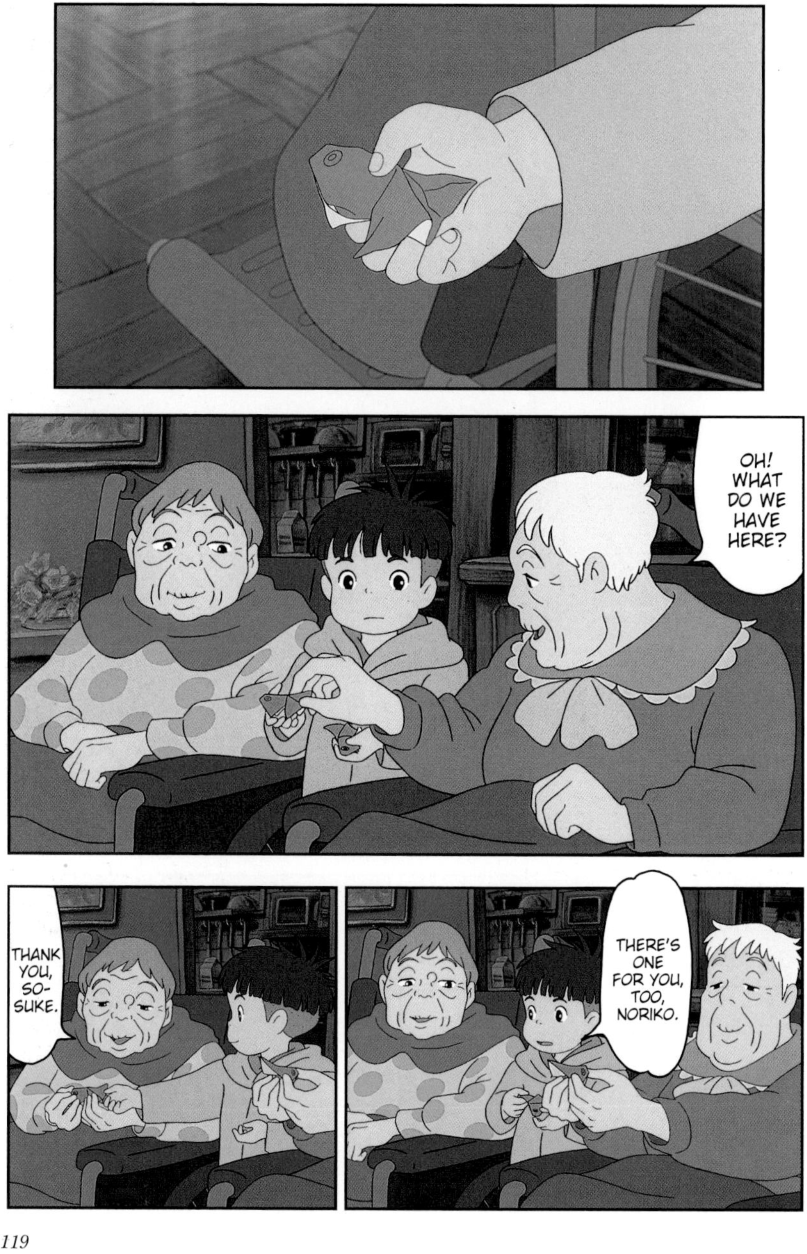
OH! WHAT DO WE HAVE HERE?
THERE'S ONE FOR YOU, TOO, NORIKO.
THANK YOU, SO-SUKE.

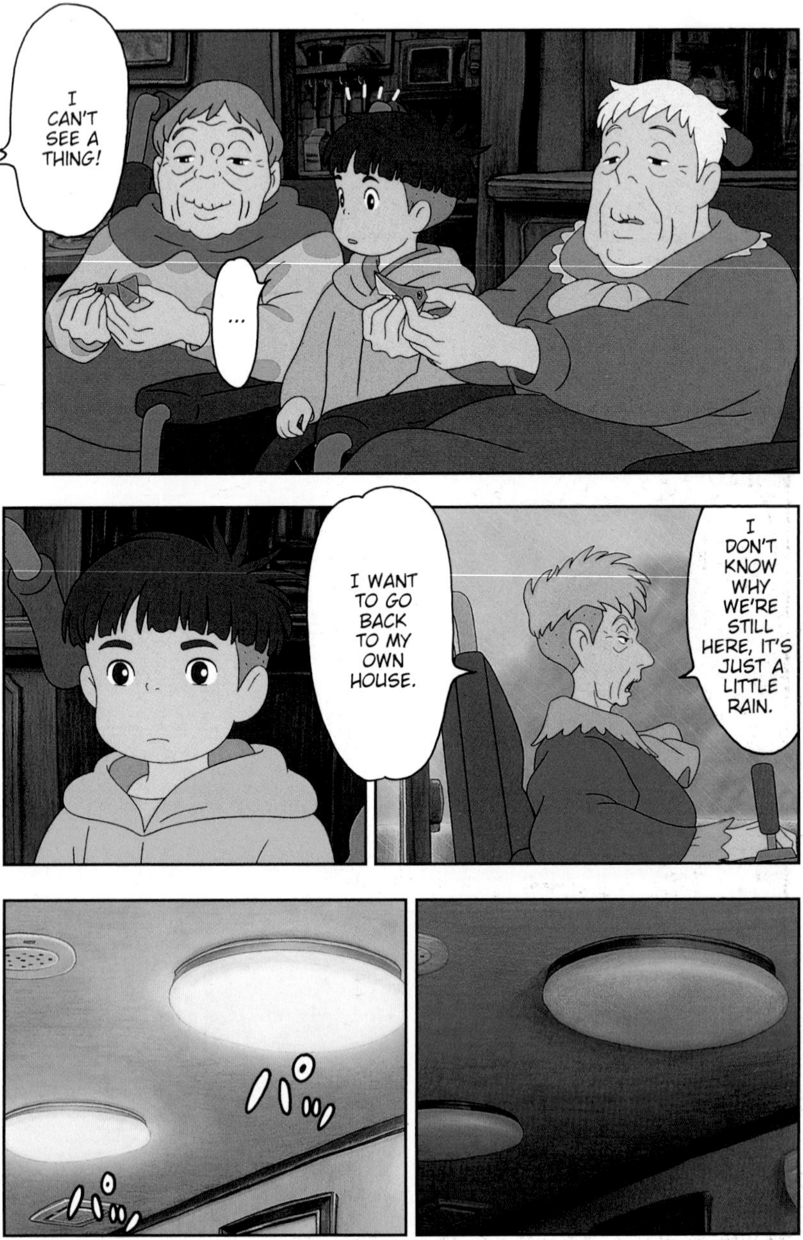
I CAN'T SEE A THING!
...
I DON'T KNOW WHY WE'RE STILL HERE, IT'S JUST A LITTLE RAIN.
I WANT TO GO BACK TO MY OWN HOUSE.

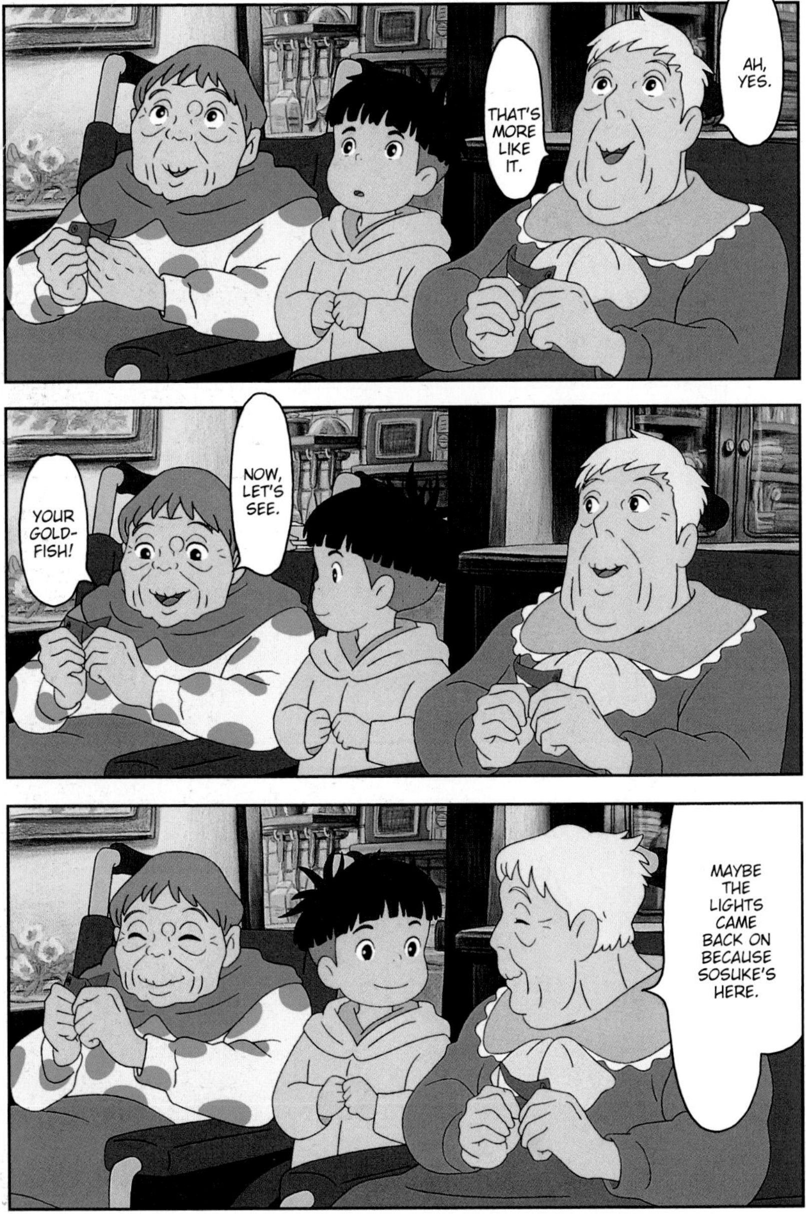
AH, YES.
THAT'S MORE LIKE IT.
NOW, LET'S SEE.
YOUR GOLD-FISH!
MAYBE THE LIGHTS CAME BACK ON BECAUSE SOSUKE'S HERE.

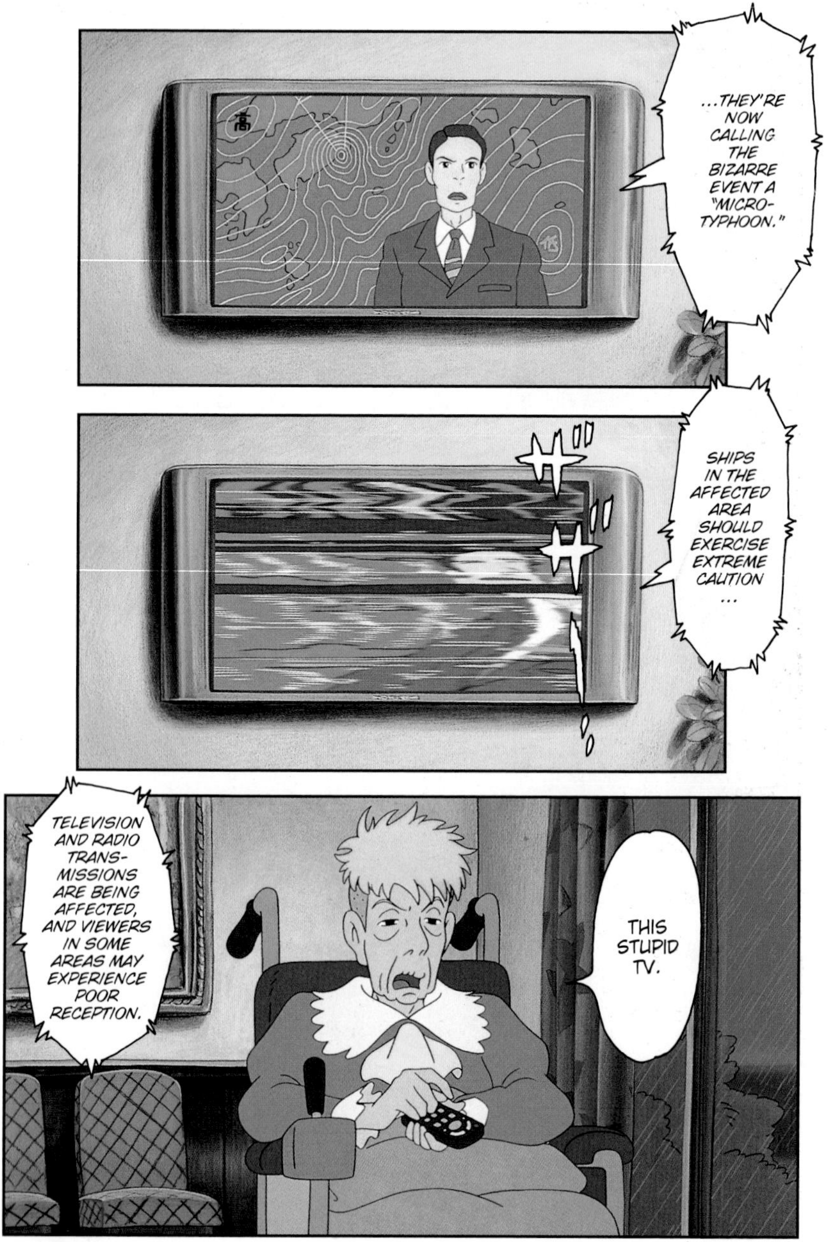
...THEY'RE NOW CALLING THE BIZARRE EVENT A "MICRO-TYPHOON."
SHIPS IN THE AFFECTED AREA SHOULD EXERCISE EXTREME CAUTION ...
THIS STUPID TV.
TELEVISION AND RADIO TRANS-MISSIONS ARE BEING AFFECTED, AND VIEWERS IN SOME AREAS MAY EXPERIENCE POOR RECEPTION.

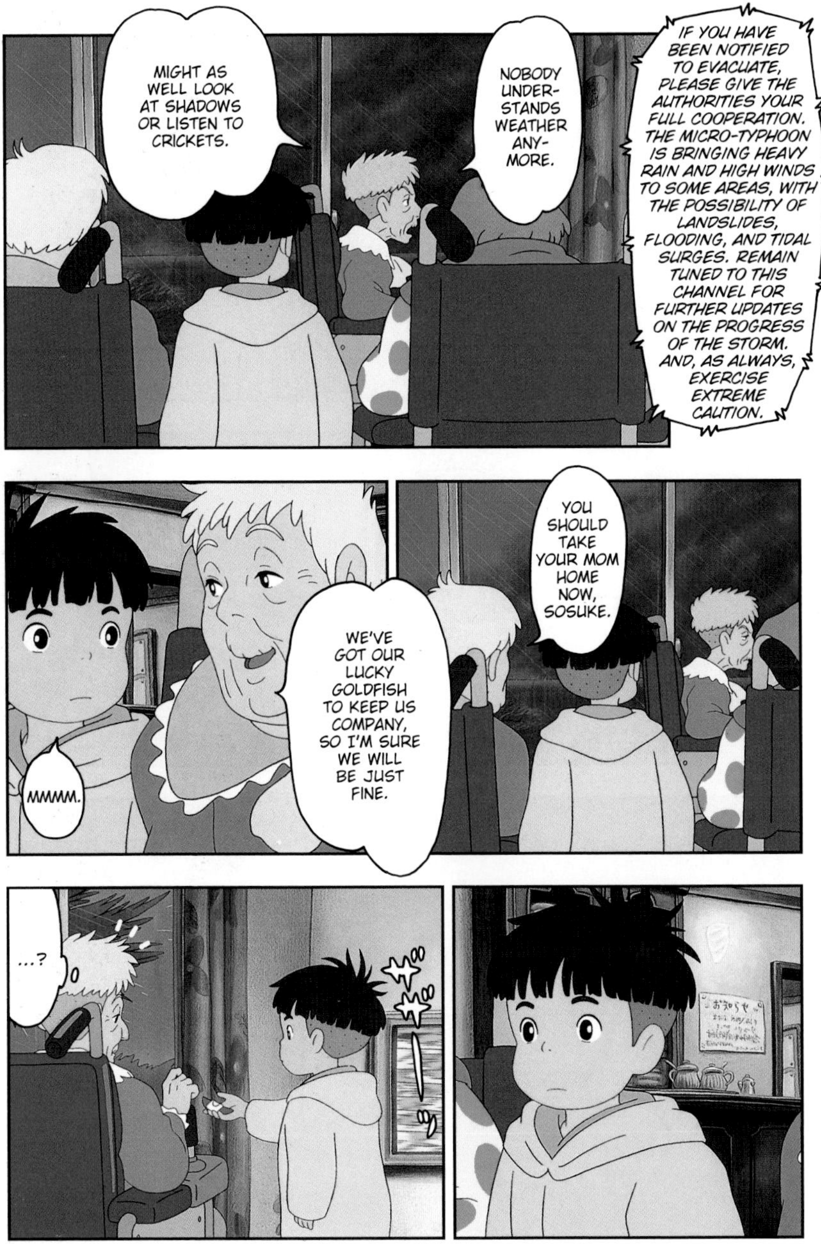

IF YOU HAVE BEEN NOTIFIED TO EVACUATE, PLEASE GIVE THE AUTHORITIES YOUR FULL COOPERATION. THE MICRO-TYPHOON IS BRINGING HEAVY RAIN AND HIGH WINDS TO SOME AREAS, WITH THE POSSIBILITY OF LANDSLIDES, FLOODING, AND TIDAL SURGES. REMAIN TUNED TO THIS CHANNEL FOR FURTHER UPDATES ON THE PROGRESS OF THE STORM. AND, AS ALWAYS, EXERCISE EXTREME CAUTION.
NOBODY UNDER-STANDS WEATHER ANY-MORE.
MIGHT AS WELL LOOK AT SHADOWS OR LISTEN TO CRICKETS.
YOU SHOULD TAKE YOUR MOM HOME NOW, SOSUKE.
WE'VE GOT OUR LUCKY GOLDFISH TO KEEP US COMPANY, SO I'M SURE WE WILL BE JUST FINE.
MMMM.
...?

THIS IS FOR YOU, TOKI.

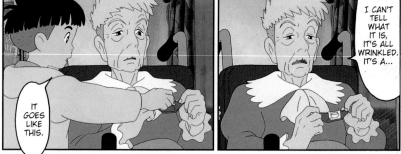

I CAN'T TELL WHAT IT IS, IT'S ALL WRINKLED. IT'S A...

IT GOES LIKE THIS.

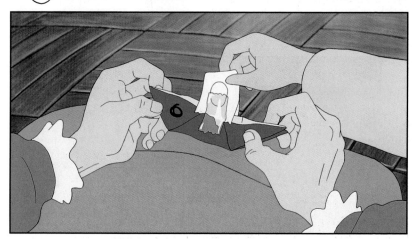

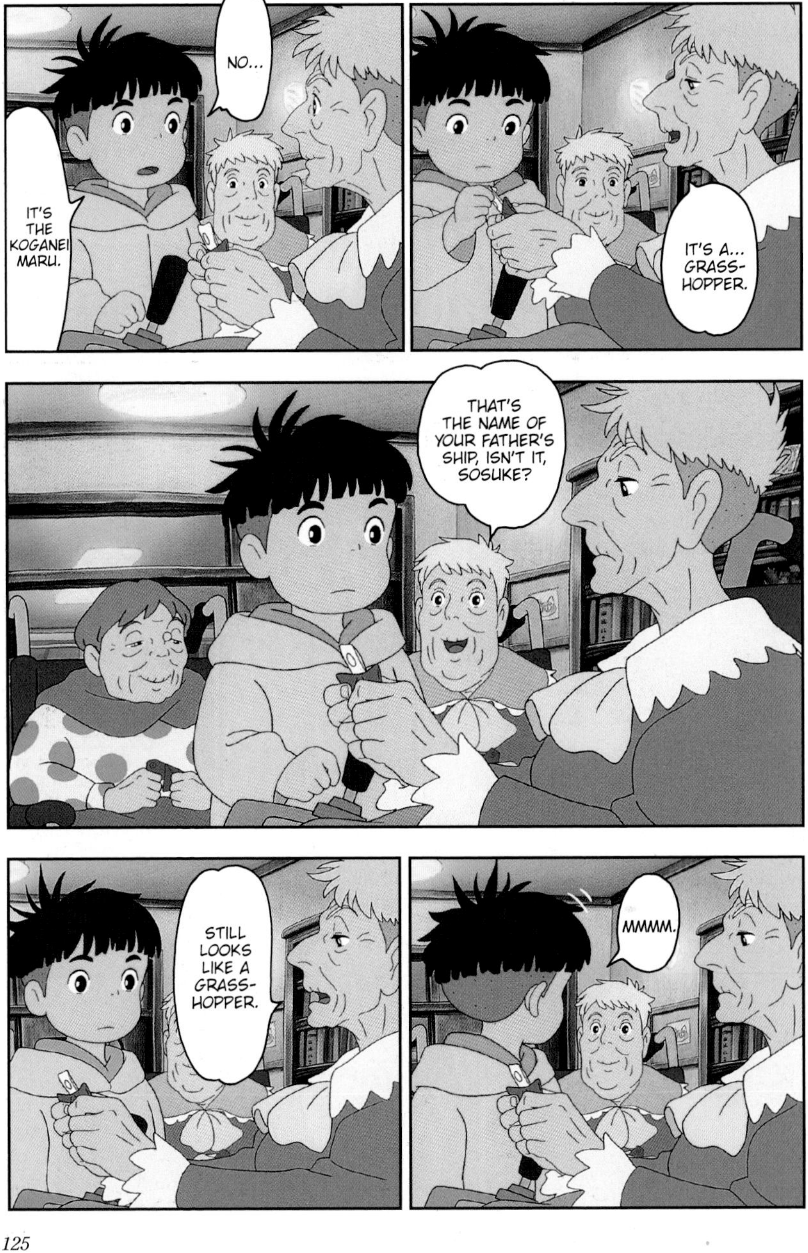
IT'S THE KOGANEI MARU.
NO...
IT'S A... GRASSHOPPER.
THAT'S THE NAME OF YOUR FATHER'S SHIP, ISN'T IT, SOSUKE?
STILL LOOKS LIKE A GRASSHOPPER.
MMMM.

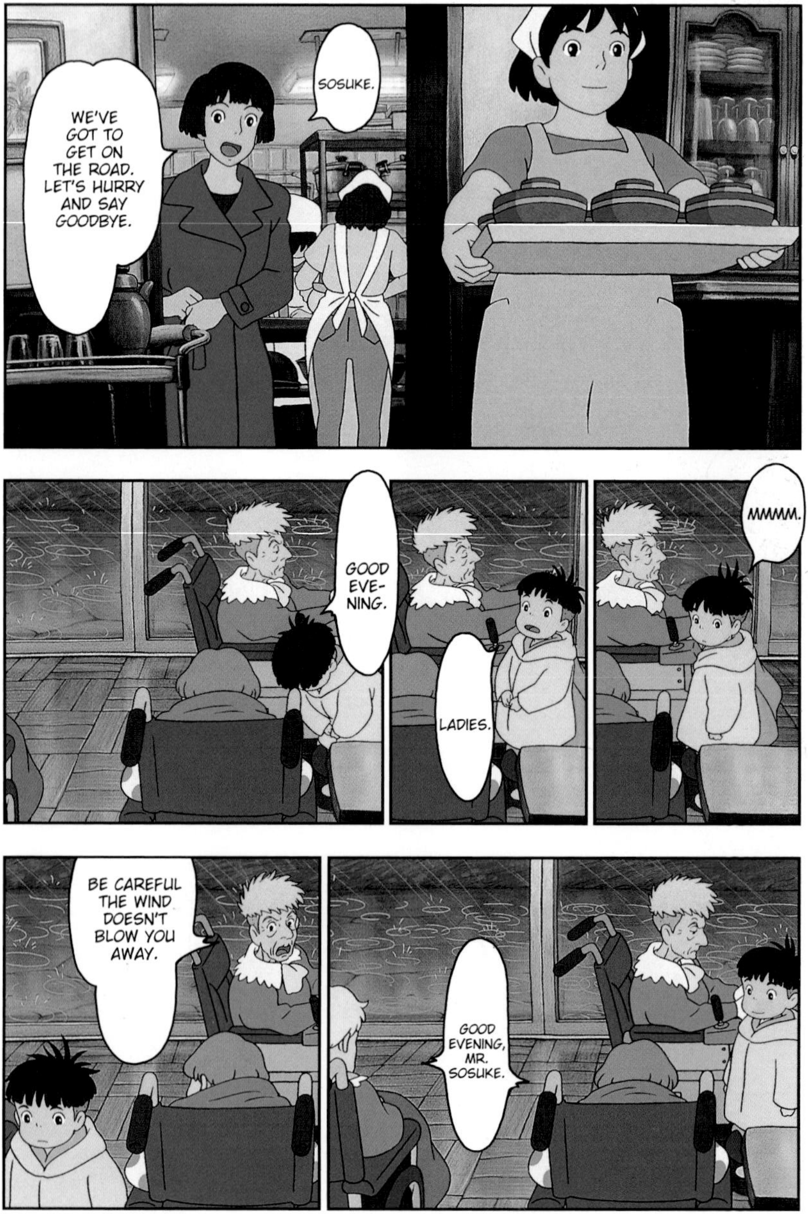
SOSUKE.
WE'VE GOT TO GET ON THE ROAD. LET'S HURRY AND SAY GOODBYE.
MMMM.
LADIES.
GOOD EVE- NING.
GOOD EVENING, MR. SOSUKE.
BE CAREFUL THE WIND DOESN'T BLOW YOU AWAY.

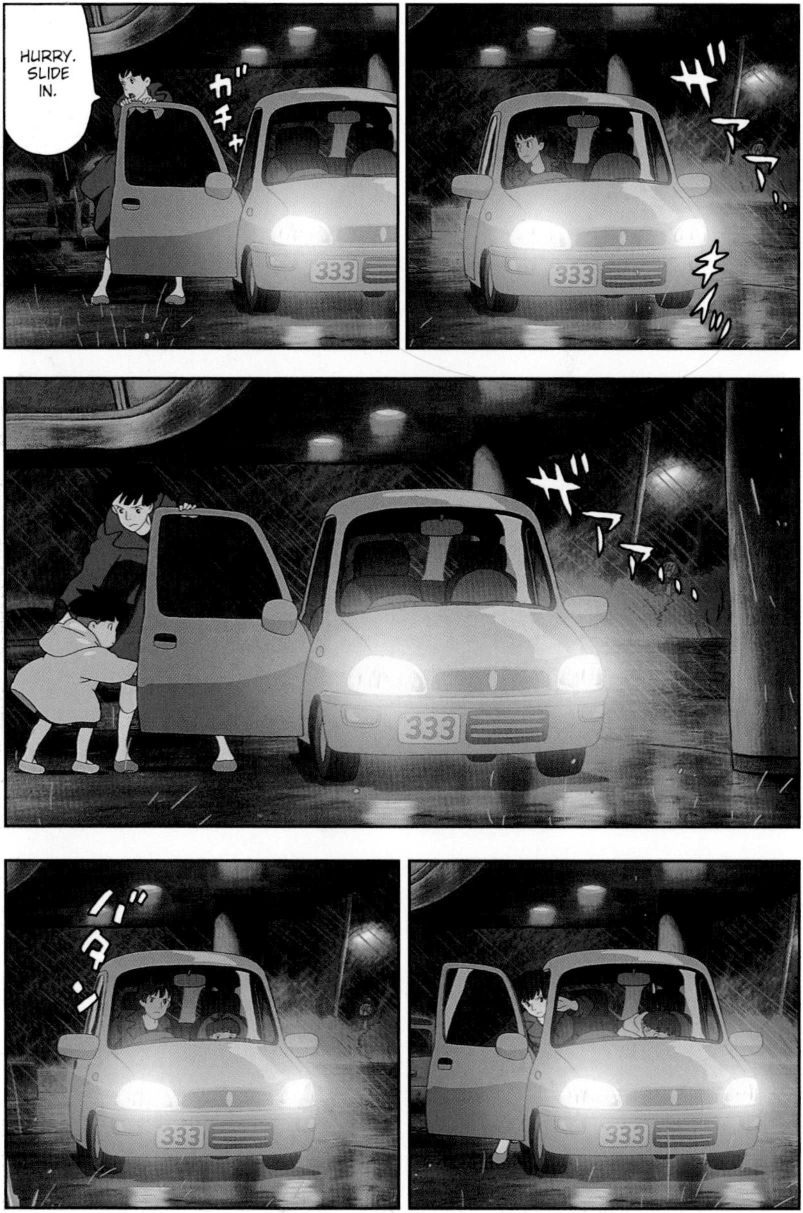
ザァァ..
キィッ
HURRY. SLIDE IN.
ガチャ
ザァァ...
バタン

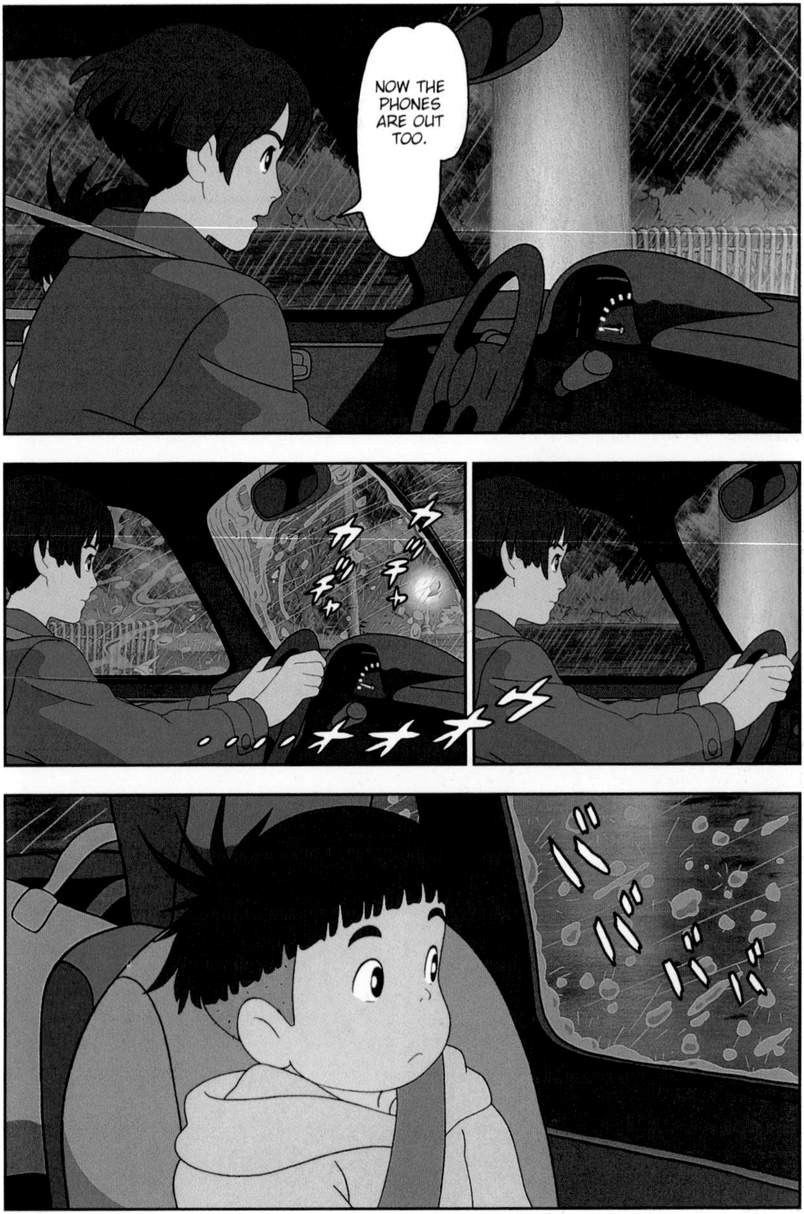
NOW THE PHONES ARE OUT TOO.

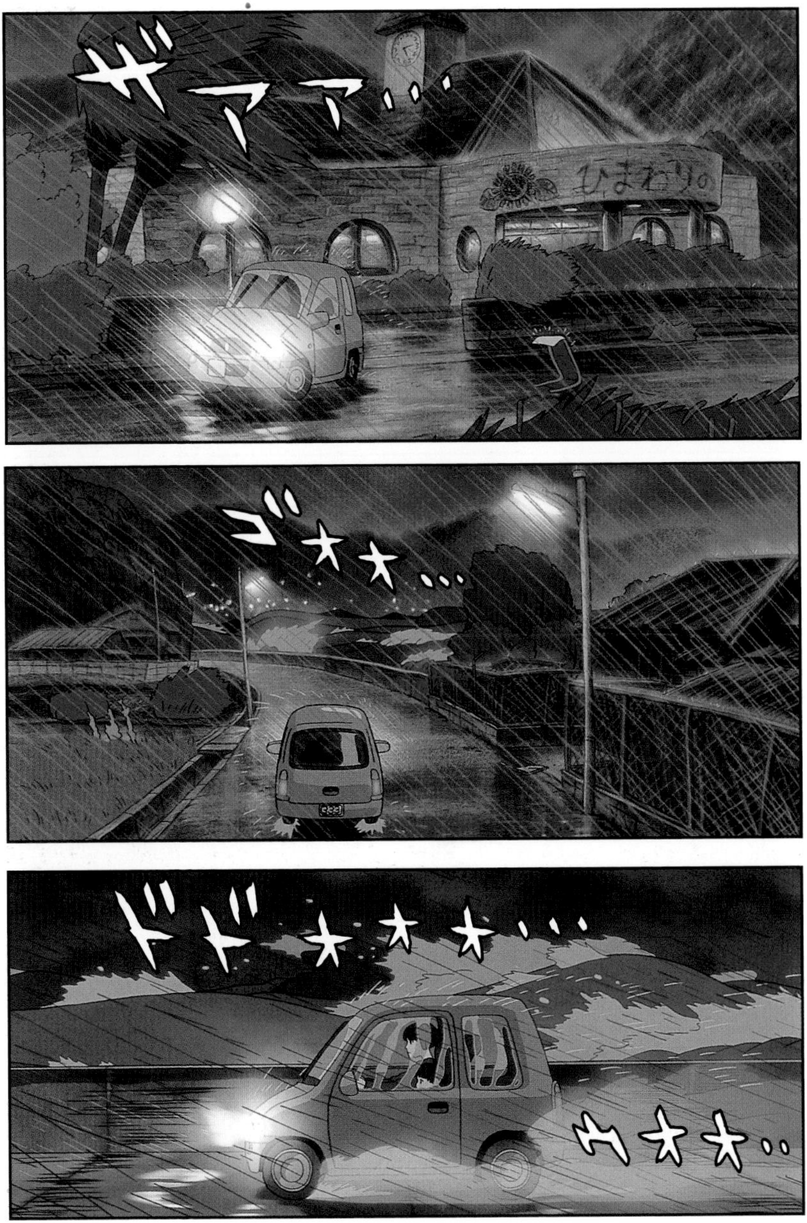
ザアア…
ひまわりの
ゴオオ…
ドドオオオ…
ウオオ‥

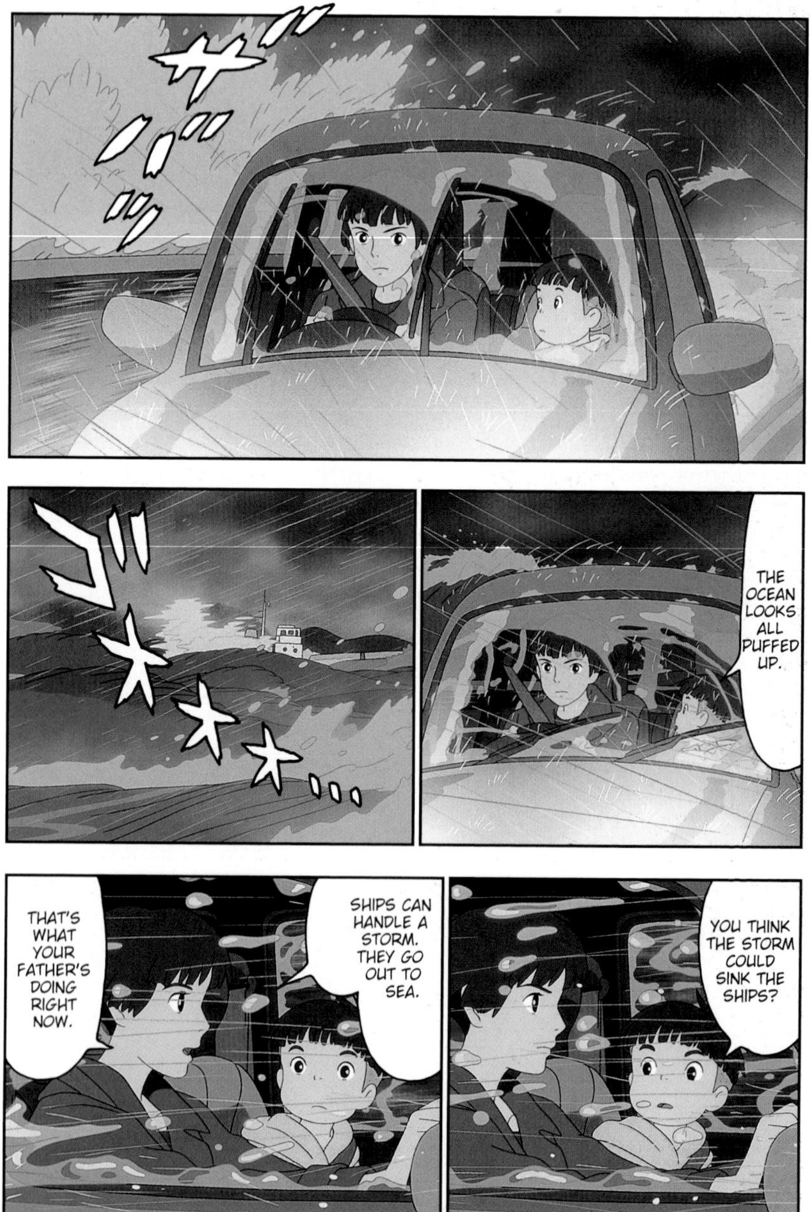
THE OCEAN LOOKS ALL PUFFED UP.
YOU THINK THE STORM COULD SINK THE SHIPS?
SHIPS CAN HANDLE A STORM. THEY GO OUT TO SEA.
THAT'S WHAT YOUR FATHER'S DOING RIGHT NOW.

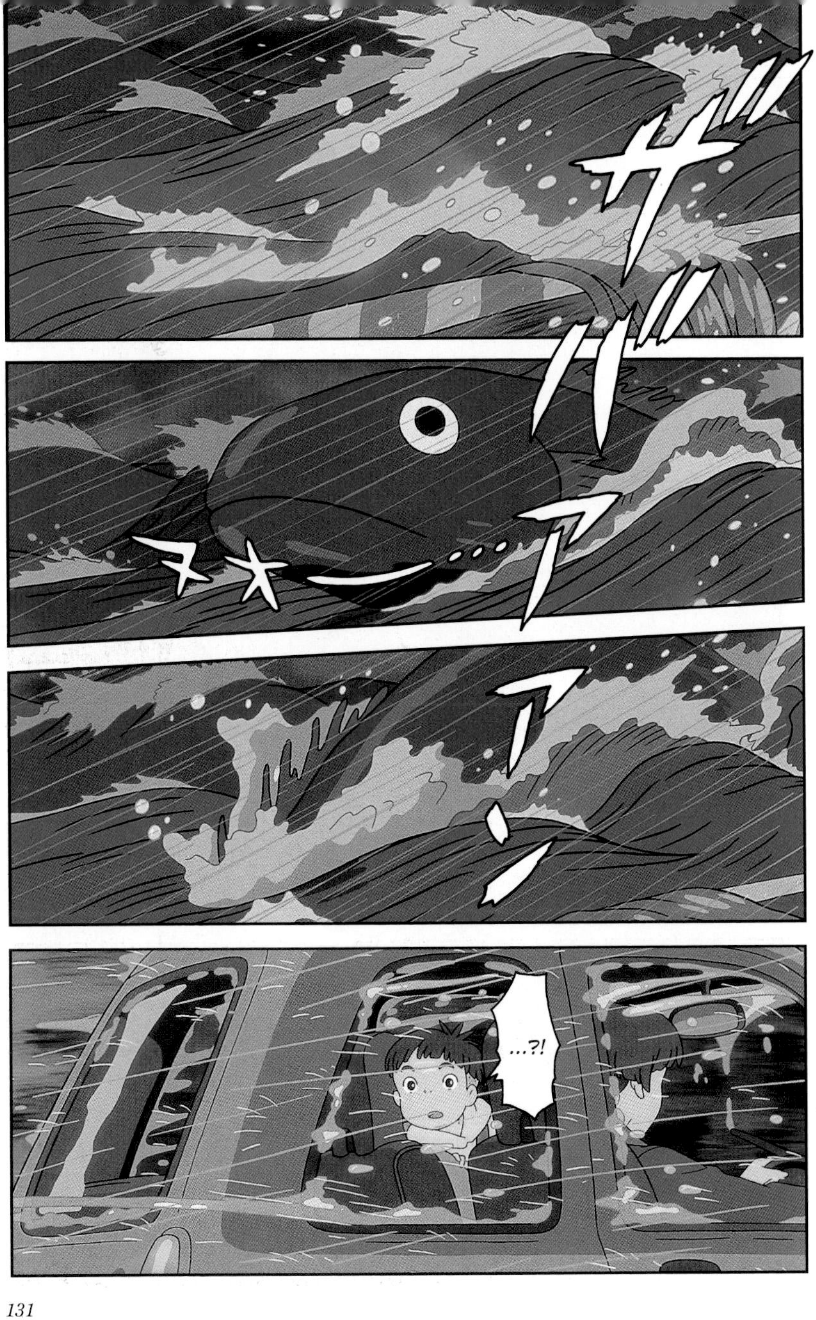
ザバアアン
ヌオー…
...?!

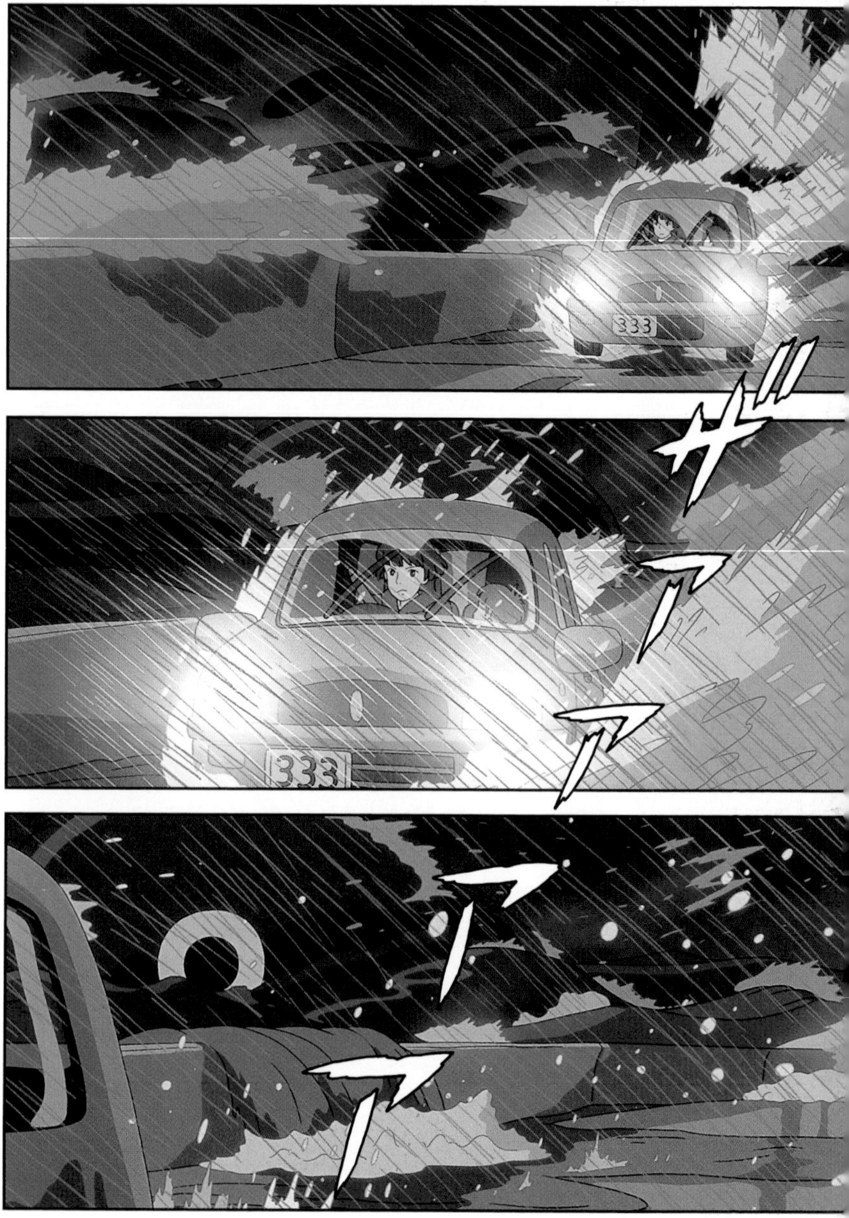
ザアアアア

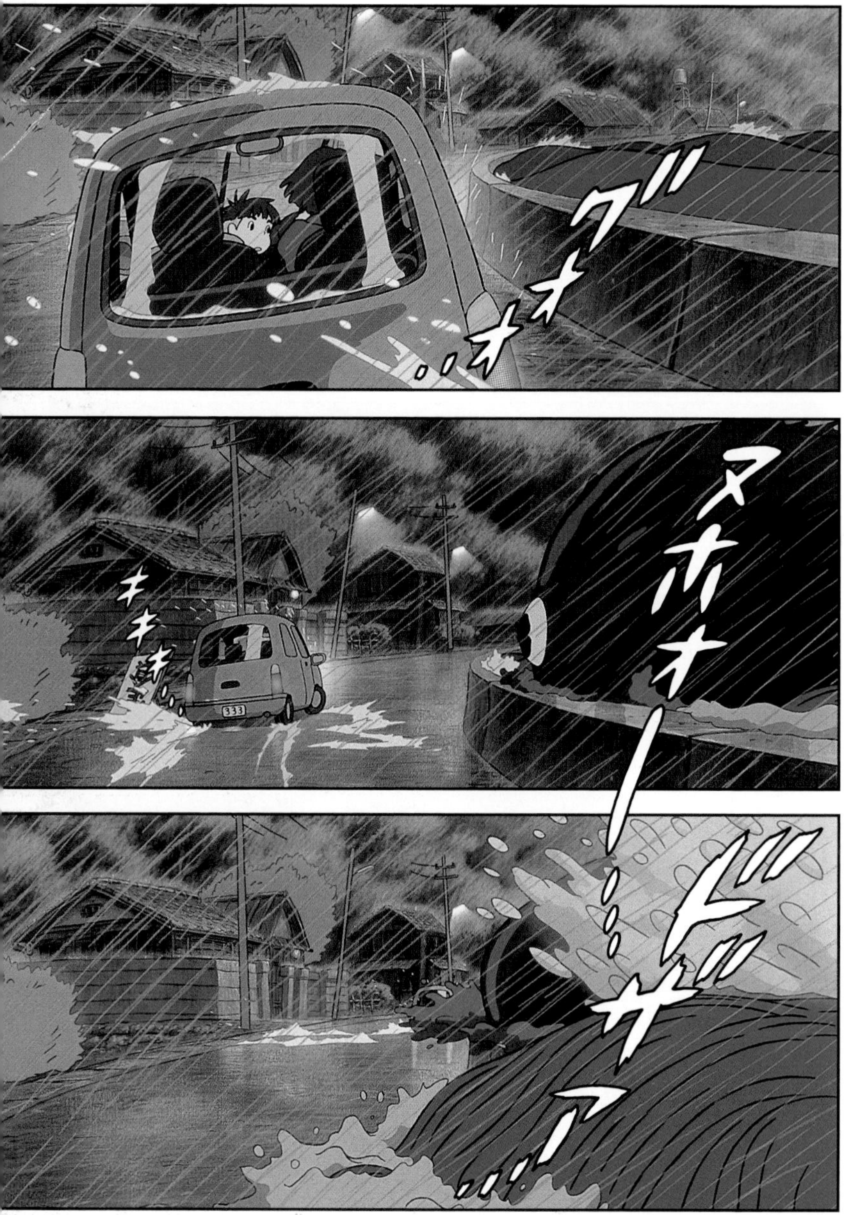
グオオ…
ヌホオー…
キキキ
ドザァ…

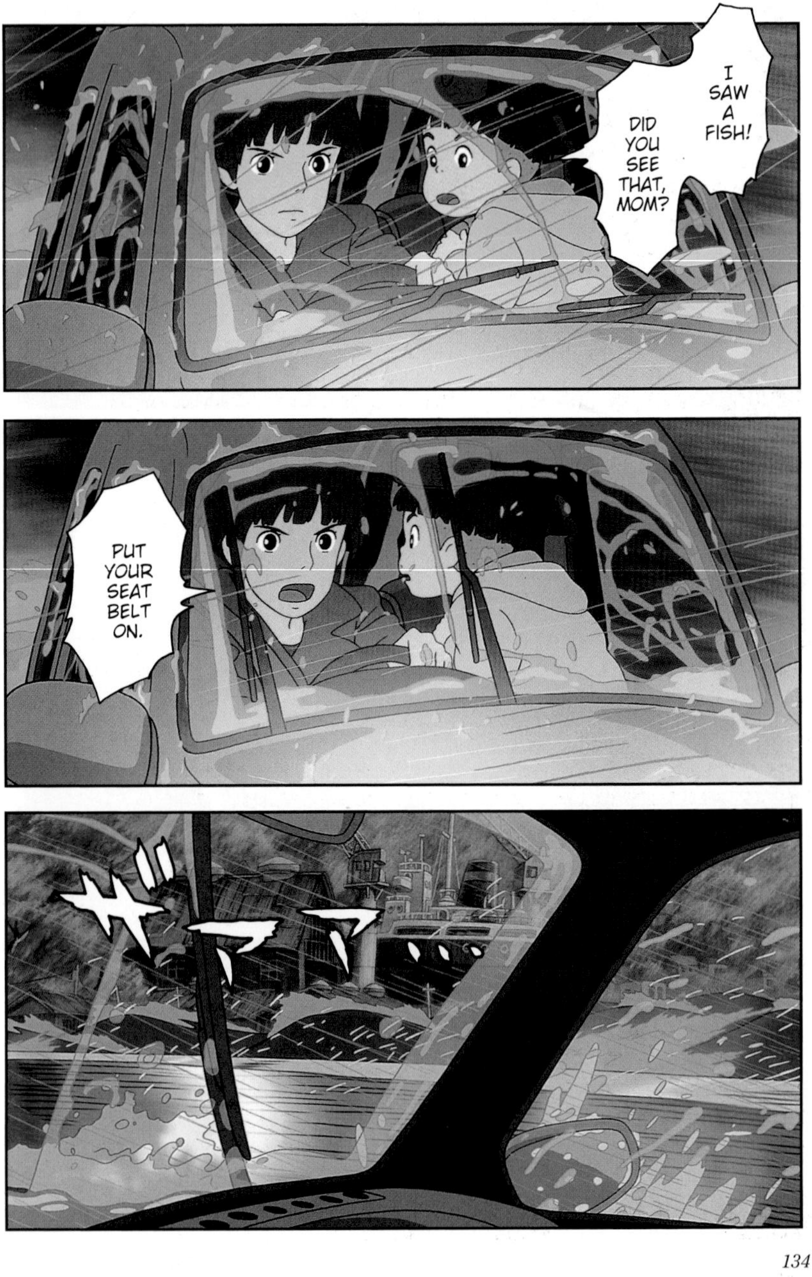
I SAW A FISH!
DID YOU SEE THAT, MOM?
PUT YOUR SEAT BELT ON.

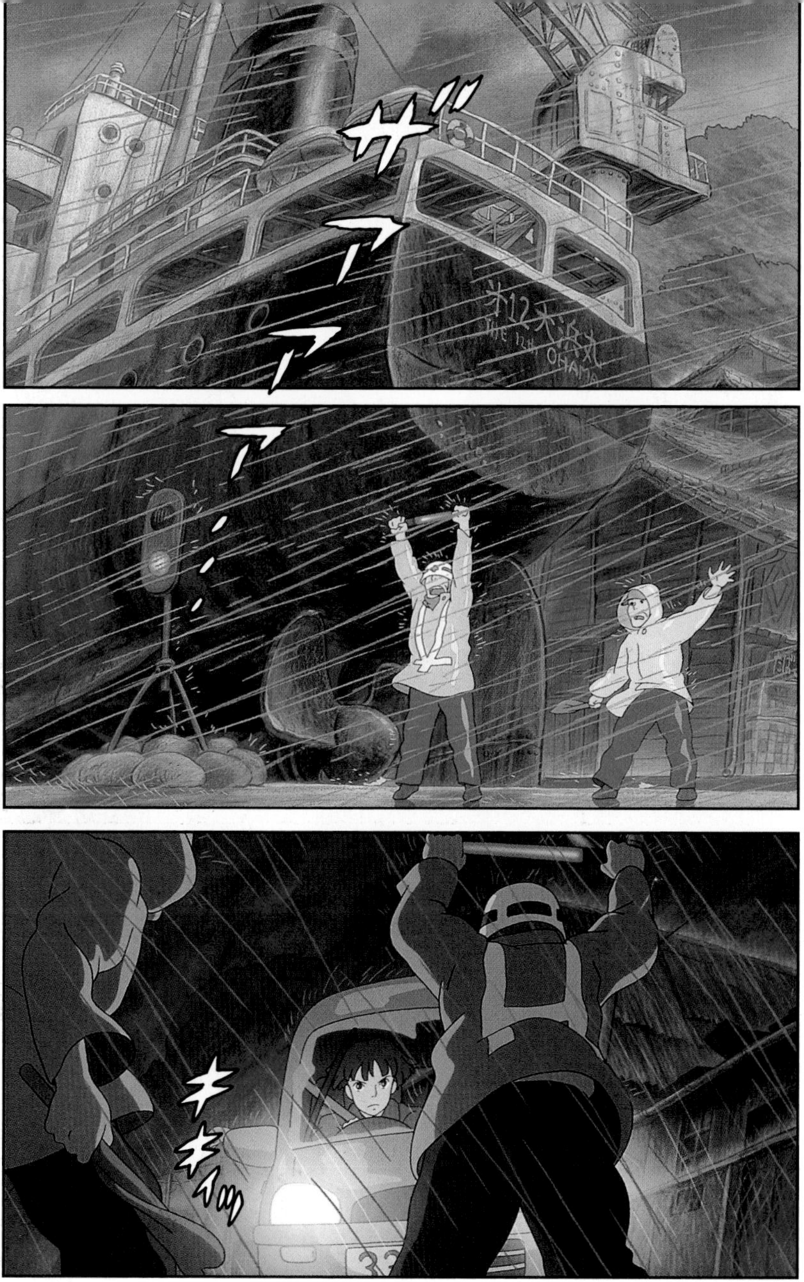
ザァアアア…
キキィッ

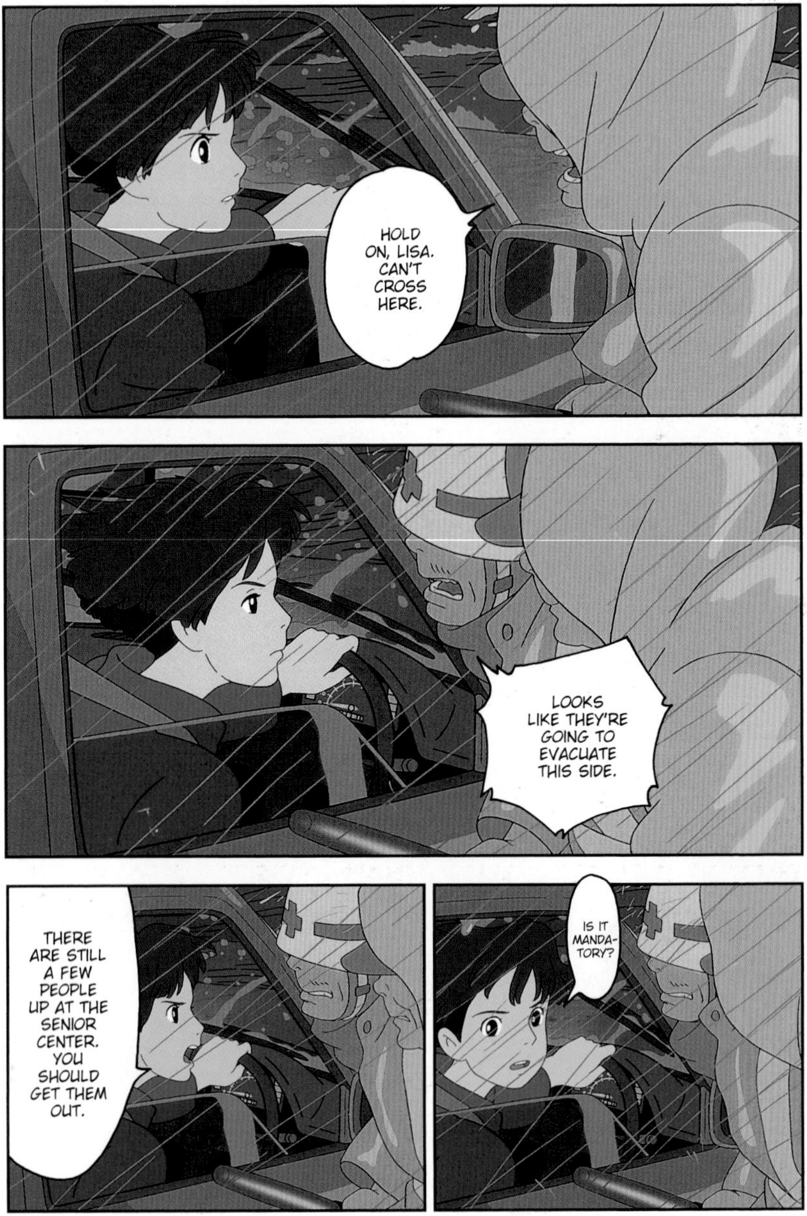
HOLD ON, LISA. CAN'T CROSS HERE.
LOOKS LIKE THEY'RE GOING TO EVACUATE THIS SIDE.
IS IT MANDATORY?
THERE ARE STILL A FEW PEOPLE UP AT THE SENIOR CENTER. YOU SHOULD GET THEM OUT.

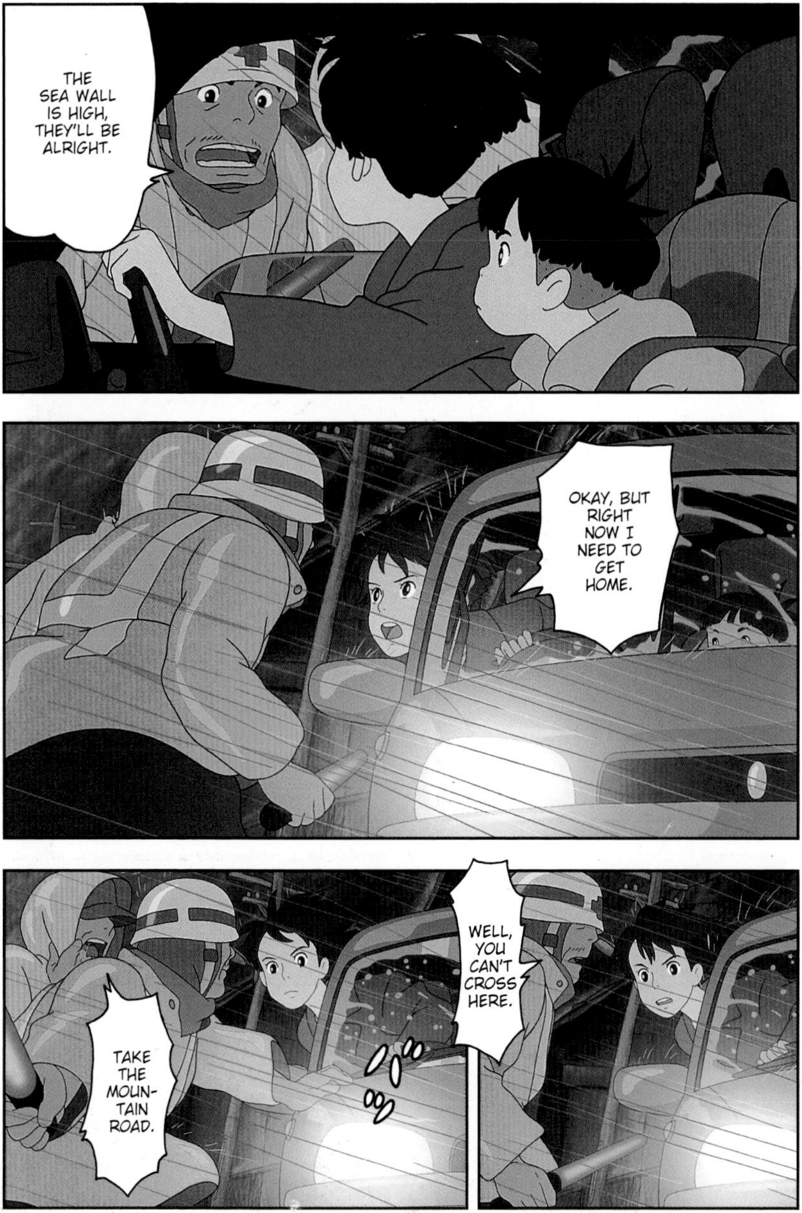
THE SEA WALL IS HIGH, THEY'LL BE ALRIGHT.
OKAY, BUT RIGHT NOW I NEED TO GET HOME.
WELL, YOU CAN'T CROSS HERE.
TAKE THE MOUN-TAIN ROAD.

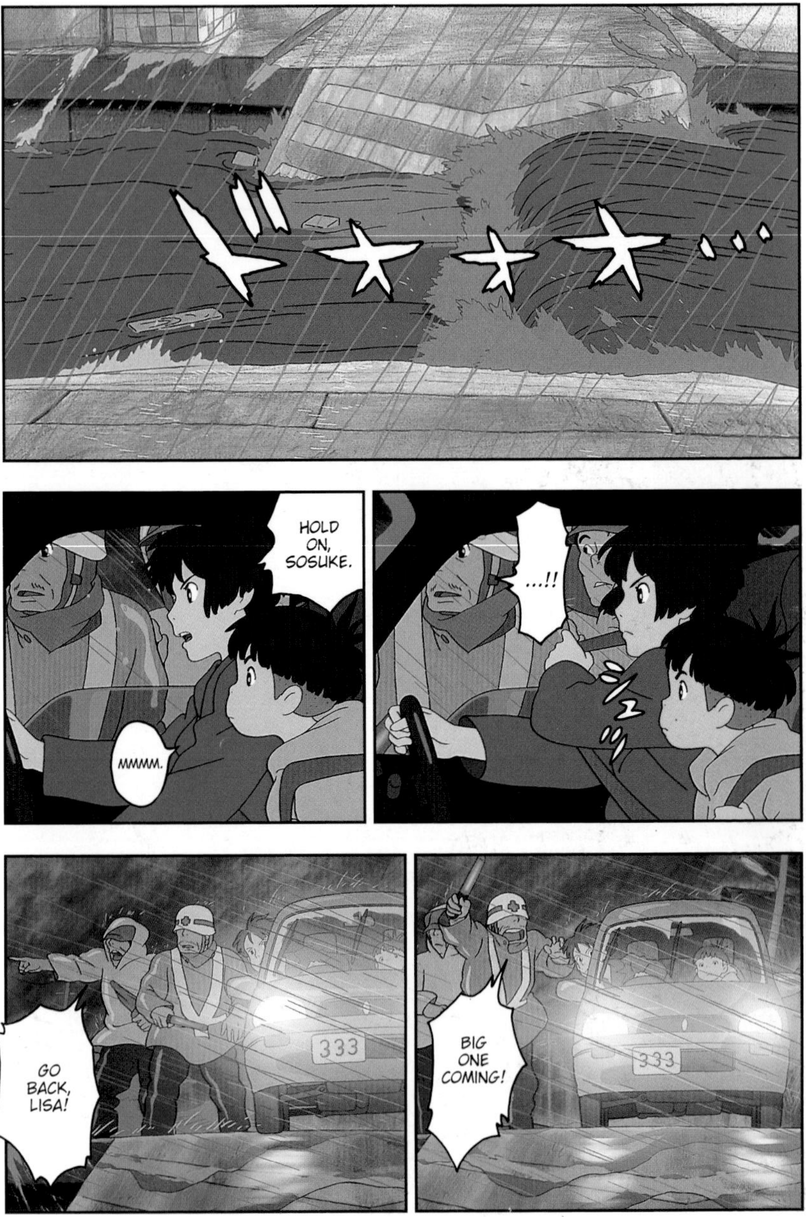
ゾォォォ…
...!!
HOLD ON, SOSUKE.
MMMM.
BIG ONE COMING!
GO BACK, LISA!

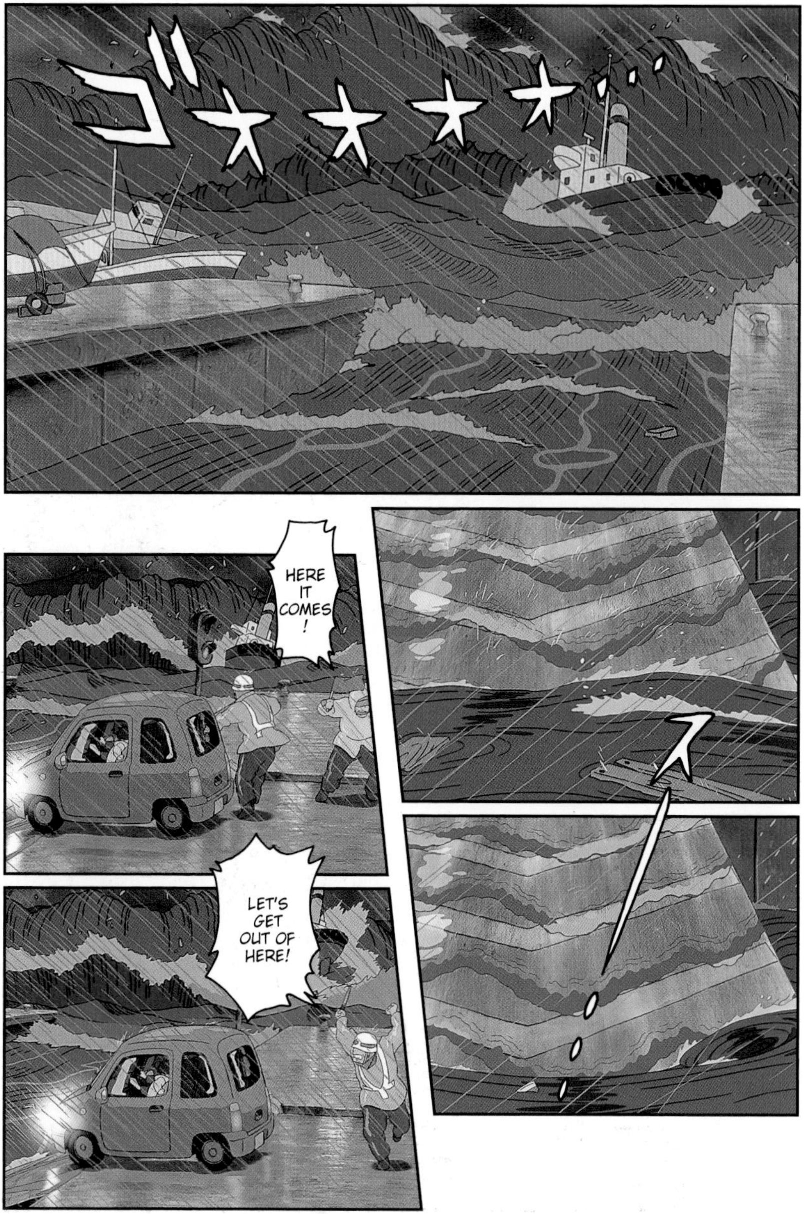

ゴォォォォ
ス
HERE IT COMES!
LET'S GET OUT OF HERE!

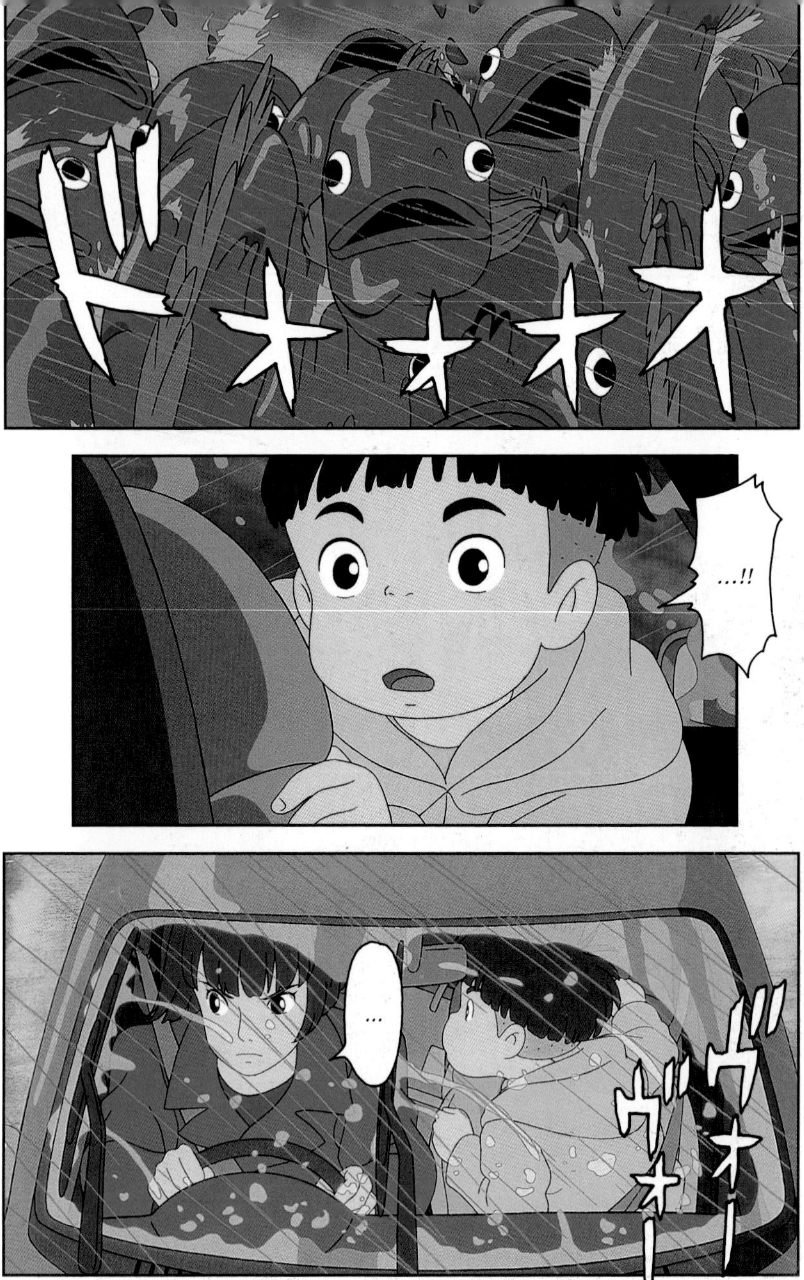
ドオォオオ
...!!
...
ヴォー
ヴォー

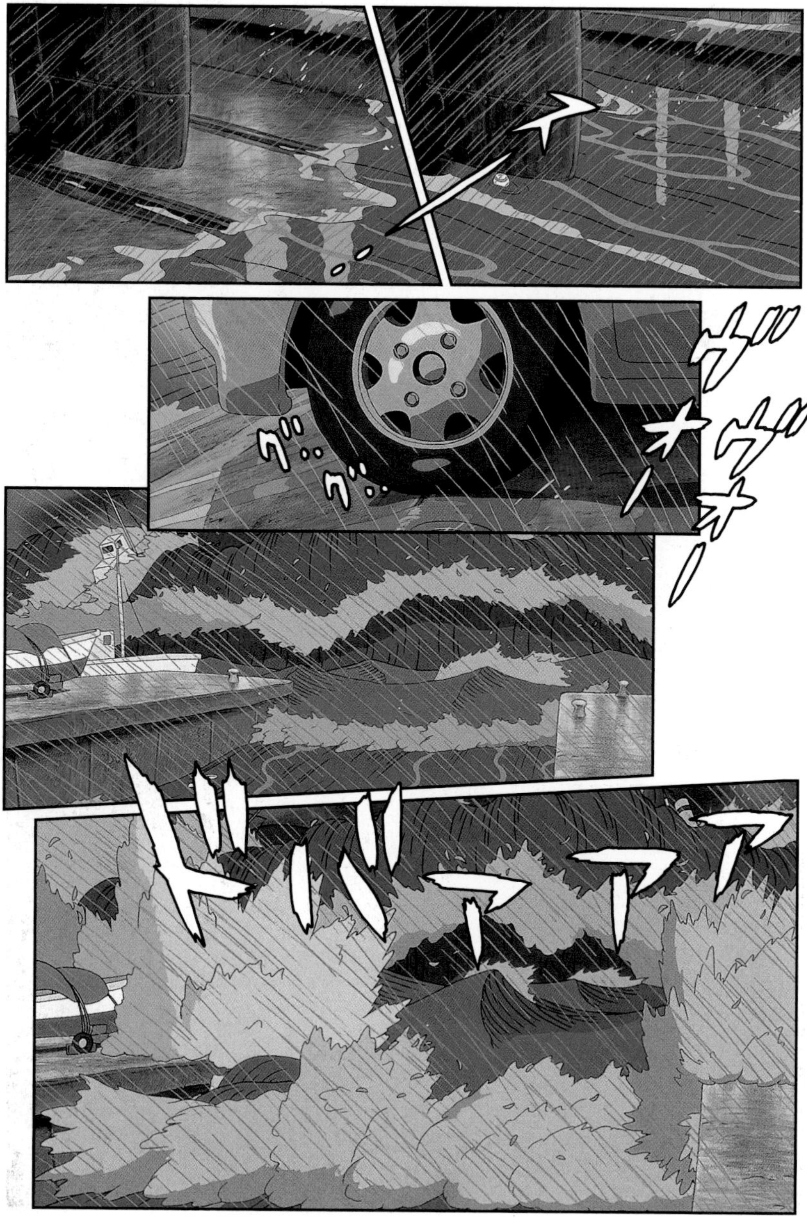
スー‥
ヴォー
ヴォー
グ‥
グ‥
ドバァーアァ

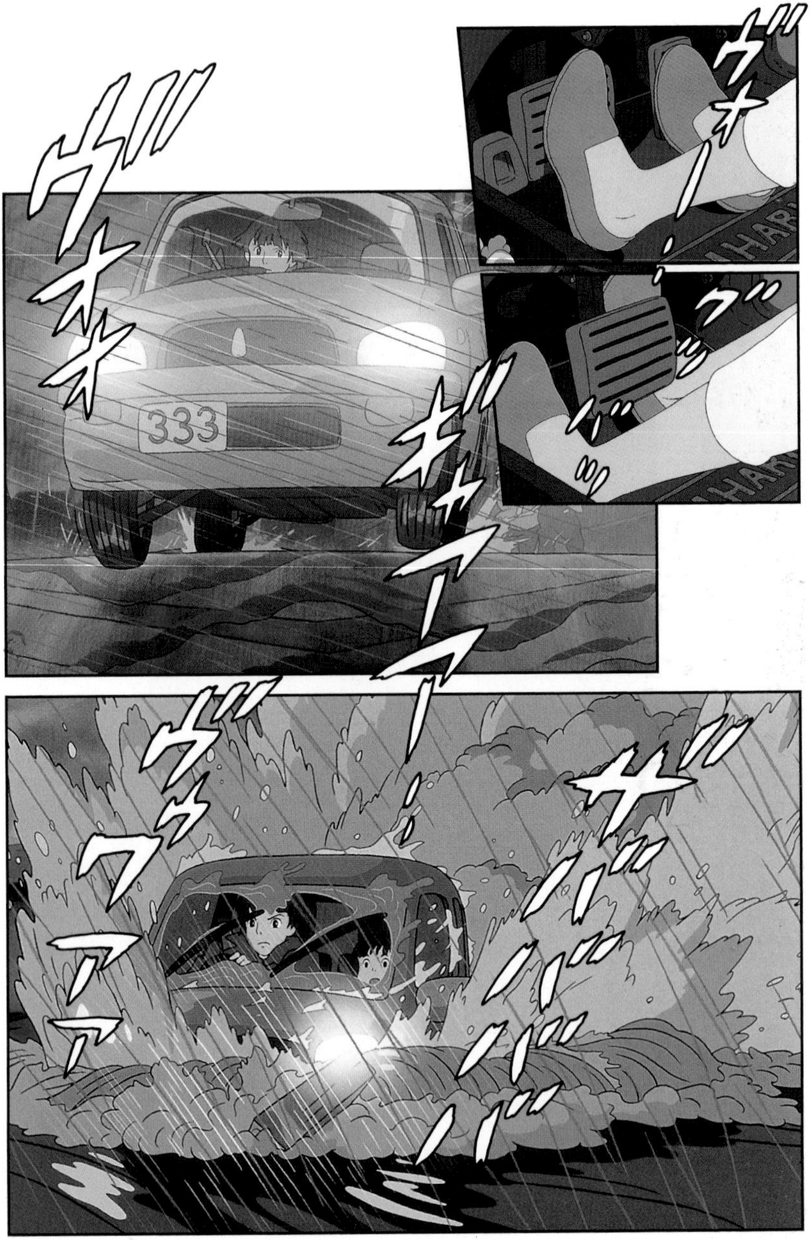
ヴォー…
ググッ
ヴォォォ
ギャアアー…
ザバババババ
ヴゥワアア

87.4	FX:	ZAAAA [swosh]
87.5	FX:	PIKA [flash]
88.1	FX:	DWOOOO [wooooosh]
88.4-5	FX:	GYUUN [gwaaa]
89.1	FX:	HYUN [shwp]
91.3	FX:	GYUUU [pull]
91.5	FX:	GYUUU [pull]
94.1-3	FX:	GWOOOO [wooooosh]
95.1-3	FX:	GWOOOO [wooooosh]
96.1-3	FX:	GWOOOO [wooooosh]
101.2	FX:	ZUNN [shwaa]
101.3	FX:	GWOOOO [wooooosh]
103.1	FX:	BOTO [blopp]
103.2	FX:	BOTO BOTO [blopp blopp]
103.3	FX:	BOTO [blopp]
104.1	FX:	ZABA [crash]
104.3	FX:	GUWA [gwpp]
104.4	FX:	GWOOOO [wooooosh]
105.1-2	FX:	DWOOOO [wooooosh]
105.2	FX:	DOBA [splshh]
105.3	FX:	GUFEEEE [boooosh]
107.1	FX:	DWOOOO [wooooosh]
109.3	FX:	ZAAAA [shwaaaa]
110.1	FX:	ZABABABA [splch splch]
110.2	FX:	ZAAAA [shwaaa]
110.3	FX:	ZAAAA [shwaaa]
111.5	FX:	PEKORI [bow]
111.7	FX:	GATA [grik]
112.1-2	FX:	ZAAAA [shwaaa]
112.3-4	FX:	ZAAAA [shwaaa]
112.5.1	FX:	BUWA [bwsh]
112.5.2	FX:	ZAAAA [shwaaa]
113.1	FX:	GWOOOO [wooooosh]
113.3	FX:	BYUUU [wiiiish]
114.2	FX:	SUTA SUTA [stp stp]
114.3	FX:	GU GU [grrr]
114.4	FX:	ZZU [slpp]
117.3	FX:	SSA [slpp]

70.4	FX:	TSUN TSUN [poke poke]
71.2	FX:	PUNYA [nib]
71.4	FX:	PUNYA PUNYA [nib nib]
71.5	FX:	PUNYA PUNYA PUNYA [nib nib nib]
72.1	FX:	ZORO ZORO ZORO [crwd crwd crwd]
72.2	FX:	PUNYA PUNYA PUNYA [nib nib nib]
72.3	FX:	PUNYA PUNYA PUNYA PUNYA [nib nib nib nib]
73.1	FX:	PUNYA PUNYA PUNYA [nib nib nib]
73.2	FX:	PUNYA PUNYA PUNYA [nib nib nib]
74.2	FX:	PANN!! [pop]
74.4	FX:	BBA [ahh]
75.2	FX:	PONN!! [plop]
75.4	FX:	UUUN [urrrr]
75.5	FX:	PANN!! [pop]
76.3	FX:	CHU [smooch]
79.1	FX:	GU [glp]
79.2	FX:	PONN [popp]
79.2-3	FX:	DWOOOO [wooooosh]
80.3	FX:	GWOOOO [woooosh]
80.4	FX:	PYURO [swpp]
80.5	FX:	GWOOOO [wooooosh]
81.1	FX:	DWOOOO [wooogh]
81.2	FX:	DWOOOO [wooogh]
81.3	FX:	DWOOOO [wooogh]
81.4	FX:	PETA PETA PETA [pitter patter]
81.5	FX:	TA [tp]
82.1	FX:	SUUUU [szzzzz]
82.3	FX:	NUUU [urrrp]
82.4-5	FX:	DWOOOO [wooooosh]
83.1-2	FX:	DWOOOO [wooooosh]
83.3	FX:	GWOOOO [wooooosh]
84.1-3	FX:	GWOOOO [wooooosh]
84.4-6	FX:	DWOOOO [wooooosh]
85.1.1	FX:	GISHI [creek]
85.1.2	FX:	ZAAAA [swish]
85.2	FX:	BWA [flood]
85.3	FX:	DWOOOO [wooooosh]
86.1-2	FX:	GWOOOO [wooooosh]
86.3	FX:	GWOOOO [wooooosh]
87.3	FX:	ZAAAA [swosh]

50.3	FX:	PONN! [pwopp]
51.3	FX:	MUGYU [grpp]
52.1	FX:	GU GU [grrrr]
52.2	FX:	BUNN!! [znnn]
52.3	FX:	BUNN!! [znnn]
53.1	FX:	GU GU [grrr]
53.2	FX:	BUNN [znnn]
53.3	FX:	GU GU [grrr]
53.4	FX:	DDA [thmp]
54.1	FX:	GOKU GOKU [gulp gulp]
54.2.1	FX:	BBA [shwa]
54.2.2	FX:	GASHAN [smash]
54.3	FX:	GUI [grpp]
54.4	FX:	GOKU GOKU [gulp gulp]
54.5	FX:	GASHAN GASHAN [smash smash]
55.2	FX:	KURU [spin]
55.3	FX:	TTA [tmp]
56.4	FX:	WOOO [whoa]
59.3	FX:	GGU [shove]
60.4	FX:	KASA KASA KASA [crawl crawl crawl]
61.1	FX:	ZORO ZORO [crpp crpp]
61.2	FX:	KASA KASA KASA [crawl crawl crawl]
61.5	FX:	KASA KASA KASA [crawl crawl crawl]
62.2	FX:	GACHA [kcha]
63.1	FX:	KATSU KATSU [thmp thmp]
63.2	FX:	KATSU KATSU [thmp thmp]
63.4	FX:	KOTSU KOTSU [thmp thmp]
64.1	FX:	GACHA [KCHA]
64.4	FX:	GU GU [grrr]
64.5	FX:	GACHA [kcha]
65.4	FX:	TOROOO [glgg glgg]
66.2	FX:	KOKU [glup]
66.4.1	FX:	BI BIIN!! [zapppp]
66.4.2	FX:	BIRI BIRI [zpp zpp]
68.2	FX:	SSA [slpp]
69.2.1	FX:	GAKO [gltt]
69.2.2	FX:	GA [gtt]
69.3	FX:	GONN [shut]

25.1	FX:	CHIKA CHIKA [blink blink]
26.1	FX:	TON [thp]
26.4	FX:	PACHI [flip]
26.5	FX:	TA TA [tp tp]
27.2	FX:	KACHI [flip]
27.3	FX:	CHIKA CHIKA [blink blink]
28.1	FX:	CHIKA CHIKA CHIKA [blink blink blink]
29.2	FX:	KACHI KACHI [click click]
29.3	FX:	KACHI KACHI KACHI [click click click]
29.4	FX:	CHIKA CHIKA CHIKA [blink blink blink]
31.1	FX:	KACHA KACHA KACHA KACHA KACHA KACHA KACHA KACHA KACHA [click clack click clack click clack click clack click clack]
31.2	FX:	CHIKA CHIKA CHIKA [blink blink blink]
31.3	FX:	BA BA BA [tda tda tda]
32.2	FX:	PUI [hmph]
32.5	FX:	KACHI [click]
33.1	FX:	KACHI KACHI KACHI [click click click]
33.2	FX:	CHIKA CHIKA [blink blink]
33.3	FX:	CHIKA CHIKA [blink blink]
33.5	FX:	TON [thp]
34.1	FX:	PPA [flip]
35.5	FX:	SSU [slpp]
36.2	FX:	GORON [roll]
36.3	FX:	GYUUU [squeeze]
36.4	FX:	BBA [flip]
38.2	FX:	PA [plink]
38.3	FX:	PA PA PA [plink plink plink]
42.1	FX:	KURU [flip]
42.3	FX:	PPU [plpp]
45.2	FX:	NIKO [grin]
45.4	FX:	KURU [flip]
47.4	FX:	PURU PURU [grr grrr]
48.4	FX:	WOOO [whoa]
49.2	FX:	PONN! [pwopp]
49.3	FX:	PONN! [pwopp]
49.4	FX:	BA [ahh]
49.5	FX:	GACHAN [crash]
50.1	FX:	WAAAA [whoaaaa]

Your Guide to *Ponyo on the Cliff by the Sea* Sound Effects!

To increase your enjoyment of the distinctive Japanese visual style of *Ponyo on the Cliff by the Sea*, we've included a listing of and guide to the sound effects used in this comic adaptation of the movie. In the comic, these sound effects are written in the Japanese phonetic characters called *katakana*.

In the sound effects glossary for *Ponyo on the Cliff by the Sea*, sound effects are listed by page and panel number. For example, 4.1 means page 4, panel 1. And if there is more than one sound effect in a panel, the sound effects are listed in order (so, 22.1.1 means page 22, panel 1, first sound effect). Remember that all numbers are given in the original Japanese reading order: right-to-left.

After the page and panel numbers, you'll see the literally translated sound spelled out by the katakana, followed by how this sound effect might have been spelled out, or what it stands for, in English—it is interesting to see the different ways Japanese people describe the sounds of things!

You'll sometimes see a long dash at the end of a sound effects listing. This is just a way of showing that the sound is the kind that lasts for a while; similarly, a hypen and number indicate the panels affected.

Now you are ready to use the *Ponyo on the Cliff by the Sea* Sound Effects Guide!

15.2	FX: TA TA TA [tp tp tp]		4.2	FX: TSUN TSUN [poke poke]
			4.3	FX: GUI GUI [urg urg]
17.3	FX: KAPO [klup]			
			6.2	FX: GATAN [dwmp]
18.1	FX: GUTSU GUTSU [glup glup]		6.3	FX: BWOO [vroom]
18.2	FX: BASA [flop]		6.4	FX: BWOOO [vroom]
18.3.1	FX: PIRORORORO [brring ring]			
18.3.2	FX: GATA [grik]		7.3	FX: BWOOO [vroom]
18.4.1	FX: PIROROROROR [brring ring ring]			
18.4.2	FX: ZAAA [shaaaa]		8.3	FX: BWOOO [vroom]
19.1.1	FX: PIROROROROR [brring ring]		9.3	FX: KYU KYU KYU [squeek squeek squeek]
19.1.2	FX: GACHA [plip]			
			10.3	FX: PERO [slurp]
20.5	FX: GACHAN [slam]		10.4	FX: GUII [vwoosh]
20.7	FX: TSUKA TSUKA [thmp thmp]		10.5	FX: KI KI KI KI [squee]
			10.6	FX: BWOOO [vroom]
21.1	FX: KACHA [click]			
21.3	FX: ZZA [shhha]		11.1.1	FX: BWOOO [vroom]
21.4	FX: GASHAN [slam]		11.1.2	FX: KI KIII [squeeee]
21.5	FX: SSHU [slllp]		11.2	FX: BWOOO [vroom]
			11.3	FX: ZAAAA [gwwrrrr]
22.3	FX: BASHI [flpp]		11.4	FX: BWOOO [vroom]
22.4	FX: KURU [turn]			
			12.3	FX: DOSA [thwomp]
23.2.1	FX: BA [fwa]			
23.2.2	FX: GATA [grik]		13.2	FX: GACHA [kcha]
23.3.1	FX: BATAN [fwpp]		13.3	FX: ZZU [drag]
23.3.2	FX: PASHU [shpa]			
23.4.1	FX : BUSHUU [shpaaa]		14.2	FX: KOTO [plop]
23.4.2	FX : BOTO BOTO [glip glip]		14.5	FX: CHIRA [glance]
24.1	FX: RIIIN RIIIN [crick crick]		15.1	FX: TA TA [tmp tmp]

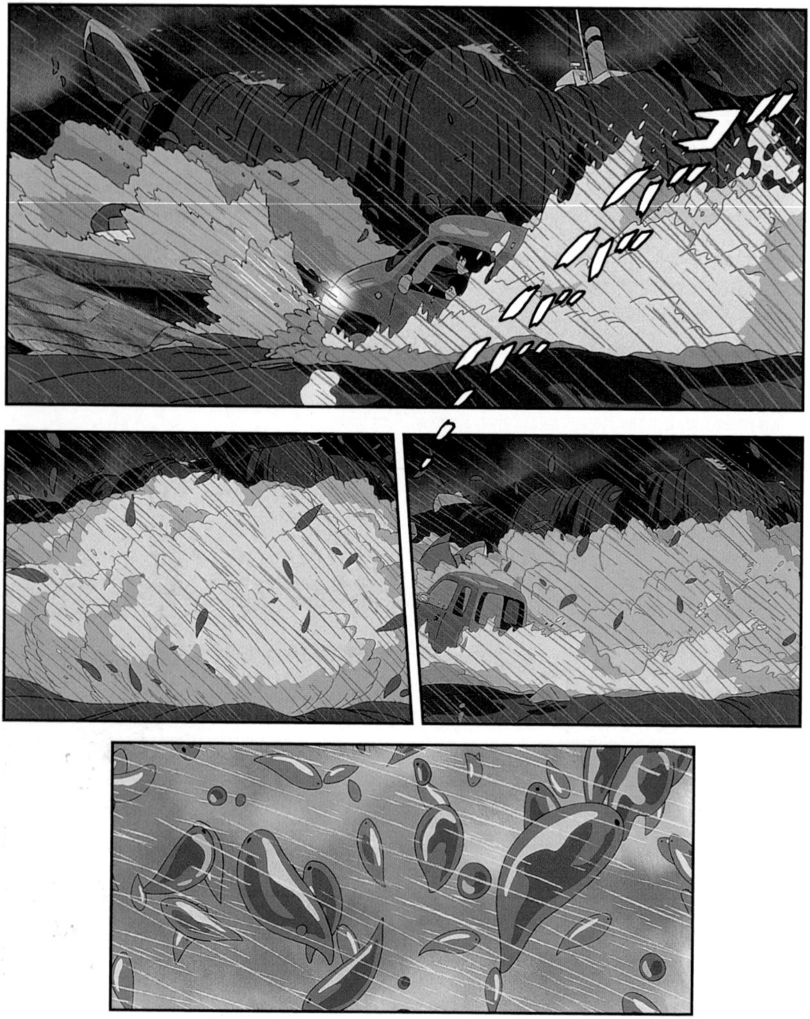
ゴ

To be continued…

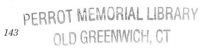

134.3	FX:	ZAAAA [shwaaa]
135.1-2	FX:	ZAAAA [shwaaa]
135.3	FX:	KI KI [squeee]
137.4	FX:	BA [popp]
138.1	FX:	DWOOO [wooosh]
138.2	FX:	SHU [slpp]
139.1	FX:	GWOOO [woooosh]
139.2-3	FX:	SUUUU [shhhhpppp]
140.1	FX:	DWOOOO [wooosh]
140.3	FX:	BWOOO BWOOO [vroom vroom]
141.1	FX:	SSSSS [shwaaaa]
141.2.1	FX:	BWOO BWOO [vroom vroom]
141.2.2	FX:	GU GU [grk grk]
141.5	FX:	DOBAAAAA [spblasshh]
142.1	FX:	BWOO [vroom]
142.2.1	FX:	GU [urk]
142.2.2	FX:	BA [tamp]
142.3.1	FX:	BWOOO [vroom]
142.3.2	FX:	GYAAA [grwaaa]
142.4.1	FX:	ZABABABABA [shpapapapa]
142.4.2	FX:	BWAWAA [vrvrrrrr]
143.1	FX:	GOBABABABA [glub glub glub]

120.5	FX:	PA PA [blpp blpp]
122.2	FX:	ZA ZAAAA [fzzzzz]
123.5	FX:	ZA ZAAAA [fzzzzz]
127.1.1	FX:	ZAAAA [shwaaa]
127.1.2	FX:	KII [squeak]
127.2	FX:	GACHA [kcha]
127.3	FX:	ZAAAA [shwaaa]
127.5	FX:	BATAN [shut]
128.3.1	FX:	KACHA KACHA [click click]
128.3.2	FX:	BWOOO [vroom]
128.4	FX:	BA BA BA BA [blp blp blp blp]
129.1	FX:	ZAAAAAA [shwaaaa]
129.2	FX:	GWOOO [wooosh]
129.3.1	FX:	DODWOOOOOOO [dwoooooosh]
129.3.2	FX:	BWOO [vroom]
130.1	FX:	ZABA [splash]
130.3	FX:	GWOOO [wooosh]
131.1-3	FX:	ZABAAAN [crash]
131.2	FX:	NWOOO [wmmp]
132.2-3	FX:	ZAAAAAAA [shwaaaaa]
133.1	FX:	BWOOO [vroom]
133.2.1	FX:	NUHOOOO [bwooooo]
133.2.2	FX:	KI KI KI [sqeee]
133.3	FX:	DOZAAA [blshhh]

This book should be read in its original Japanese right-to-left format.
Please turn it around to begin!

PONYO

Volume 2 of 4

Original story and screenplay written and directed by
Hayao Miyazaki

Translated from the original Japanese by Jim Hubbert
English-language screenplay by Melissa Mathison

Film Comic Adaptation/Mai Ihara
Lettering/Rina Mapa
Design/Carolina Ugalde
Editor/Megan Bates
Editorial Director/Masumi Washington

VP, Production/Alvin Lu
VP, Publishing Licensing/Rika Inouye
VP, Sales & Product Marketing/Gonzalo Ferreyra
VP, Creative/Linda Espinosa
Publisher/Hyoe Narita

Gake no Ue no Ponyo (Ponyo on the Cliff by the Sea)
© 2008 Nibariki - GNDHDDT
All rights reserved.
First published in Japan by Tokuma Shoten Co., Ltd.
PONYO title logo © 2009 Nibariki-GNDHDDT
The stories, characters and incidents mentioned in this publication are
entirely fictional.

Printed in Singapore

Published by
VIZ Media, LLC
295 Bay St.
San Francisco, CA 94133

First printing, August 2009

PARENTAL ADVISORY
PONYO is suitable for all ages.
ratings.viz.com

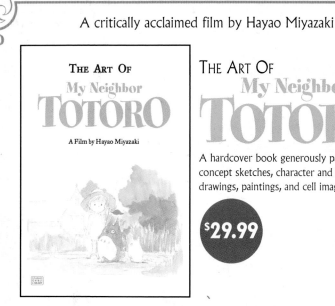

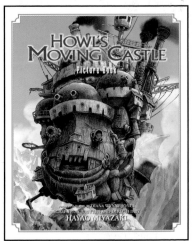

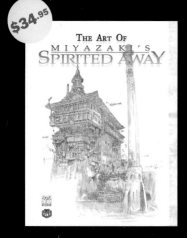
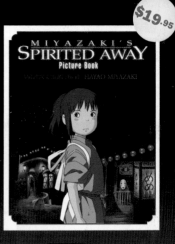